AF879165

What Is the CURE for America?

What Is the CURE for America?

Star Parker

Creators Publishing
Hermosa Beach, CA

What Is the CURE for America?

Cover art by Little Shiva, littleshiva.com

CREATORS PUBLISHING
737 3rd St
Hermosa Beach, CA 90254
310-337-7003

ISBN (print): 978-1-949673-96-8

First Edition
Printed in the United States of America
1 3 5 7 9 10 8 6 4 2

A Note From the Publisher

Our goal is to make you think. We want you to react. We want you to respond.

Since 1987, the writers we represent and publish start discussions, arguments and even controversies. Love them or hate them, you can't ignore them.

Beginning with print and evolving into digital, Creators has been at the forefront of the media industry. We have been disrupting the status quo since our company was founded on the premise that creators should own their work, characters and ideas. Decades later, we continue to evolve as society pushes forward and technology changes.

At Creators, we support creators.

—Creators Publishing

Contents

Health Care 115

Culture 149

Introduction

"What is the CURE for America?" highlights the vision and insights of Center for Urban Renewal and Education (CURE) President Star Parker. As a nationally syndicated columnist with Creators, Star has shared her unique perspectives with readers on a weekly basis for many years.

In a column entitled, "Today's Great Black Dilemma" (March 2020), Star boldly confronts the challenge facing black Americans. "Once the challenge that black Americans faced was the scourge of racism and the acts of evil white men. Today's great challenge for blacks is to shake off the culture of the welfare plantation and the destructive rhetoric of evil black liberals who want to keep them there," she says.

Star calls out Black Lives Matter for sowing anger and division in our culture and the "Poor People's Campaign" for encouraging greater dependency on government.

She believes our nation has strayed from the vision Dr. Martin Luther King Jr. articulated in his 1963 "I Have a Dream" speech. Critical race theory flies in the face of King's dream that all Americans be judged not by the color of their skin but by the content of their character.

The indictment of the woke movement is that America is the problem. King offered up America as the solution.

Star says King talked about the "magnificent words of the Constitution and the Declaration of Independence."

"I have a dream that one day this nation will rise up and live out the true meaning of its creed: 'We hold these truths to be self-evident, that all men are created equal.'"

The problem, as King explained, is not America or the

eternal truths that were brought to bear in its founding. The problem was the failure of the nation to live up to the challenges of its great founding principles. Dr. King appealed to the nation to realize the dream of its founding fathers. Not to crush it and bury it, as we hear today.

In his Farewell Address to the nation in 1796, America's departing first president, George Washington, observed: “It is substantially true that virtue or morality is a necessary spring to popular government.”

Washington elaborated by saying, “reason and experience both forbid us to expect that national morality can prevail in exclusion of religious principle.”

Like our first president, Star Parker believes for a democracy to function properly, it must be guided by moral principles. And the guidelines and rules by which we define what is moral are framed by principles of the Bible.
Rather than our democracy following prior moral principles, our moral principles now are defined by our democracy. What we deem to be moral—good and evil, right and wrong—now arrives to us not from heaven but from Hollywood.

Star Parker weaves these messages together to highlight the serious challenges that confront our nation, but she also offers a path to prosperity and happiness.
In the pages that follow, Star addresses a wide range of issues and national controversies. She affirms leaders who adhere to timeless principles, but does not shy away from calling out those who seek to lead us astray.

Economics

Nipsey Hussle and the Opportunity Zone Dream

May 15, 2019

A basic law in physics says that energy cannot be created or destroyed. It can only be changed from one form to another.

The same rule, I think, applies to society.

There is a given amount of human energy. Is it going to be directed creatively? Or destructively?

We see both at play in the life and death of rapper Nipsey Hussle.

Hussle was a born entrepreneur. According to a newspaper account, it's what earned him his nickname.

He was polishing shoes at age 11 to earn money. Then began his music. And then he moved into investments.

And then, at age 33, he was gunned down in front of his clothing store, Marathon Clothing, on the site of a strip mall in South Los Angeles that he and real estate developer David Gross had planned to develop through the new Opportunity Zone initiative.

Opportunity Zones became law as part of the Tax Cuts and Jobs Act of 2017.

The idea was to provide for trillions of dollars of capital sitting in various types of investments—stocks, real estate, etc.—to be redirected into investments in economically distressed areas around the nation by allowing the gains to be realized tax-free.

The Treasury Department designated 8,700 zones across the USA that could qualify, which included the strip mall where Hussle's clothing store was located in South LA.

Hussle and Gross purchased the mall and planned to set up the "Our Opportunity" fund to develop the property into residential units and shops.

Their concept was to incorporate small investors through crowdfunding to partner with larger investors. This would enable residents of the local community to participate as investors and purchase homes in the residential units.

Hussle's concern was that the Opportunity Zone initiative might be successful in directing capital to distressed neighborhoods, but investors coming from outside the community would have little interest in the locals.

The vision of Hussle and Gross was that the Opportunity Zone initiative be a community development initiative as well as a purely economic development initiative.

According to Sean Parker, the first president of Facebook, and one of the visionaries of Opportunity Zones, "Instead of having government hand out pools of taxpayer dollars, you have savvy investors directing money into projects they think will succeed."

Hussle and Gross added the crucial additional dimension to structure the deals to assure participation of and benefit to the local communities.

This is public policy at its best and most creative. Structure policies that will encourage personal initiative and creativity. This is the way we will fix the broken parts of America that have been left behind.

What we then witnessed was what happens when the destructive energy within the community proves too powerful for the creative energy.

Hussle was shot and killed.

According to the Los Angeles Times, Hussle's murder was one of 29 that have occurred so far this year in South Los Angeles.

Hussle's story is a microcosm of the racial challenges of the nation.

How do we overcome the destructive energy and transform it to creative energy?

Hussle was showing the way. But his efforts fell short of overcoming the too-vast destructive energy long hovering in South LA and that hovers in similar neighborhoods across America.

From what I read, David Gross will continue their work and move forward with the Our Opportunity fund. Good news.

The complex history of black America, coupled with poor welfare state policies, has left a legacy of hard, destructive energy in our inner cities.

More social entrepreneurs, like Nipsey Hussle and David Gross, and political leaders like Sen. Tim Scott, who championed the Opportunity Zones initiative from its inception and is now traveling across America to get it implemented, can turn things around.

With the right policies and the right people, the creative energy will overcome the destructive.

Left-Wing Fake News Hurts the Nation

Jan. 9, 2019

Left-wing media stalwarts such as Newsweek, Huffington Post and Salon launched a barrage of fake news after I appeared on "Fox and Friends" recently to discuss new Agriculture Department rules tightening work requirement on food stamps.

Unfortunately, the now all-too-common disinformation campaigns from the left, distorting or simply lying about what our president says or does, or what conservative commentators like me say, just simply hurts our nation.

The oxygen of freedom is information. When citizens get fake news instead, they become slaves to the agendas being pushed by politically motivated media machines.

The Huffington Post headline read, "'Fox and Friends' Guest Says People On Food Stamps Watch Porn Instead of Working."

You can imagine the mail I got from those outraged by my supposedly heartless remarks about our nation's less fortunate.

But I didn't say what the left-wing media foghorns reported in their headlines. As result, not only were many misled, but also they weren't informed about what I did say about two major problems confronting our nation.

One, there are great inefficiencies in our food stamp program, which, at $65 billion in federal spending annually, is one of our largest federal welfare programs. And two, the nation has a major problem of millions of able-bodied prime-age males who have dropped out of the work force.

The proposed rules from the Agriculture Department would tighten down on the latitude states have in providing waivers for existing work requirements for receiving food stamps.

Is this aimed at clamping down on the less fortunate and the needy? Certainly not, and I explicitly said so in the "Fox and Friends" interview. Twice I said the "crisis is not the poor." It's about "able-bodied, non-working, mostly males."

The Agriculture Department rule explicitly states that the target is "able-bodied adults without dependents between 18-49" and does not apply to the "elderly, disabled or pregnant women."

Estimates are that the total number that will be affected is 775,000. We're talking about 2 percent of the 40 million people currently receiving food stamp benefits. With the average annual expenditure per person at $1,500, moving these able-bodied individuals into the work force would save $1.2 billion in food stamp expenditures per year and add 775,000 productive citizens to the work force.

According to The Wall Street Journal, "Some seven to nine million food-stamp recipients capable of work report no income."

American Enterprise Institute scholar Nicholas Eberstadt has written about our national crisis of prime working age, 25-55, non-working men.

The labor force participation rate, or LFPR, reported by the Bureau of Labor Statistics consists of those working or actively seeking work as a percentage of the population.

In 1965, as Eberstadt reports, the LFPR of prime-age working males was 96.7 percent. Today, it is 89 percent. So almost 8 percent fewer men aged 25-55 are working or actively seeking work today compared with 1965.

Eberstadt calls this "an ever-growing army of jobless men no longer even looking for work—over 7 million between 25 and 55, the prime of working life."

He notes that one defining characteristic of these millions of men who have dropped out of the workforce is an absence of family. They are either not married or if they have children, they don't live with them.

What are these work dropouts doing?

They spend 800 more hours per year watching TV and movies than unemployed men, 1,200 more hours than working men and 1,400 more hours than working women.

Thirty-one percent admit to illegal drug use, compared with 8 percent of working men.

We have a huge problem that carries a great moral and economic cost to the nation.

But all this doesn't interest the left-wing media. They'd rather just broadcast that I said the poor are "watching porn."

Socialism Has Already Hurt America

Feb. 13, 2019

President Donald Trump was principled and politically astute to address, in his State of the Union, the horrors taking place now in Venezuela, and then to declare:

"Tonight we renew our resolve that America will never be a socialist country."

Venezuela is indeed a poster child for what happens when a nation's economic machinery falls under political control.

Over the last five years, per The Wall Street Journal, Venezuela's economy shrank by 35 percent and poverty tripled from 48 to 87 percent.

According to Gallup, 71 percent of Venezuelans say they can't afford food, 47 percent say they can't afford shelter, just 15 percent say they are satisfied with the availability of quality health care, and 35 percent say they are satisfied with their standard of living.

Thirty-six percent of Venezuelans, 51 percent of those between 15 and 29, say they would leave the country permanently if they could.

But if it is so clear that socialism is a formula for economic disaster, why does the idea still conjure up support?

In a Gallup poll of last year, 57 percent of Democrats, compared to 16 percent of Republicans, say they have a "positive view of socialism."

Economist and New York Times columnist Paul Krugman says it's semantics.

Krugman mocks Trump, saying that "there is

essentially no one in American political life who advocates such things" as government control of industry, as is the case in Venezuela.

When Democrats say "socialism," says Krugman, they really mean "social democracy"—a market economy with a social safety net and use of the tax system as an equalizer.

The issue really isn't how we technically define socialism. The issue is really the extent to which we are free.

What difference is it really if a firm is privately owned, but the government has vast latitude to regulate what it does? Or if a private firm pays me but government taxes away a large chunk of what I earn?

Venezuela is, of course, the extreme case. Total collapse as result of political despots taking over everything.

But socialism is not like good wine, which, in moderation, might not hurt and might even be beneficial.

Every step in which economic freedom is cut back bears costs.

We see what is happening now, as the U.S. economy surges back to life as a result of cutting back regulation and taxes.

But our nation has not totally escaped the Venezuelan phenomenon.

America has entire communities in distress for the same reasons that Venezuela has fallen apart—political control over economic affairs. Life in our poor communities is in the grip of socialism, not capitalism.

Government housing, government health care, government schools, government welfare programs.

There are 31 million people living in areas of high economic distress, now designated as "opportunity zones." The average poverty rate in these zones is 28.7 percent. The average household income is 40 percent below the national average, and 36.5 percent of prime-age adults are not working. Fifty-six percent of these 31 million are non-white minorities.

The president's new opportunity zone initiative, providing tax incentives to direct investment capital into these neighborhoods, aims to change realities with the same passion that the president spoke against socialism for the rest of the country in his State of the Union address.

How do countries wind up going in the wrong direction?

British playwright George Bernard Shaw captured it when he said, "A government that robs Peter to pay Paul can always depend on the support of Paul."

Political demagogues tap into the frustrations of those who are struggling, or tap into the ambitions of those who long for power, and sell them Hollywood dreams—and lies—of a better life. Once they convince them to turn over power, the nightmare begins.

Life has no shortcuts. Freedom, hard work and personal responsibility are the one and only path to prosperity.

Change Social Security to a Program of Ownership

April 3, 2019

I have been an advocate for years of changing our Social Security system to a program of ownership rather than government taxing and spending.

To those walking around with the idea that Social Security is some kind of pension in which you have been investing for years—forget it.

Current retirees get their money from payroll taxes paid by those currently working. It's a government tax-and-spend program.

The problem is that because Americans are living longer (good news) but having fewer children (bad news), the number of working Americans per retiree keeps shrinking. The only way to keep the program going is raising taxes or cutting benefits as the worker-to-retiree ratio continues to shrink.

D-Day, when the whole thing is now projected to collapse, according to Social Security Trustees, is 2034—just 15 years away. Revenues projected for that year will cover only 79 percent of the funds needed for payout to retirees.

Keeping the finances in balance will require a 21 percent benefit cut, a 27 percent tax increase or some combination.

But the problem really isn't just one of demographics and arithmetic. It's a problem of principles.

After President Franklin D Roosevelt signed Social Security into law in 1935, its constitutionality was challenged. That case, Helvering v. Davis, in which the

Supreme Court found Social Security constitutional, changed the landscape of America regarding our sense of the role of government.

Prior to this, the welfare state, so much a part of our lives today, where government taxes one set of citizens and redistributes to another, was not understood to be among the powers the constitution grants to the federal government.

Helvering v. Davis changed all that and opened the door to any federal program that could be deemed in the "general welfare."

Once, the lion's share of federal spending was defense. Today, defense comprises only 15 percent of the federal budget, with most of the $4.2 trillion of federal spending going to entitlement and welfare programs, which are key drivers of our massive federal deficits and debt accumulation.

Invariably, when I convey that Social Security is an entitlement program, I get indignant letters from people saying they paid taxes all their working life to qualify for this benefit.

Some 62 million are now collecting Social Security benefits. According to Gallup, 57 percent of retirees say Social Security is a "major source" of their retirement income.

But none of these tens of millions are in the system by choice.

Government forces them to pay in. Government determines what they will get. And government determines the conditions under which they will get it.

And government has changed the rules innumerable times, and now it is about to change them again—if we allow it.

The extent to which Americans have conceded the moral dignity and economic benefits of ownership, allowing government to take control of their lives, has hurt our country.

Countless studies have shown that investing the equivalent of one's payroll tax in a personal retirement account over a 45-year working life would produce far higher returns than Social Security now delivers. Now those Social Security returns are about to get worse with the changes necessary to get the system back in balance.

Equally important, you own your personal account. It's your personal wealth that you control and watch accumulate, and that you can pass on to heirs.

This is particularly important to low-income Americans who have no other platform for accumulating and bequeathing wealth.

According to Gallup, 36 percent of African Americans compared with 60 percent of white Americans own stock in some form.

Bringing a culture of ownership to low-income Americans can be transformational.

Nothing could be more American than to reform and transform our broken Social Security system to a system of personal ownership, saving and wealth accumulation.

Alabama and Georgia Abortion Laws on Right Track

May 22, 2019

When we talk about "pro-life" in our national discussion about abortion, "life" is understood to be about the unborn child in the mother's womb.

But it would serve us well to expand our understanding about what "pro-life" means.

We should understand that respecting the sanctity of life is key to the values and behaviors in general that sustain and nourish all our lives today and create the necessary conditions for our future.

A just-released report from the National Center for Health Statistics, a unit of the Centers for Disease Control and Prevention, reports that the total number of births in the United States in 2018 was down 2 percent from 2017 and is the lowest number of births in the country in 32 years.

It also reports that the general fertility rate—the number of births per 1,000 women aged 15-44—was also down 2 percent and is at a record low.

The total fertility rate needs to be 2,100 births per 1,000 women to keep our overall population at steady state—not shrinking. It now stands at 1,728 per 1,000 women.

If the alternative to "pro-life" is so-called "pro-choice," the mindset of legal abortion on demand, the latter is capturing, and destroying, American society. We are choosing to extinguish ourselves.

It turns out that "reproductive freedom," the banner under which "pro-choice" operates, translates into the freedom to not reproduce.

University of Southern California demographer Dowell Myers calls the declining birthrates we are witnessing a "barometer of despair."

Birthrates decline, according to Myers, when people are not optimistic about the future.

How about the general collapse of the marriage institution?

In 1960, 72 percent of Americans 18 and above were married. By 2016, this was down to 50 percent.

At a conference at the Vatican in 2014, Rabbi Jonathan Sacks, former chief rabbi of the United Kingdom, called marriage "the single most humanizing institution in history."

He said that life begins "when male and female meet and embrace."

"Morality," he continued, "is the love between husband and wife, parent and child, extended outward to the world."

A society in which sanctity of life is respected is a society that appreciates that we are all part of something larger than ourselves. When we lose this awe, this appreciation for the sacred, we disconnect from one another and disappear into our separate selves.

Love, marriage, children and our future begin to recede.

It's a spiritual tragedy with profound and destructive practical implications for society.

The Census Bureau projects that in 2035, for the first time, the number of Americans over the age of 65 will exceed the number of Americans under 18.

As society ages, the number of retirees per each working American increases—what is called the dependency ratio.

We are already seeing the implications with huge deficits in our social security and Medicare programs, where payroll taxes finance retirement and health care costs of the elderly.

A healthy pushback is starting to occur at the nation's grassroots.

States are getting aggressive to stop the destructive abortion culture. Most recently, Alabama and Georgia have enacted laws making abortion that is legal under federal law illegal in the state.

This puts state law on a collision course with federal law.

Whether this will wind up at the Supreme Court with a revisiting of the Roe v. Wade decision remains to be seen.

We should be praying it will happen.

The current abortion culture that has been defining America since the Roe v. Wade decision in 1973 is part and symptomatic of an America whose future is in danger.

We must fight for restoration of a pro-life culture in our country that respects the sanctity of life and will restore the American family, children and our future.

No, Democrats, America Works

July 3, 2019

With the first round of Democratic Party debates behind us, Americans have now heard from their candidates why they think they should run the country.

One theme permeates the messages of all these Democrats.

America is not fair, and they aspire to be president to make things fair.

Elizabeth Warren: "When you've got an economy that does great for those with money and isn't doing great for everyone else, that is corruption, pure and simple. We need to call it out. We need to attack it head on."

Kamala Harris: "For too long, the rules have been written in the favor of the people who have the most and not in favor of the people who work the most. ... on day one, I will repeal that tax bill that benefits the top 1 percent and the biggest corporations of America."

Bernie Sanders: "Well, President Trump, you're not standing up for working families ... 83 percent of your tax benefits go to the top 1 percent. That's how we beat Trump: We expose him for the fraud that he is."

There are, of course, more candidates and more issues. But this generally sums it all up.

Per the Democrats, America is rigged for the wealthy; everyone else is a getting a raw deal; and we need government to straighten everything out.

The challenge for President Trump and Republicans in the upcoming elections is to make clear to voters that the Democrats' message is not true and to communicate what is true.

Who are these wealthy Americans who, according to Democrats, control everything?

The answer is that those who are wealthy are changing all the time, because contrary to what we hear from Democrats, America works.

Every year, Forbes Magazine publishes a list of the 400 wealthiest Americans.

In 2018, 43 percent of those on this list were not on it 10 years before.

Forbes notes who among these 400 inherited their wealth and who are self-made.

In 1984, according to Forbes, less than half of those on the list were self-made.

In 2018, 67 percent "created their own fortunes."

"Over the past 30-plus years," says Forbes, "the number of Forbes 400 members who have forged their own path, using entrepreneurial capitalism as a means to attain a vast fortune, has increased dramatically. This tells us many things, but one should stand taller than the rest: The American Dream, it seems, is alive and well."

What about all the tax unfairness that Democrats tell us about?

According to the Tax Foundation, in 2016, the latest data available, taxpayers earning in the top 1 percent paid 37.3 percent of all federal taxes. Those earning in the top 5 percent paid 58.2 percent of all federal taxes. Those earning in the bottom 50 percent paid 3 percent of all federal taxes.

At less than 250 years old, the USA is one of the planet's youngest countries. Yet at $20.5 trillion gross domestic product, its economy is by far the world's largest. It's 60 percent larger than China's, the second-largest economy, and more than 400 percent larger than Japan's, the third-largest.

Those who want to lead the country should be talking about what has created America's enormous wealth and success, how to keep it going and how to assure that as many Americans as possible participate.

Freedom and entrepreneurial capitalism have been the mother's milk of the magnificent American success story. The poor are not poor because the rich are rich or because the system is rigged. If we want to help them, let's honestly examine why they are not participating and try to help them help themselves.

Certainly, many things don't work as well as they could. Health care, education, housing, our entitlement programs. Almost invariably, their dysfunction comes from too much government, not too little.

If Republicans convey these truths in 2020, they will win.

Minimum Wage Laws Are a Terrible Idea

July 17, 2019

Democrats in Congress have again brought the minimum wage to the national political stage.

Legislation moving forward in the House, H.R. 582, the Raise the Wage Act, would increase the national minimum wage from the current $7.25 per hour to $15 per hour in increments spanning the next five years.

Minimum wage is a highly partisan issue, reflecting the very different ways the two parties view economic reality.

When the Pew Research Center surveyed voters during the 2016 presidential campaign, 82 percent of Hillary Clinton supporters favored raising the federal minimum wage to $15 per hour, while only 21 percent of Donald Trump supporters favored the idea.

What drives the difference between the parties?

Some would like to say it's because Republicans are pro-business and Democrats are pro-worker. Some would like to say it's because Republicans are for the wealthy and Democrats are for those with low income.

But I reject this take on things.

The thrust of all my work focuses on improving the lot of low-income Americans.

And I think the minimum wage is a terrible idea.

I operate a business, albeit a nonprofit business.

How do I decide how much to pay employees? I determine what I can afford and then try to get the best people I can at that wage.

Suppose what I decide I can afford is not enough to attract the kind of person I am looking for. I won't get any applicants. I've got to figure out how I can pay more, or if it is viable to hire people less qualified and hope they will learn on the job and then not quit if their salary does not grow with their performance.

In short, these are dynamic and highly personalized calculations between a business owner, workers and the marketplace.

How can it possibly work if the government gets involved telling me what I should pay people? It can't work, and it doesn't work.

Minimum wage advocates want to claim that it's different on the lowest rung of the pay scale. But no, it's not different.

Every employer pays as much as he or she can to get the best possible workforce.

If the government sets a floor on what can be paid for a certain kind of job, either the job won't be filled; someone overqualified will do it; or automation will substitute.

There's tons of research on the minimum wage. But the bottom line is common sense. All employers will hire the best workforce they can afford. If government limits what they can afford, the workforce will be constrained.

A new report from the Congressional Budget Office confirms the common-sense conclusion. Although a $15 minimum wage would lift some 1.3 million out of poverty, at the same time, 1.3 million jobs would be lost—in the mid-range scenario. And 3.7 million jobs would be lost in the worst-case scenario.

This is even giving Democrats pause.

But what is even missing from this analysis is how many would benefit from minimizing government interference in the marketplace altogether, rather than government stepping in and manipulating and distorting the marketplace.

The bread and butter of Democratic politicians is convincing voters that they can make their lives better by expanding government and getting it more involved in private lives.

But data convincingly shows that the most prosperous nations are the ones with the freest economies.

Democrats also cause collateral damage by getting many Americans to believe what isn't true—that politicians can make their lives better.

The headline of a Wall Street Journal report from a few days ago reads, "A Record Expansion's Surprise Winners: The Low-Skilled." The subheadline reads, "As unemployment remains at near generation lows, the fortunes of low-wage workers have improved markedly."

Want to help those struggling at the bottom? Reduce regulations. Cut taxes. Minimize government interference. And unleash the creative human potential of the free marketplace.

Ownership, Not Government Spending, Will Shrink Wealth Gap

July 31, 2019

With the next round of Democratic presidential candidate debates upon us, we will surely hear more about government activism to fix racial inequalities.

Inequality is real and needs attention.

According to the Urban Institute, average white household wealth in 2016 was $171,000 compared with average black household wealth of $17,409.

Sen. Cory Booker wants government to make deposits into savings accounts for low-income children to the tune of up to $50,000 each.

Sen. Kamala Harris proposes $100 billion in government subsidies for black homeownership.

These kinds of proposals may win some black votes, but should they? Will they really make blacks and the nation better off?

Government anti-poverty spending is not exactly a novel idea. We've been doing it since the 1960s, totaling, by some estimates, over $20 trillion since then. Has it achieved anything?

Changes in the poverty rate are barely discernible. And the wealth gap has just gotten bigger.

Per the same Urban Institute data, the wealth gap between white and nonwhite households was $45,188 in 1963, $92,045 in 1983 and $153,591 in 2016.

If a history of spending massive sums of taxpayer funds without results is not enough to discourage this approach, how about asking where the money will come from?

This fiscal year, the federal government will spend $4.5 trillion, $3.5 of which will be financed by tax revenue, leaving a trillion-dollar deficit to finance through borrowing.

According to the latest "Long Term Budget Outlook" from the Congressional Budget Office, "Large budget deficits over the next 30 years are projected to drive federal debt held by the public to unprecedented levels—from 78 percent of gross domestic product (GDP) in 2019 to 144 percent by 2049."

And, CBO continues, "The prospect for such high and rising debt poses substantial risks for the nation ..."

Sometimes it might be reasonable to take a risky plunge into debt, if the investments being made with the funds raised have high potential return and payoff.

But we're talking here about plunging the nation deeper into debt to spend money in ways that have always failed. Does this make sense to anyone other than politicians who might get in office as a result of buying votes?

There is a way out of the darkness, but it takes principles and courage.

Low-income America isn't suffering because of insufficient government dependence but because of insufficient independence—ownership. And here we can use government policy to make things better.

Per the Urban Institute, the average savings in retirement accounts in 2016 was $157,884 in white households and $25,212 in black households. Black families, according to the report, "have less access to retirement savings vehicles and lower participation when they have access."

The headline in a recent Wall Street Journal column

reads, "Counter Inequality With Private Social Security Accounts."

The authors, Jeff Yass and Stephen Moore, propose Own America Accounts, private retirement accounts to where workers could shift 10 percent of their paycheck from Social Security.

The average annual return on Social Security over the last 40 years has been about 1 percent per year, according to Yass and Moore, and stocks returned 6 percent per year.

With Own America Accounts, an average American could have retired in 2016 with between $1 and 2 million in savings over a 40- to 45-year working life, per Yass and Moore.

Furthermore, Social Security is yet another dysfunctional government program. Social Security trustees project that in just 16 years, there will be insufficient funds to meets obligations. So a bad deal will get even worse when our politicians try to "save the system" by raising taxes, raising the retirement age or cutting benefits.

At minimum, make Own America Accounts available to low-income Americans, and help them build wealth through ownership rather than more government dependence.

Cuccinelli Right to Keep the Focus on Freedom

Sept. 4, 2019

The left-wing media is having a field day distorting acting U.S. Citizenship and Immigration Services Director Ken Cuccinelli's comments regarding the famous poem emblazoned on the base of the State of Liberty.

Discussing the Trump administration's new "public charge" rule, an NPR host asked Cuccinelli if the poem's words "give me your tired, your poor" are also part of the American ethos.

"They certainly are," said Cuccinelli. "Give me your tired and your poor who can stand on their own two feet and will not become a public charge."

The new "public charge" rule will expand the government's latitude to reject permanent resident status—green cards—to immigrants seeking government aid, such as foods stamps, housing and Medicaid.

Those media hosts pouncing on Cuccinelli show little interest in the crowning phrase of the poem, "yearning to breathe free."

CNN's Erin Burnett cherry-picked words from the poem: "wretched ... poor ... refuse."

"That's what the poem says America is supposed to stand for," charged Burnett.

Maybe that's what America is about to a left-wing CNN host. But to me and tens of millions of Americans, America is about "yearning to breathe free."

Cuccinelli explained to Burnett, who ignored him, that the first immigration law excluding those who would likely become a public charge was passed in 1882, the year before Emma Lazarus wrote "The New Colossus."

Immigration is just part of the larger discussion dividing us so deeply today. Is "freedom" what primarily defines our nation, or is it welfare and redistribution of income?

And if it's "freedom," what does this mean?

Here is the great free market economist and Nobel laureate Milton Friedman: "Why is it that free immigration was a good thing before 1914"—according to popular opinion—"and free immigration is a bad thing today? ... Because it is one thing to have free immigration to jobs. It is another thing to have free immigration to welfare. And you cannot have both."

"If you have a welfare state," continues Friedman, "in which every ... resident is promised some minimal level of income ... whether he works or not, produces it or not, well, then it really is an impossible thing" to have free immigration.

In 1900, three years before Emma Lazarus' poem was posted on the Statue of Liberty, 2.8% of the nation's gross domestic product was taken by the federal government. Today it is 23.2%, almost one quarter of our nation's economy taken and largely redistributed by the federal government.

Those immigrating to the United States in 1903, when "The New Colossus" appeared on the State of Liberty, were the "tired ... poor ... huddled masses yearning to breathe free." What America offered them was freedom, work, opportunity.

They came, learned the language, became part of the country and its culture, and participated in building the great and prosperous nation that America was to become in the 20th century.

It's not to say that many who aspire to come to America today are not motivated by these things. But because welfare is so available now, in contrast to 1903, we must be careful. Not only is it costly to us but, despite the claims of progressives, rarely is it compassionate. I know from personal experience we should be offering those escaping oppression a free life, not more government.

It is simple prudence to make sure that new arrivals to the country become producers and taxpayers rather than consumers of government benefits. The Congressional Budget Office has just sounded its latest alarm that the national debt burden is headed to "unprecedented levels," posing "substantial risks" to the nation.

I wish these media hosts trying to get such mileage from "The New Colossus" were equally anxious to look for faithfulness to other songs and poems that are part of our national culture.

Songs like the one composed in 1918 by Jewish immigrant Irving Berlin, with the words:

"God Bless America,
"Land that I love.
"Stand beside her,
"And guide her,
"Through the night with a light from above."

Secretary Ben Carson's Innovation in Homeless Policy: Thinking

Sept. 25, 2019

Ben Carson, the neurosurgeon-turned-secretary of housing and urban development, has written many books.

One of them is called "You Have a Brain."

The book is not about neurosurgery. The title is a quote from his single mother, who raised him and his brother and led them out of lives of poverty to successful careers.

When one of the lads would confront a problem and turn to their mother, she would say, "You have a brain—use it."

This simple bit of wisdom should be employed with greater frequency in public policy debate and discussion in our country.

Carson is once again under attack by liberals, who are distorting perfectly legitimate observations he made regarding concerns of admittance of transgender women into federally funded women's homeless shelters.

The press headlines read that Carson made "hateful" remarks demeaning transgender individuals.

Predictably, with no serous investigation into what Carson actually said or meant, a host of Democrats are calling for his resignation.

Carson, in discussions with staff, said he was conveying concerns he heard from women at homeless shelters regarding "big, hairy men" who "would come in and have to be accepted into the women's shelter even though it made the women in the facility very uncomfortable."

Carson went on to clarify and said: "Our society is in danger when we pick one issue (such as gender identity) and say it does not matter how it impacts others because this one issue should override every other common-sense consideration. I think we have to look out for everyone, and we need to use our intellectual capabilities to find common good rather than attempting to always stir up controversy through identity politics."

Part of the concern of Democrats is that the Department of Housing and Urban Development under Carson's leadership is looking to modify a 2012 Obama-era HUD rule, the Equal Access Rule, which bars federal housing discrimination on the basis of sexual orientation or gender identity.

But this is case in point for Carson's appeal to "use our intellectual capabilities to find common good," or, in his mother's words, "You have a brain—use it."

Regardless of one's convictions about gender identity, it is reasonable to accept a rule against discrimination in federal housing.

But discrimination is different from forcing women in homeless shelters to share all facilities with transgender women.

It seems to me appropriate to the idea of "you have a brain—use it" to propose, as HUD has proposed, that "programs which permit single-sex or sex-segregated facilities (such as bathrooms or temporary, emergency shelters... that require ... shared sleeping quarters or bathing facilities)" take into consideration an individual's sex for the purpose of admitting the individual to the facility.

According to one HUD staffer, as reported in The Washington Post, such a policy "prioritizes someone's discomfort over another person's right to shelter."

I have news for this HUD staffer. No one has a "right to shelter" at taxpayer expense. To the extent to which these facilities are provided, it is done under the good graces and consent of taxpaying American citizens, not because anyone has a "right" to these facilities.

And Secretary Ben Carson is entirely and absolutely correct that implementing policy in our deeply value-fractured country requires careful thought to balance all competing interests.

Only liberals, blinded by their own bias, self-absorbed with their own self-righteousness, can be so intolerant and insensitive to others and pretend this is the high ground and tolerance.

These same warriors for the transgender cause claim that 1 in 3 transgender individuals have experienced homelessness.

If this is so common, work to establish facilities specific to these individuals.

But forcing women to sleep and share bathrooms with men who have decided they are women is heartless indifference to the trauma this causes to the women.

Let's appreciate the wisdom of Ben Carson and his mother.

"You have a brain—use it."

Marriage and Pregnancy Reduce Crime

Dec. 4, 2019

There's a general assumption in public policy discourse that economic policy and social policy are separate universes.

When economic policy is the topic, we think about taxes, government spending, business, jobs, etc. When social policy is the topic, we think about marriage, family, children, abortion, etc.

But, in reality, the line between economic policy and social policy is ambiguous, if it exists at all.

In recent years, for instance, family structure has gotten increasing attention as an important factor to consider in policy discussions about poverty.

Now we have a new academic paper by economists—Maxim Massenkoff and Evan Rose, both doctoral candidates in economics at the University of California, Berkeley—that makes it even clearer that what we generally think of as social policy can fall into the realm of economic analysis.

The paper—"Family Formation and Crime"—examines the connection between the incidence of pregnancy, childbirth and marriage, and the incidence of crime.

The conclusion, in the words of the authors: "Our event-study analysis indicates that pregnancy triggers sharp declines in crime rivaling any known intervention. For mothers, criminal offending drops precipitously in the first few months of pregnancy, stabilizing at half of pre-pregnancy levels three years after the birth. Men show a smaller, but still important 25 percent decline beginning at the onset of pregnancy, although domestic violence arrests spike for fathers immediately after birth."

Marriage, according to the authors, "is a stopping point, marking the completion of a roughly 50 percent decline in offending for both men and women."

The analysis, again per the authors, is "by far the largest such study ever conducted in the United States." They tapped information on over a million births and, using data in the state of Washington, matched records on "criminal offenses, births, marriages, and divorces."

George Mason University economist Alex Tabarrok discusses the work on his enormously popular blog, Marginal Revolution.

Tabarrok notes his own research on crime deterrence, which shows that in the case of three-strikes laws, the prospect of an additional 20 years to life imprisonment reduced criminal recidivism by 17%. Compared with this, notes Tabarrok, "the effect of pregnancy is astoundingly large."

Of course, demonstrating statistical correlation and explaining why the occurrences correlate are different things. Why is incidence of pregnancy followed by significant drops in criminal activity in both women and men?

What is it about birth and marriage that contributes significantly to reducing crime?

Tabarrok conjectures it's about "socializing and civilizing both men and women."

I would speculate that it is similar to why, when a pregnant woman sees an ultrasound image of the child developing within her, she is less likely to abort that child.

It's a wake-up call to the awe and mystery of life, which produces a sense of meaning and personal responsibility.

It follows that we ought to be concerned about the decline in Americans' sense of importance of marriage and children.

In a newly published survey from Pew Research Center, 57% of men and 46% of women said “having a job or career they enjoy” is “essential for a ... fulfilling life.”

Compared with this, only 16% of men and 17% of women said marriage is “essential for a ... fulfilling life.”

And only 16% of men and 22% of women said children are “essential for a ... fulfilling life.”

I love my work and agree that satisfying and meaningful work is rewarding. But I think something is wrong when Americans are saying work is three times more important for a fulfilling life than marriage and children.

The public policy implications of this research showing a drop in crime after pregnancy are not clear. But what is clear is we should be thinking more about how our culture can do a better job conveying the importance of marriage and children.

Young Democrats Lose Interest in Freedom

Feb. 19. 2020

I happened to listen the other day to then-Sen. John F. Kennedy's opening remarks in his debate with then-Vice President Richard Nixon during the 1960 presidential election cycle.

Kennedy, the Democratic Party candidate, recalled that Abraham Lincoln, in the 1860 presidential election cycle, said the great question facing the nation was whether it could exist "half-slave and half-free."

In the 1960 election, said Kennedy, the issue was "whether the world will exist half-slave or half-free."

"Whether it will move in the direction of freedom, in the direction of the road that we are taking ... will depend in great measure upon what we do here in the United States," he said.

How things change. The Democrats' candidate in 1960 headlined freedom as the issue defining his campaign. Now, 60 years later, Democrats are moving down the road to nominating a socialist, pushing freedom as an American ideal out of the picture.

It is astounding that many Democrats are ready to cast aside the core value that has defined our nation, for which so many have fought and died.

One major part of the story is our youth.

Support for the two parties is divided by age.

In 2016, a majority of those under age 44 voted for Hillary Clinton. Fifty-five percent of those ages 18-29 voted for her, compared with 37% for Donald Trump. Trump received the majority of those 45 years and above.

It is our youth that is enamored with socialism and the socialist candidate.

In a recent Pew Research Center poll, 40% of Democrats ages 18-29 expressed preference for Sen. Bernie Sanders to be their party's candidate, compared with 25% of those 30-49, 13% of those 50-64 and 10% of those 65 and over.

In a Gallup poll, 51% of those ages 18-39 expressed a positive view of capitalism and 49% a positive view of socialism. Among those 40-54, 61% were positive about capitalism compared with 39% for socialism. And those 55 and over, 68% were positive about capitalism compared with 32% for socialism.

What's driving these young Democrats to the far left?

Niall Ferguson of Stanford University's Hoover Institution and consultant Eyck Freymann suggest, in an article in The Atlantic, "The Coming Generation War," that the capitalist America that worked for earlier generations is not working for these youth.

"They face stagnant real wages" and carry a large burden of student debt, they say.

It's a generation "to whom little has been given, and of whom much is expected," they continue.

I think it is just the opposite. It is a generation to whom much has been given and from whom little is expected.

When Kennedy ran for president in 1960, America's youth still faced a military draft. In 1960, 72% of Americans over 18 were married, compared with 50% today.

According to Pew, 78% of those ages 18-29 say it is acceptable for an unmarried couple to live together, even if they don't intend to get married.

Over the decade 2009-2019, there was a drop of 16% among those ages 23-39 who identify as Christian and an increase of 13% of those self-identifying as religiously unaffiliated.

And that age group doesn't vote. Since 1980, the percentage of eligible voters in their 20s who voted in presidential elections has averaged between 40% and 50%, compared with 65% to 75% of those over 45, Ferguson and Freymann report.

We have a generation of American youth today who have grown up in a culture of legal abortion and same-sex marriage, with little sense of responsibility to God and country.

Freedom is about personal responsibility, and these youth do not seem to be interested. They appear, rather, to be very open to the idea of turning their lives over to be run by a 78-year-old socialist.

Such values among our youth do not bode well for our future.

Meanwhile, the best near-term solution is keeping the nation under Republican control.

Democratic Establishment Tries to Bail Out Biden

March 4, 2020

South Carolina Democratic voters have revived Joe Biden's candidacy.

Maybe I should say that South Carolina Congressman Jim Clyburn has.

According to exit polls, 61% said Clyburn's endorsement of Biden was an "important factor" in their decision, and 27% said it was "the most important factor."

Clyburn explained Biden is his friend and has been a reliable vote for government programs that blacks like.

He also argued that with Biden on the ticket, reelection prospects for congressmen and congresswomen running for election down ticket would be better.

"We need to keep the House speakership under Nancy Pelosi," said Clyburn.

Now, the whole Democratic establishment is piling on to endorse Biden and push out Bernie Sanders. But are they being straight with us?

It goes back to my column of a few weeks ago: "It doesn't matter which Democrat wins."

Despite Sanders' socialist declarations, the realities that would result under him or under Biden are barely distinguishable.

The country is already well down the path to socialism. And without major reforms to take things in a different direction, it will only become more so.

The saying popularized by Karl Marx, summing up the ethos of communism, was, "From each according to his ability, to each according to his needs." That is, those with political power get the final say regarding who has what.

In our own country, we call these transfer payments. Government takes from one set of taxpayers and redistributes through government programs to others.

According to American Enterprise Institute economist Mark Perry, in 1950, transfer payments made up of less than 20% of the federal budget. By 2012, they were 70%.

Former Senate Banking Committee chairman Phil Gramm and former Bureau of Labor Statistics assistant commissioner John Early summarized the extent to which government now redistributes our economic resources (that is, how much socialism we already have) in a recent Wall Street Journal opinion column.

Per Gramm and Early, "More than 80% of all taxes" are paid by households with incomes in the top 40% and "more than 70% of government transfer payments" go to households with incomes in the bottom 40%.

We're talking about programs like Social Security, Medicare, Medicaid and food stamps—all told, around 95 federal programs.

The average household income in the bottom 20% is $4,908, say Gramm and Early. That household, they say, receives $45,389 in government transfers.

Without reforms, American socialism will just expand.

Unfunded liabilities—the projection of shortfall in current taxes to meet future requirements—of Social Security and Medicare are around $50 trillion, per trustees of the programs. That's more than twice our annual GDP.

Government needs to take more taxes to keep these programs going. That is, more socialism.

What are the chances that President Biden would

introduce reforms to bring more market forces into the picture? Did you say zero?

So a President Sanders or Biden, in the end, wouldn't be much different. At least Sanders is honest.

However, for a sitting senior congressman like Jim Clyburn, voting for Biden means his buddy of some 30 years would be sitting in the White House. Any question of whom he would prefer?

You might ask, “Doesn't all this government make us a more moral society?” Consider that when the War on Poverty began in 1967, 70% of those in households in the bottom 20% were working. Now it is 36%—about half.

The difference between socialism and charity is that the latter is voluntary, individualized and motivated by personal caring. Charity aims to lift up the unfortunate and usually originates with people of faith.

Socialism is an atheistic institutionalized system that pretends to solve human challenges through politics. It's why, in the end, it destroys the human spirit. This is the real problem in our poor communities.

So Bernie or Joe? There's little difference.

Democrats Blackmail a Nation in Crisis

March 25, 2020

I quoted Maj. Gen. George S. Patton in my column last week: "A good plan violently executed now is better than a perfect plan executed next week."

I'm repeating it because it is so relevant to the coronavirus crisis.

No one thinks the stimulus bill the Senate is trying to pass, which Democrats have sabotaged, is a perfect plan. There is something in it for everyone to criticize. But when the house is burning down, the job is to put the fire out as quickly as possible. A moment delay to look for a better way to do it can result in absolute destruction.

As Senate Majority Leader Mitch McConnell put it: "This is not a political opportunity. It's a national emergency."

Even calling this a stimulus bill is a misnomer.

It is more accurate to call this a bridge loan to ourselves.

Anyone who has operated a business understands that a bridge loan makes it possible for you to cross a valley between a difficult situation you are in, providing an opportunity to work through difficulties so you can get to the other side and once again function in a healthy way.

The assumption of a bridge loan is that you are, at the core, OK. Once you get through the storm, you will be OK again.

Bridge loans are not given to businesses that are deemed failing to begin with.

Before this health crisis hit, our economy was strong.

Our country is fundamentally strong. But we've taken an unusual and hard physical blow.

This is not like other economic crises, where the collapse was the result of some major flaw in our existing institutions or the way we are managing our affairs.

This crisis is the result of shutting down our economy because of an immediate health threat.

Economies function as buyers and sellers meet in the marketplace. If you tell buyers and sellers they are prohibited from showing up in the marketplace, everything will collapse.

This is where we are.

We need financing so businesses, particularly small businesses, can get to the other side, so that when we stop this scourge, hopefully sooner rather than later, they will not be wiped out, and will be able to get going again and pick up where they were before.

We also need to provide cash flow to individuals so those whose livelihood is cut off or limited can pay their bills and make it to the other side.

This is what this legislation is about. Period.

It's hard to believe that as we try to throw a lifeline to our economy, House Speaker Nancy Pelosi, Senate Minority Leader Chuck Schumer and their Democrats want to condition it on signing off on their left-wing agenda: the Green New Deal; tests on gender, race and ethnicity for business; government dictates on how businesses manage their financial affairs and how much they pay their executives. Sen. Elizabeth Warren, who has never run a business or met a payroll, wants to force minimum wage when companies are shedding their workforce in order to stay afloat.

It's like telling a patient on life support that he must sign off on gender-neutral restrooms before we agree to connect his ventilator.

Rep. Alexandria Ocasio-Cortez, who called this bill a "crony capitalist slush fund," recently helped kill the deal that would have brought a new Amazon headquarters to New York—the same Amazon that is now adding 100,000 new workers.

I don't like companies turning to Washington as the first reaction to a crisis. But it's Democrats who have played a central role in creating the welfare-state culture that has debilitated the nation.

But this isn't time for this discussion. This is a time for immediate action to save ourselves before mortal damage is inflicted, so we can live to see a better day.

Personal Retirement Accounts Will Help in Next Crisis

May 6, 2020

Congress passed and President Donald Trump signed into law the CARES Act to provide emergency measures to help us get through the economic crisis caused by the COVID-19 shutdown.

A crucial objective was to provide funds to the many individuals who suddenly found themselves cash-strapped and unable to pay bills because, through no fault of their own, they were out of work.

Two major provisions are $1,200 cash payments for individuals, and relaxing rules to allow withdrawal from or loans against IRAs, 401(k)s and other defined benefit retirement plans without penalties or tax consequences.

The cash payments received most of the attention. But the provisions for getting cash from retirement plans were a highly desirable addition. Ideally, it's best to be able to manage through a crisis with your own resources rather than government money.

If there is anything foreseen, it is that the unforeseen will always be part of our lives. We all should manage our personal affairs with this in mind. Living day to day, week to week, paycheck to paycheck is not how anyone should be managing their life.

You might say: "I'm working two jobs. I spend practically nothing on entertainment, and I still barely make it to the end of the month."

And here is where the right government policy can help you be freer to manage your own life.

I've been writing for years that Americans should be allowed to invest their payroll tax in their own personal retirement account. The payroll tax is what's used now to finance Social Security.

Many still think that Social Security is some kind of retirement investment plan. No, it's just another government tax and spend program.

Every year, retirees get Social Security payments. The funds come from the payroll tax that practically every working American pays.

It seemed like such a good idea when then-President Franklin D. Roosevelt signed it into law in 1935. Every working American would pay a small tax, and those funds would immediately go out and provide retirement income to retirees.

But back then, there were more than 40 Americans working for every retiree.

Today, our world is much different. Fewer are getting married. Fewer are having children. And the miracles of modern medicine give us a much longer life.

So instead of 40 working for every retiree, today there are around three.

According to the annual report issued by the Trustees of the Social Security Administration, in 2035, just 15 years from now, Social Security will only have funds to cover 76% of the benefits promised to retirees.

Either taxes must be raised, or benefits must be cut. Who wants either?

Doing so would make a bad deal even worse. According to a study commissioned by the Committee to Unleash Prosperity, the average annual return of Social Security over the last 40 years was about 1%. Over the same period, the stock market returned more than 6% annually.

According to the Federal Reserve, only 43.6% of working households earning $40,000 or less annually say they have any retirement savings. This means the only retirement provision the rest have is the payroll tax being taken out of their paycheck designated for Social Security.

Social Security Trustees are now telling those who are 52 years old or younger and expect to retire at 67 that they can expect just 76% of their benefits.

Now that President Trump is talking about the payroll tax as a policy tool to deal with this crisis, we should act.

Let's allow working Americans, or at least those earning $40,000 or less, to divert their payroll tax into their own retirement account.

They will get independence and have far more wealth when they retire.

And when the unforeseen is upon us again, when there is another crisis, they won't have to pray that the government will send them money. They will have their own savings, which they can tap into to get themselves through the crisis.

We're All on Welfare Now

May 13, 2020

I'm pleased to read that Republican leaders in the White House and on Capitol Hill want to take a pause before enacting more coronavirus stimulus spending.

Thinking about the coronavirus debt that my grandchildren will have to endure is already starting to keep me up at night.

But what really had me in cold sweats was when I found myself anxiously waiting for a Paycheck Protection Program loan, or PPP loan, to provide assistance to my struggling company.

I pondered, with deep angst, that after shedding myself of welfare dependency some 35 years ago, suddenly I find myself back in business with government.

Back when I was on means-tested welfare programs, the rules were "Don't work. Don't save. Don't get married," and my rich uncle in Washington would reach into someone else's pocket and provide me security and stability on his government plantation.

Now politicians are setting up commissions and oversight to allegedly assure compliance with the rules for the trillions of coronavirus stimulus dollars allocated.

I say allegedly because, sadly, it is largely a show with a storyline that we tell ourselves, pretending that politicians can design trillions in spending programs that are targeted and efficient and can be overseen to assure that it's all done right.

The PPP program consists of $659 billion in loans that will go to millions of businesses around the country.

Each of these businesses is unique. What does my Washington, D.C., nonprofit have in common with a dry cleaner or a restaurant? What does my organization of 12 employees have in common with a business of 500, the largest that qualifies for PPP loans?

Yet, the rules for using the PPP loan are the same for everyone.

The loans can become grants if 75% of the funds are used for payroll and the business is staffed as it was before the crisis.

But the way we are going to get out of this crisis is creativity, doing things in new and different ways.

Many businesses, including my own, will not and should not be the same. There should be a lot of change and reinventing going on.

Yet the condition for the government money is that you run your business as government tells you how to run it, and that you continue to operate it as you did before—both very bad ideas.

Also consider that the PPP was one part of the $2 trillion CARES Act package. Another part included a $600 weekly payment to the unemployed, over and above unemployment insurance.

So while the PPP demands that employers restore their workforce, many in that workforce are now being subsidized by government to stay out of work.

Of course, we are in unique circumstances that require government action. But the issue is not whether government should act but how.

All this could have been done without vast new expenditures and government micromanagement of our lives.

The point was to get cash to individuals and businesses to get through the crisis without interfering with individual autonomy.

This could have been done through a tax holiday, where individuals were sent back their 2019 taxes. If a business paid $30,000 in taxes in 2019, refund it.

And/or, as Peter Wallison of the American Enterprise Institute suggested, short-term credit forbearance could have been provided. Deferral of rent payments, mortgage payments, car payments, utilities, etc., could have been permitted, providing for payment later at a special low interest rate.

Brian Riedl at the Manhattan Institute estimates that what we've spent so far in this crisis will add another $8 trillion to our national debt, which was already approaching the size of our entire economy.

We've made a big mistake by dealing with a cash flow crisis by introducing massive new government spending, debt and political intervention into our personal lives.

Let's wait before doing more of the same.

COVID-19 to Elections 2020

May 20, 2020

With the House passage of Speaker Nancy Pelosi's $3 trillion Heroes Act, COVID-19 policy has now officially transformed into presidential politics 2020.

Let's recall that prior to the crisis, the nation appeared quite pleased with the leadership that President Donald Trump was providing.

The economy was growing at a brisk pace, with job creation robust and unemployment rates at historic lows.

In February, Gallup's monthly measure of national satisfaction hit 45%, the highest since 2004. During former President Barack Obama's eight years, it hovered between 20% and 30%.

Then the coronavirus hit.

The national satisfaction index dropped to 30%. The latest for May creeped up to 32%.

Coronavirus politics really has telescoped the core debate that was going on in the country before it.

Are we a nation driven by government or by people?

The theme of President Trump's 2016 campaign was draining the Washington swamp and returning America to its citizens, and he had been governing—tax cuts, deregulation—true to this theme, with great results.

COVID-19 has taken things in the opposite direction.

Shutdown policies and massive government action returned focus to government.

Few would argue that there was any alternative.

The question is: What now?

Drilling down further into the Gallup satisfaction poll,

we find that practically all the drop has been with Republicans.

Before the crisis, satisfaction among Republicans was at 80%. Now it's 48%. Among Democrats, there has been hardly any change.

From April to May, the percentage of Republicans saying the coronavirus is the most important problem facing the country dropped from 47% to 35%. Among Democrats, there was practically no change: 46% in April and 45% in May.

The number of Republicans saying the economy/jobs is the most important problem increased from 13% in April to 17% in May. Among Democrats, again there was practically no change: 6% in April and 7% in May.

It seems clear that Republicans are restless to start returning the country to freedom and Democrats are happy to leave leadership with government.

Pelosi's Heroes Act is responding to this.

We're already in uncharted territory regarding government.

Prior to this crisis, trillion-dollar deficits were news.

Back in 2018, a group of leading scholars from Stanford University's Hoover Institute—including former Secretary of State George Shultz, former Council of Economic Advisers Chair Michael Boskin and former Treasury Undersecretary for International Affairs John Taylor—authored a piece in The Washington Post titled "A Debt Crisis is on the Horizon." They warned of the dangers of the deficit increasing from $800 billion to a trillion and national debt increasing from $15 trillion to $20 trillion.

The Congressional Budget Office now estimates that the fiscal 2020 deficit will be $3.7 trillion.

This was recently updated by Brian Riedl of the Manhattan Institute with an estimate of $4.2 trillion. Riedl projects deficits for the next 10 years averaging almost $2 trillion per year. He estimates national debt reaching $41 trillion by 2030, or 128% of our gross domestic product.

Despite these mind-boggling figures, Nancy Pelosi wants to serve up to the nation another $3 trillion in spending, including a trillion to bail out states, extending the $600 weekly benefit above unemployment insurance, a new round of cash payments to individuals—including payments to undocumented workers—billions in housing assistance, etc.

We're at the fork in the road, and this fork will define presidential politics in 2020.

Has government done the major part of its thing to help us get through the coronavirus crisis, or are we going to keep moving to a new welfare state and socialist America?

Sentiments gleaned from the polls show the Republicans are ready to start turning things back to individuals.

Democrats? The Heroes Act says it all.

Government or freedom? This is the question pointing to November.

Opt out of Social Security for Racial Equity

Feb. 10, 2021

A recent Reuters headline read, "Yellen, Rice tout economics as key to fixing American inequality."

According to Susan Rice, President Joe Biden's new domestic policy adviser, "The evidence is clear, investing in equity is good for economic growth."

Our new Treasury secretary, Janet Yellen, says, "I believe economic policy can be a potent tool to improve society. We can—and should—use it to address inequality, racism ..."

I couldn't agree more.

According to the Federal Reserve's most recent Survey of Consumer Finances, the median wealth of white families is $188,200, compared with $24,100 for Black families.

To the extent that change in government policy can lift the median wealth of Black families, I am for it. The good news is there is such an opportunity.

I have been writing about it for many years. We should give working Americans the option to opt out of Social Security and use the taxes they are paying into it to invest in their own personally owned retirement account.

We'll achieve more racial equity by allowing low-income Americans the opportunity to have more equity in—ownership of—America.

A big reason for the huge wealth gap between white and Black families is the huge gap in ownership of equities—stock—between white and Black families.

According to the Pew Research Center, 61% of white families have either direct or indirect ownership in stocks. Only 31% of Black families do.

Per the Federal Reserve, among white Americans ages 35 to 54, 65% have at least one retirement account. Among Blacks in this age range, only 44% do.

It is true that median Black household income is also lower than median white household income, meaning Blacks on average have less to save and invest. Which is why giving the option to opt out of Social Security is so vitally important.

Every working American pays 12.4% of their income to Social Security, half taken out of their paycheck and half paid by their employer.

This is a tax, not an investment. The government then uses this tax revenue to recycle and make payments to those currently retired, who themselves paid taxes during their working life.

The Committee to Unleash Prosperity, working with the nonpartisan Tax Foundation, recently calculated what working families at different income levels would have earned at retirement if they could have invested their payroll tax rather than paying into Social Security.

For instance, a low-income couple who started working in 1971 and retired in 2015, where one earner earned 45% of the national median income and the other 25%, would have gotten an annual Social Security benefit of $21,035. If that same couple could have invested 10% of their paychecks in a stock fund over the same period, using actual historic data for this 45-year period, they would have had $738,360 at retirement that could produce $40,610 annual income for them—almost double what they would get from Social Security.

They would also have the benefits of ownership. They could bequeath what remains to their heirs.

Per the Federal Reserve, 29.9% of white Americans say they have benefited from inheritance or some other family gift. Only 10.1% of Black Americans say they have received an inheritance or family gift.

If Black Americans do not feel part of and invested in the nation, as they should, one reason is that they are disenfranchised by the same government that claims it wants to help.

So, Secretary Yellen, policy adviser Rice, how about getting on board with me? How about showing Black Americans, and all Americans, that you really want to level the playing field?

The Social Security Trustees report that by 2034, the system will have insufficient funds to meet obligations.

Ownership, rather than more government, is the answer.

Now we just need courageous leadership.

A Message to Delta CEO Bastian From a Delta Diamond Flyer

April 7, 2021

The controversy surrounding the new voting law in the state of Georgia raises important issues regarding the governance of our country and the role of corporations.

Corporations are big and have a lot of economic clout, so there is justified concern about them abusing this economic power.

It's why there are such strict lobbying laws in Washington. We want to make sure that corporations don't step over the line of representing their legitimate interests in legitimate ways.

Corporations such as Atlanta-based Delta are now falling over themselves to see who can be the most zealously out front and condemn Georgia's new voting law.

After President Biden, who called the new Georgia law "Jim Crow on steroids," suggested that Major League Baseball pull the All-Star Game out of Atlanta, MLB Commissioner Rob Manfred wasted little time to announce plans to do just that.

But isn't the key issue about the "democracy" of the voting law? And wasn't Georgia's law passed by a democratically elected state legislature and signed into law by a democratically elected governor? Who are these multinational businesses to condemn what Georgians passed into law by their own state democracy? Who is Major League Baseball to use its economic clout to punish Georgians for a voting law that was passed legitimately and legally through the machinery of their own democracy?

According to Statista, 32% of Major League Baseball fans are Republicans, 38% are Democrats, and 30% are independents. Manfred reportedly earns $11 million in compensation to serve this diverse group of fans what they want—great baseball. One widely quoted businessman now claims Atlanta will lose $100 million in tourist revenue as a result of pulling the game. Who is hurt here, and why?

When CEOs speak out in the name of their company, they are not speaking as private citizens but as an employee of their company. They are paid to serve customers and produce value for owners—shareholders.

I happen to have Delta Million Miler Status and Diamond Medallion Status. I make considerable effort to adjust my flight plans so I can maintain this status.

It does not please me at all to discover that Delta CEO Ed Bastian does not spend every waking minute of his time on the job making sure customers like me get the best service possible.

Somehow, Bastian and other corporate CEOs have mistakenly concluded that they are being paid tens of millions for their opinions on voting law and matters concerning black Americans. As a black American and Delta Diamond traveler, I disagree with everything I have heard from Bastian on both these matters, and I urge him to spend his time on what he is paid to do.

Here's what famed economist Milton Friedman had to say on the subject in his classic text "Capitalism and Freedom": "The view has been gaining widespread acceptance that corporate officials ... have a 'social responsibility' that goes beyond serving the interest of their stockholders ..."

He continues: "Few trends could so thoroughly

undermine the very foundations of our free society as the acceptance by corporate officials of a social responsibility other than to make as much money for their stockholders as possible."

In 2019, Delta had 91,000 employees worldwide and around 30,000 in Atlanta. As private citizens, the 30,000 who live in Georgia can exercise their political proclivities as they choose. In this way, Delta influences local politics. However, the common interest of all Delta employees worldwide is the economic welfare, the business, of the firm that pays them.

No doubt it is the left-wing activism of groups like Black Lives Matter, and the Democrats with this agenda who now control the White House and Congress, that has motivated CEOs to step out on Georgia's voting law.

In doing so, they are abusing the economic power of their firms and, as a result, damaging the economy and the political integrity of our nation.

Biden's Era of Big Government

May 5, 2021

When I began my work 25 years ago, my vision for fixing our poor, broken communities was driven by my belief in America and what made it successful.

It's what I call the 3 C's: the principles of Christianity, the virtues of capitalism and the rule of law outlined in our Constitution.

After the civil rights movement, big government was deemed necessary to turn poor communities around.

When then-President Johnson affixed his signature to the Civil Rights Act of 1964, the given assumption was that, although there was new law protecting freedom—civil rights—for all, low-income Black Americans were not prepared to be free and capable of being free.

A new era of big government ushered welfare-state socialism into these communities.

Despite tens of trillions of federal expenditures targeted toward these communities since the 1960s, poverty rates are practically unchanged. But major new problems were created—mainly the decimation of families. Single-parent homes and out-of-wedlock births have tripled.

Today's Democrats want to blame racism for the persistence of problems in low-income communities. In some respect, they are right. It is their own racism that refused and refuses to accept that low-income Americans can and must be free.

Now, today, President Biden and his party aspire to the opposite of what I have fought for.

Instead of wanting to bring the capitalism of the

healthy parts of America to the broken parts of the country, they want to bring the failed welfare-state socialism of the broken parts of the country to the rest of the country.

The $6 trillion spending blowout of the first 100 days of the Biden administration, sold under the guise of COVID-19 recovery, has been about using the COVID-19 crisis to sell a new era of welfare-state big-government socialism that will fundamentally change our country forever.

The U.S. economy was already well underway to recovery in the latter half of last year, and in the first quarter of 2021, it surged 6.4%, taking our gross domestic product almost to where it was pre-COVID-19.

Contrary to the president's rhetoric, the case for the connection between prosperity and freedom is about facts, not ideology.

Each year, the Fraser Institute publishes its Economic Freedom of the World report, which consistently shows that nations with more economic freedom—smaller government, lower taxes, less regulation—have the highest incomes and lowest poverty rates.

In his address to Congress, the president assured the American people that he can finance all this big government by getting the wealthy and big corporations to pay their "fair share."

But facts about who foots the tax bill tell a different story than the president's ideology-colored stories.

According to the nonpartisan Tax Foundation, which used the latest data available from the IRS, in 2018, the top 1% of all taxpayers paid 40.1% of all taxes. The top 50% of taxpayers paid 97.1% of all federal taxes. And the bottom 50% paid the remaining 2.9%.

What about corporations? Again, facts tell a different

story.

Corporate income taxes simply punish labor with lower wages and punish customers with higher prices. Boston University economist Laurence Kotlikoff estimates that a zero percent corporate tax rate, which would focus taxes only on individuals, would increase wages 12%.

Giving the nation a civics lesson worthy of one of our failing public schools, President Biden used in his address the opening words of the preamble to the Constitution—"We the People ..."—to justify big government.

But that preamble says that the Constitution was established to "secure the Blessings of Liberty to ourselves and our Posterity."

Sen. Tim Scott, in his response to the president, noted what he experiences, and what I have experienced all my working life: that Blacks who speak about freedom and biblical values are met with derision and ridicule from the left.

Scott spoke truth. America is about freedom under God. Achieving this is today's great challenge.

Birth Dearth About Values, Not Economics

May 12, 2021

The Centers for Disease Control and Prevention reports that births in the USA reached another historic low in 2020.

For the sixth consecutive year, the birth rate dropped—this time by 4%. The average annual drop in the five previous years was 2%.

The rate at which American women are having babies is way below the rate necessary to keep the population steady-state—that is, for the population not to shrink.

A steady-state population requires a total fertility rate of 2.1 children per woman. In 2020, it was 1.64.

Needless to say, for politicians, there is no problem that does not have a government solution, and the birth dearth is no exception.

Both President Joe Biden and Sen. Mitt Romney have plans for bolstering American families. The president's American Families Plan proposes to spend a modest $1.8 trillion. Romney is pitching his Family Security Act, which proposes per-child government payments up to $1,250 per family per month.

Romney writes in The Wall Street Journal, "Young people are marrying less and having fewer kids in part because they don't feel confident about their job prospects and financial security."

But if less marriage and fewer children are the result of today's economic stress, why is it that in 1960, the fertility rate was 3.58—more than double today's 1.64—yet today's real per capita income, per the Federal Reserve Bank of St. Louis, is over three times higher than it was in 1960?

According to the Institute for Family Studies, in 2018, 35% of Americans ages 25 to 50 had never been married. In 1970, only 9% in this age range had never been married.

Is this because times got harder? I don't think so. Per capita income in 2018 was 2.4 times higher than it was in 1970.

I don't think our young people are avoiding marriage and children because of concerns about financial security.

I think they are avoiding marriage and children because they don't want marriage and children.

In a Pew Research survey conducted in 2019, 16% said having children is essential for a man to have a fulfilling life, and 16% said marriage is essential for a man to have a fulfilling life, while 57% said "having a job or career they enjoy" is essential for a man to have a fulfilling life.

Regarding women, 22% said having children is essential for a fulfilling life. Seventeen percent said marriage is essential for a fulfilling life. And 46% said "having a job or career they enjoy" is essential for a fulfilling life.

What does it all mean?

In 1960, 9.1% of our population was over age 65. By 2019, 16.2% of the population was over 65.

A graying population, due to fewer and fewer children, means a shrinking portion of the population that is working and producing, and increasingly large numbers of elderly and retirees whom those working must support.

Consider our Social Security system, where retirees' benefits are drawn from the payroll tax paid by working citizens. In 1945, there were 41.9 working citizens for every retiree. By 1950, this was down to 16.5 to 1. By 1990, it was

3.4 to 1. And as of 2013 (the latest data available), it was 2.8 to 1.

Trustees of Social Security report that by 2034, 13 years from now, the system will only have sufficient revenue to pay 76% of the benefits due to retirees.

Per the Kaiser Family Foundation, in 2016, those age 65 and over constituted 16% of our population yet represented 36% of all health care spending.

The collapse of marriage, family and the national birthrate is the result of the secularization of our culture. Faith and values have been displaced by materialism and egotism.

How do we turn it around? As a starter, let's have more parental choice in education so parents can get their children out of public schools and into religious schools, where they can learn values that sustain life.

Bogus Claims From the Poor People's Campaign

July 14, 2021

The Poor People's Campaign has announced a "season of nonviolent, moral direct action," targeting the U.S. Senate with disruptive activities every Monday, July 12 through Aug 2.

According to the campaign's co-chair, the Rev. William Barber II, "The Senate must end the filibuster, protect and expand voting rights, and pass a minimum wage of $15 an hour."

Barber is getting national attention. Even President Joe Biden recorded a video expressing his support.

Concern about poverty is something we all share.

What bothers me is that the factors driving poverty, according to the research of my organization and others, are ignored by the Poor People's Campaign. And the issues on which they choose to focus either have nothing to do with the reality of poverty or actually make things worse.

It may surprise Barber that the Senate filibuster is a powerful tool to protect minority interests.

He is either confused or disingenuous when he claims abolishing the Senate filibuster is about protecting "democracy."

It is not democracy he cares about, but Democrats, who now control the government, being able to pass every piece of far-left, big-government legislation they want. The only thing that stands in their way is the 60-vote requirement of the Senate filibuster.

The history of our American democracy is that

government changes hands all the time. When Republicans are running the show, as they will again, Barber will direct his heavenly prayers to save the filibuster so that Democrats can prevent Republicans from doing whatever they want.

It is the filibuster in the Senate that prevents passage of the For the People Act, the voting and election reform legislation, House Resolution 1, that passed in the House without a single Republican vote.

Although HR 1 is being labelled as "voting rights" legislation, it addresses many more aspects of election law than just voting. The legislation eviscerates actions that Republican states have moved on to reduce voter fraud, such as voter ID laws and stopping vote harvesting. But it also moves the federal government into a host of other areas, such as defining political speech and the organization of the Federal Election Commission.

The issue here is not to debate election law but to ask what this has to do with poverty and why it is such a priority for the Poor People's Campaign.

In the current Congress, there are 60 African American senators and House representatives. In 1964, there were five.

Per The Wall Street Journal's Jason Riley, in 1970, nationwide, there were fewer than 1,500 Black elected officials. Today, there are more than 10,000.

In the 2008 and 2012 presidential elections, Black turnout was higher than white turnout.

Yet in 2019, the average Black poverty rate was more than 2 1/2 times higher than the white poverty rate.

There is little evidence that Black poverty has persisted over the last half-century because Black Americans have not been able to accumulate political power or express their will on election day.

Regarding minimum wage, economic logic and economic facts show that the higher the minimum wage, the more low-wage jobs disappear. Raising the minimum wage is a great tool to make poverty worse, not better.

What can make a difference?

In 2019, the average poverty rate among American households was 9%. The average poverty rate in Black households headed by a married couple was 6.4%, per Statistica.

However, the average poverty rate in Black households headed by a single woman was 29.5%, and 41% of Black households were headed by single women.

But the Poor People's Campaign has nothing to say about the data connecting family breakdown and abortion to poverty.

Many Americans do understand this connection, including my organization, CURE. So, when the Poor People's Campaign storms the Senate over the next four weeks with bogus claims, we hope our elected officials will heed other voices.

Ben & Jerry's Takes Liberal Distortions Global

July 28, 2021

Ben & Jerry's, noted for its ice cream made from "contented cows," has produced not such contented consumers in many circles following its announcement to stop selling its ice cream in Israel's West Bank and in East Jerusalem.

Although the announcement calls these areas "occupied territories," more accurate would be to describe their status as "disputed" territories regarding Israel's sovereignty.

These are areas captured by Israel after the Six-Day War in 1967.

Let's keep in mind that Israel has been in a battle for survival since its founding in 1948.

Israelis are survivors, not conquerors. If not for incessant hostility by its Arab neighbors, the Six-Day War, in which these territories were captured, never would have taken place.

But the point here is the consistency of the confused minds of liberals, that now Ben & Jerry's shows knows no borders.

The history of the company is proudly recounted on the firm's website, relating how Ben Cohen and Jerry Greenfield started it in 1978 with a $12,000 investment ($4,000 borrowed) and a $5 correspondence course in ice-cream making.

Prominent in telling their story is their emphasis on how important "core values" are to them.

But the “core values” they ignore are the values that made their success possible.

Those are the values of freedom and capitalism that make possible starting a small business and building it into a multimillion-dollar enterprise.

In all likelihood, the grandparents of Cohen and Greenfield immigrated to the United States one or two generations before they were born, most likely from Europe. Like most Jewish immigrants, they came to America for freedom and opportunity.

Had their grandparents remained where they were, the chances that their grandchildren would be worth hundreds of millions of dollars today are zero.

Yet their grandchildren, who have achieved so much, do not include freedom and capitalism among the values that they list as important to them.

Greenfield has been a supporter of socialist Sen. Bernie Sanders.

And last year, after the George Floyd incident, the firm announced on their website, “We Must Dismantle White Supremacy.”

The announcement reminded their consuming public of the firm's commitment to Black Lives Matter.

This is the Black Lives Matter that I wrote about last week that attributes poverty in Cuba not to the communists who run the place but to the United States of America.

Like so many wealthy liberals, although freedom and capitalism made them rich, they want to deprive those who do not have those very values that could make the same possible for them.

But Ben & Jerry's is not satisfied promoting moral relativism and big government in the U.S., limiting opportunity for the poor in America; they want to bring the same misguided worldview to the Middle East.

Over 100 years ago, when Jews started returning to their ancient homeland, there was nothing there. As author and businessman George Gilder has written, from 1921 to 1943, the new Jewish immigration increased the number of enterprises in the region fourfold, the number of jobs tenfold and the amount of capital investment one-hundredfold.

Today, Israel's $43,610 per capita GDP is more than 10 times the average of their neighboring countries. This growth has benefited Arabs as well as Jews.

But the liberal mind knows no logic. Only its distorted worldview.

Ben & Jerry's is not interested in condemning mismanaged neighboring Arab countries for not providing opportunity for their own citizens. They reserve their protest for the one country in the region, Israel, that is working for both Jews and Arabs, due to hard work, creativity, and economic freedom and opportunity.

Ben & Jerry's wants to spread their left-wing values across the globe, limiting opportunity for the world's poor.

Like all those from the left, the company damages exactly those who it claims to care about and want to help, all in the name of "core values."

Democrats Spend Big, and We Pay, for Their Socialist Dream

Sept. 15, 2021

In 1983, Tom Cruise starred in the film "Risky Business." It's about wealthy parents in Chicago who go on vacation and leave the house under the stewardship of their high school-age son.

In short order, the boy throws a wild party, and the rest of the film is about the chaotic fallout.

It's the closest thing I can think of to capture current reality in Washington as the kids—the Democrats running the White House and Congress—throw their big party and breathlessly spend their parents' money (in this case, our money), knowing that the party will be over when adults return.

The $3.5-plus trillion spending binge that Democrats are rushing to pass is not following a period of austerity. Record spending and debt have been piled on since the Obama years, using government to spend its way out of a government-induced economic collapse. And then we had the COVID-19 challenge and massive new government spending to get out of that.

Per the Cato Institute's Chris Edwards, in 2001, the amount of federal debt per U.S. household was $30,684. By 2011, this was up to $84,470, and now it is at $179, 082. If the Democrats succeed with their $3.5 trillion binge, federal debt per U.S. household by 2031 will be up to $288,047.

Of course, this needs to be financed by taxes as well as borrowing, and the result will be higher taxes on corporations and on capital gains.

Perhaps you recall that the year after Donald Trump was elected president, a major tax bill was passed cutting corporate taxes, and the result was an economic surge from which all income classes in the country benefited. This will be reversed. Higher taxes mean slower growth.

It's not like we're looking at essential expenditures that must be made for our national well-being. Most of this spending is not about fixing roads and bridges and strengthening our military.

Most of it is to build the socialist paradise that Senate Budget Chairman Bernie Sanders and House Speaker Nancy Pelosi dream about: new household entitlements, new employer mandates, Medicare benefits expansion and all kinds of corporate welfare subsidies in the name of the Green New Deal and industrial policy spending.

But let's get to perhaps the most fundamental point.

These are so-called political leaders that pretend to care about America's poor.

The last thing that America's poor need is a slowed-down, sluggish economy, larded down by massive new government.

Furthermore, our federal government sets a horrible example for financial management for all American households. You don't take on new debts when you haven't dealt with the debts that are currently on your doorstep.

On Aug. 31, the latest annual reports from the Social Security and Medicare Trustees landed on the desks of Pelosi and the president of the Senate, Vice President Kamala Harris.

These reports show both programs gushing red ink and hovering on bankruptcy.

By 2034, just 13 years from now, Social Security will

have cash flow to meet just 78% of its obligations. Its overall projected shortfall over the next 75 years is $19.8 trillion.

The Medicare Hospital Insurance Trust Fund will be bankrupt by 2026. In 2020, of the $925.8 billion in Medicare spending, only $430.3 billion was paid for by payroll taxes and premiums. The rest was borrowed, amounting to almost 16% of the federal deficit.

But not a word about this while Democrats push for massive new spending and debt.

Not only not a word, but they want to layer on new entitlements to Medicare, already gushing red ink, that will cost, per The Wall Street Journal, another $360 billion over the next decade.

The good news is President Joe Biden's approval rate is falling, meaning that adults are paying attention. Hopefully we can hold on until the adults return in 2022, before the kids destroy everything.

America Is Still Working

Sept. 29, 2021

The Census Bureau has just issued its latest annual report, "Income and Poverty in the United States: 2020," and American Enterprise Institute economist and blogger Mark Perry has extracted and summarized its highlights, as he does every year.

Perry's work is always illuminating because the data shows how much healthier the country is socially and economically than anyone would believe who listens to the naysayers on the left, who want to transform America into a giant, socialist welfare state.

Contrary to what we hear from Democrats and the left-leaning media, Americans continue to move up and earn more.

And those who don't fail to do so for reasons that are entirely in their control, as I will explain later.

In 2020, 33.6% of American households had income of $100,000 or more, 40.3% had income between $35,000 and $100,000, and 26.2% had income of less than $35,000.

In 1967, only 10.9% of American households had earnings of $100,000 or more (in constant, inflation-adjusted dollars). That is, from 1967 to 2020, the percentage of American households earning $100,000 or more has tripled!

Compared with 1967, the percentage of middle-income earning households—$35,000 to $100,000—has shrunk, 53.9% in 1967 compared with 40.3% in 2020.

The percentage of middle-income households has shrunk because more households have moved into the upper-income category.

The percentage earning $35,000 has shrunk from 35.2% in 1967 to 26.2% in 2020.

Perry then drills down into the data and looks at household income and household demographics to see how they correlate.

His conclusions:

"Specifically, high-income U.S. households have more income-earners on average than lower-income households, and individuals in high-income households are far more likely on average than individuals in low-income households to be well-educated, married, working full-time, and in their prime earning years. In contrast, individuals in lower-income U.S. households are far more likely than Americans in higher-income households to be less-educated, working part-time, either very young (under 35 years) or very old (over 65 years), and living in single-parent or single-member households."

We get a much different picture here than the message that politically correct woke culture, which has attained such influence over recent years, has transmitted.

Any individual's fate in America is very much in their own hands and the result of how much personal responsibility they want to take in their own life.

Major factors that correlate with earning power—education, work, family—start with personal decisions and personal responsibility.

Readers might recall the incident I reported last year when my organization, CURE, posted billboards in various low-income communities saying that if you want to get out of poverty—finish school, go to work and get married.

Black Lives Matter protested and got the billboard

company to remove our message.

That's not to say that there is not public policy work that needs to be done. But it's not what we hear from the left. The work to relieve poverty and improve upward mobility is work that removes obstacles for individuals to take personal responsibility for their lives.

Obstacles like our union-controlled, government-controlled public school systems. Parents should control their child's education, not government and union bureaucrats.

This week, my organization, CURE, is releasing its first State of Black America report, published in partnership with the Claremont Institute.

The report points to the strength of American principles and points to cultural and institutional obstacles that contribute to the perpetuation of poverty—too much government and too much politics—as factors that pull us away from those principles and truths.

The Census Bureau's "Income and Poverty in the United States: 2020" report shows that America is still working.

It can work even better if we strengthen, not weaken, as the left wants, the great principles of a free nation under God that defined our founding.

Progressives Versus Independent Contractors

Oct. 20, 2021

Despite being a politician all his life, and never having worked in a blue-collar job, President Joe Biden declared, "I'm a union man," when he announced his presidential campaign at a Teamsters union hall in Pittsburgh in April 2019.

What our president really loves is big government and political power, and there is no more reliable money trough for Democrats than unions.

According to OpenSecrets, which tracks political spending, Biden's campaign received $27.5 million in contributions from unions, compared with $360,000 from unions that went to former President Donald Trump's campaign.

So, it is no surprise that the president and his party are now unfurling legislation aimed at protecting unions. It's called the PRO Act—Protecting the Right to Organize.

The bill passed in the House, but with little prospect of it making it on its own in the evenly split Senate, Senate Democrats have buried it in the budget reconciliation bill that can pass with a simple majority and is not subject to filibuster.

What certain unions want is to take the country in the opposite direction where it needs to go in this new era of global competition and technology-enabled freelancing. But other unions, like those that represent truckers and journalists, are concerned about independent contractors being run out of their jobs.

Among the various major provisions of the PRO Act is effective nationalization of California's AB5 law that passed in 2019. This law makes hiring independent contractors much more difficult and specifies that contractors must be reclassified by businesses that hire them as employees, unless they meet specific and rigorous standards allowing them to stay independent.

The PRO Act takes direct aim at the powerful new technology-enabled trend referred to as the “gig economy.” These are freelancers and entrepreneurs of many different stripes who are buying into the flexibility of this new high-tech economy.

But entrepreneurship and flexibility are exactly what big-government politicians and certain special interest unions don't want.

Proposition 22 passage in November 2020 provided protection for app-based transportation and delivery firms, such as Uber, Lyft and DoorDash, from AB5.

But this still leaves many independent contractors subject to the law. This includes many truckers who are independent operators and are impacted by these onerous new requirements.

Truckers are seeking relief through the courts, now principally through the California Trucking Association moving its case to be heard in the Supreme Court. Meanwhile, truckers have gotten a court injunction to hold up their need to submit to AB5 requirments.

Another significant provision of the PRO Act would be the effective elimination of right-to-work laws that exist today in 27 states.

Right-to-work laws enable workers in unionized workplaces that do not wish to join the union and pay dues to opt out. The PRO Act eliminates this option and forces all workers to pay union dues.

Considerable academic research points to positive economic results in right-to-work states in the way of higher employment growth, higher productivity, higher population growth and higher personal income growth compared with states without right-to-work laws.

The Census Bureau reports annually on net population outbound and inbound for every state.

In the most recent report, 9 of the 10 states with the highest population inbound were right-to-work states, and 8 of the 10 states with the highest population outbound were forced-unionization states.

It is no accident that today, the number of American workers in unions is about half what it was 40 years ago.

We are entering into new times. Sweeping change was already taking place before COVID-19 hit us. Now our post-COVID-19 economy is reemerging with new realities.

For our marketplace to get where it needs to go, we must embrace change, embrace the new, embrace entrepreneurship and flexibility. These are all things progressives don't want. If the PRO Act becomes law, today's challenges regarding labor and supply shortages will just get worse.

It's time to embrace the new.

Build Back Better—Wasting Trillions

Nov. 17, 2021

As Democrats regroup to try to pass their $2 trillion Build Back Better Act, pressure grows for shining the light of fiscal responsibility on all this.

Given President Joe Biden's crashing approval ratings, there is some hint that the American people smell a rat.

One sign of the smell of that rat is the alarming escalation of the rate of inflation to where it hasn't been in over 30 years.

Let's start with the announcement from the Treasury Department a week ago that the revenue measures built in to finance the $2 trillion in spending will not only not add to the nation's existing fiscal deficit but will reduce it.

The headline from the Treasury department reads "Preliminary Estimates Show Build Back Better Legislation Will Reduce Deficits." The document shows an estimate of $2.151 trillion in revenue raising measures against $2 trillion in spending.

However, the University of Pennsylvania Wharton School of Business has its own model, overseen by a professor with extensive experience in the Congressional Budget Office and the Treasury Department. According to the Wharton model, Build Back Better will add $500 billion to the federal deficit.

Treasury says the Build Back Better cuts the deficit by $151 billion. Wharton says it increases it by $500 billion. Not exactly a trivial difference.

Who do we believe?

The Congressional Budget Office will also weigh in.

But it still leaves us with the question of who to believe.

It isn't about one place having better economists than the other.

The problem is that it is impossible to make meaningful forecasts with such huge amounts of funds, all of which are highly politicized.

Anyone who has ever run a business knows what I am talking about.

I run a small business with revenues of a few million dollars a year. Even at a few million dollars a year, it is a great challenge to do accurate projections.

If it is hard at a few million, how about at $6.5 trillion, which is where the federal budget stands this year?

The corporation with the largest revenue in the country is Walmart. It's about $560 billion, or about 10% of the federal budget.

I am sure if you ask any analyst in Walmart's budgeting department, they will tell you how hard it is to project. But aside from the amounts we're talking about, there is another huge difference between what is going on in any private business, at Walmart, and at the federal government.

In private business, we are spending our own funds. In a big corporation like Walmart, they are spending their shareholders' funds. Every single individual spending and investing these funds is held personally responsible. If they are irresponsible, they get fired.

But where is the personal responsibility for the trillions being spent by the federal government?

The 100 Democrat progressives who are pushing so hard for this $2 trillion in spending have zero personal responsibility to assure that these funds are spent in an effective and responsible way. It is all politics. They dream up programs that sound so beautiful. But the realities of these programs submit to no responsible individual scrutiny.

Americans work too hard for their income on which they are paying taxes to have these funds expropriated by those who have political power but no personal responsibility.

In addition, inflation is also a tax. When the government doesn't explicitly take the funds through taxes and prints the money to meet obligations, this shows up as inflation, which then hits every working American.

In 1900, federal government nondefense spending amounted to 1.8% of our economy; in 1950, it was 10.4%; in 2000, it was 14.8%; and in 2021, it was 28.5%.

Far too much of your money and mine is being taken by politicians to wastefully spend.

Hopefully the $2 trillion won't make it into law.

Saule Omarova Shouldn't Be Overseeing our Banks

Nov. 24, 2021

It is ironic when Democrats complain about sensational use of language.

Thanks to progressives, practically every white person in America has been labelled a racist.

But now Democrats are screaming because Republican Sen. John Kennedy suggested that Saule Omarova, whom President Joe Biden has nominated to head the Office of the Comptroller of the Currency—the nation's top banking regulator—might be a communist.

Kennedy opened his questioning of Omarova at her Senate Committee on Banking, Housing and Urban Affairs confirmation hearing asking if he should call her "professor or comrade."

Distinct from the labels and charges we regularly hear from progressives, there is substance to the senator's suggestion about Omarova's proclivities.

No, it's not that she was born in Soviet-controlled Kazakhstan, or that her degree is from Moscow State University, or even that her doctoral thesis is entitled "Karl Marx's Economic Analysis and the Theory of Revolution in the Capital."

It is about how she views the world.

This is someone who will oversee our nation's banking system that wants to "end banking as we know it" and transfer vast parts of it to government control.

Maybe we must read Omarova's doctoral dissertation to get a handle on the fine points of what we call communism.

But if turning our financial services system over to government control is not communism, suffice it to say it certainly is not what America is supposed to be about.

She proposes that the Federal Reserve, the least accountable entity in the federal government, take over a vast swath of private banking functions, with private banking accounts being replaced by accounts run by the Fed.

If there is a microsecond where you might think this is a good idea, look at what's happening now to prices at the gas pump and at the supermarket, where we see inflation at a 30-year high. Consider where this is coming from.

Yes, the Federal Reserve. Journals and newspapers burst with warnings from private economists over recent years that Federal Reserve monetary policy will lead to inflation, and Fed Chairman Jerome Powell has been poo-pooing these warnings.

Now it's happening. And this is who professor/comrade Omarova thinks should be taking over the full scope of our financial lives.

If you think turning over your financial security to the wise stewardship of the Federal Reserve is a good idea, consider that the Federal Reserve was created in 1913 with motivations not that different from those of Omarova. The whole idea then was that giving a government entity control over our monetary system would bring stability.

Under this great government stabilizing influence, we have been through the Great Depression of the 1930s, double-digit inflation and interest rates in the 1970s, and, most recently, a severe financial meltdown in 2008.

Since the Fed's creation in 1913, per economist and blogger Mark Perry, the consumer price index has increased by "27.25 times which has caused the U.S. dollar to lose 96.3% of its value/purchasing power." The 1913 dollar is today worth 3.67 cents.

There are notable other areas where Omarova wants much more government power, such as giving government planners vastly more power over climate control policy—to the extent of intentionally driving small oil and gas businesses to bankruptcy.

Maybe why so many Democrats, including our president, take offense at Kennedy's communist labeling is because they take his accusations personally.

The Wall Street Journal calls the Build Back Better multitrillion dollar spending frenzy, just passed in the House, "the biggest expansion of the entitlement state since the 1960s, and maybe ever."

We have two competing views in America today. One sees private property, individual freedom and personal responsibility as the answer to our problems. The other sees it as the source of our problems.

The first view I call American. The second—well, if not communist, certainly it is not American.

Please, Senators, do not confirm Saule Omarova to oversee our nation's banking system.

Democrats Spend Low-Income Americans Into Poverty

March 30, 2022

I have been writing for years about how progressive policies championed by the Democratic Party and served up under the guise of caring about low-income Americans wind up hurting these very communities.

The latest chapter in this saga is the newly unleashed round of inflation, the worst our country has seen in 40 years.

Two important points here are that first, we can lay responsibility for this inflation directly at the doorstep of the Biden administration, and second, those being hurt most by this inflation are the very low-income Americans that this administration claims to care so much about.

A recent report from the Federal Reserve Bank of Minneapolis focuses on the disparate impact of inflation on different communities, causing the most damage to low-income Americans.

According to the report, although one number for inflation is reported nationally, different households do not equally take the brunt of this.

According to a Gallup survey from late 2021, 45.5% of all Americans reported experiencing "severe" or "moderate" hardship caused by inflation.

However, the story changes dramatically when broken down by income. Among those with incomes of less than $40,000, 70.7% say they are experiencing "severe" or "moderate" hardship. And 46.5% of those earning from $40,000 to $99,999 and 28.3% of those earning $100,000 or above reported experiencing "severe" or "moderate" hardship.

The report offers various explanations about why inflation hits lower-income households harder. These include the fact that lower-income households have a lower percentage of interest-bearing assets, meaning their world is mostly cash. And inflation takes its highest toll on cash.

Higher-income households have more flexibility in adjusting behavior than do lower-income households. And lower-income households tend to be renters rather than homeowners, and rent is more volatile in an inflationary environment.

The tragedy is that inflation is not a surprise attack. We know what causes inflation. Like many physical diseases, we know what their causes are, and those that become victims do so not out of lack of knowledge, but out of irresponsible behavior.

Despite the fact that we know the damage that smoking causes, or excessive drinking, or improper diet, people still do it.

We know that inflation is caused by pouring excessive money into the economy. If today an apple costs $1, and tomorrow the government prints another dollar, without producing another apple, the price of an apple will jump to $2.

Economists were widely reporting that the Biden administration was spending too much money and that this profligate spending was being enabled by the Federal Reserve.

Harvard economist and former Treasury Secretary Lawrence Summers wrote in The Washington Post last May, almost a year ago, "The inflation risk is real," noting that the problem is “overheating, and not excessive slack.”

This in the wake of the Biden administration's $1.9 trillion relief spending and the beginning of trying to pass the $4 trillion Build Back Better program, stopped by the courageous renegade senator from West Virginia, Joe Manchin.

Meanwhile, the Federal Reserve, under the leadership of chairman Jerome Powell, in its statement at the end of last April, was still predicting 2% inflation and calling the current jump in prices “transitory.”

In July of 2021, economists Steve Hanke of Johns Hopkins University and John Greenwood of Invesco predicted in The Wall Street Journal that, “By the end of the year, the year-over-year inflation rate will be at least 6% and possibly as high as 9%.” It reached 7.9%.

Yet, in November, President Joe Biden renominated Powell to a second term as Federal Reserve chairman, despite his gross mismanagement that led to the inflation we are now experiencing. Biden, in his statement, praised Powell for his “decisive action” and “steady leadership.”

Low-income Americans trying to stay above water in this new flood of inflation are probably less grateful to Biden and Powell for this so-called leadership.

Consumer Financial Protection Gone Awry

April 13, 2022

The crises of recent years tend to erase from memory those that preceded them.

One, as you may recall, was the financial collapse of 2008—a collapse deemed by many as the worst since the Great Depression.

That collapse swept into power a government like the one we have now—the White House and both houses of Congress controlled by Democrats.

Newly elected President Barack Obama appointed then-Rep. Rahm Emanuel as his chief of staff, who made popular the saying, "Never let a serious crisis go to waste."

Indeed, the new Democrat administration followed this advice and used the financial crisis as an opportunity for a major expansion of government.

Democrats wasted no time to ascribe the financial collapse to business greed and insufficient regulation of banks and other financial institutions. In 2010, the 2,300-page Dodd-Frank Act was passed—with no Republican votes in the House and three in the Senate—adding 400 new regulations on financial institutions.

Included in this tsunami of new financial regulation was the creation of a new independent agency—the Consumer Financial Protection Bureau. The agency, originally the brainchild of Sen. Elizabeth Warren, was conceived with her view, shared by Democrats on the far left, that disparities in financial results between different communities must be due to racism and discrimination. So, needed, in their view, was an all-powerful bureaucrat in Washington to level the playing field.

Now our financial institutions—banks, securities firms, credit unions, payday lenders, etc.—fall under the purview of the Consumer Financial Protection Bureau and must submit to its scrutiny and oversight.

The CFPB has just announced sweeping new changes in its "supervisory operations to better protect families and communities from illegal discrimination"

Firms must make available to CFPB "their processes for assessing risks and discriminatory outcomes, including documentation of customer demographics and the impact of products and fees on different demographic groups."

We might summarize this as financial markets gone woke.

Can a government bureaucrat really determine why a banker did or did not make a loan, and should the heavy hand of government be involved here?

Can it be the same thing when government intervenes in how financial institutions do their business as when government intervenes regarding who sits at a lunch counter?

We can learn something about this from the financial crisis of 2008.

According to the work of American Enterprise Institute's Peter Wallison, the crisis was not the result of insufficient regulation of business but of government excess.

It all started, according to Wallison, with government mandated Affordable Housing Goals in 1992. These mandated that the two giant government-backed mortgage companies—Fannie Mae and Freddie Mac—set a quota of

30% of all mortgages they acquired from mortgage originators to be targeted to low- and moderate-income borrowers.

By 2008, this was up to 56%.

In order to meet these quotas, lending practices were dramatically relaxed. Down payment requirements dropped from 10% to 3%; credit score requirements were relaxed, as were debt-to-income requirements for borrowers.

By 2008, according to Wallison, just before everything collapsed, "More than a majority of all mortgages in the U.S. financial system was sub-prime, required low or no down payment, or were otherwise risky."

With the collapse of lending standards, housing demand and prices went through the roof, and then the bubble exploded.

Who suffered the most in the ensuing recession? Per Pew Research, "Blacks and Hispanics have borne a disproportionate share of both job losses and housing foreclosures." The low-income Americans government most wanted to help were those who were hurt the most.

Today, Democrats are back at it.

CFPB Director Rohit Chopra is gearing up to use his almost unilateral power to show he knows better than business and the marketplace what is good for consumers.

Surely, once again, those who will suffer the most will be our struggling low-income citizens.

Students Must Take Responsibility for Their Debt

May 4, 2022

Lending money is not, as they say, rocket science.

According to the Federal Reserve Bank of St. Louis, in the last quarter of 2021, of the total of all outstanding business loans from all commercial banks, 1.08% were delinquent.

Per the Federal Reserve Bank of New York, as of second quarter 2021, a little over 2% of the $1.4 trillion outstanding in auto loans were delinquent.

Yet in the student loan market, totaling around $1.6 trillion, not that different from the total size of the auto loan market, an average of 15% are in default at any given time, per the Education Data Initiative.

It should be clear what the problem is.

Auto lenders make sure that those to whom they lend can and will pay back the loan. They are careful because if the borrower defaults, the lender loses.

But if, tomorrow, President Joe Biden or Sens. Elizabeth Warren or Bernie Sanders decide that it is not fair that there are Americans without new cars and managed to get government guarantees for auto loans, is there any doubt that there would be a dramatic rise in defaults on car loans?

Those lending wouldn't care who they lend to because they wouldn't take the loss on a default. You and I, we taxpayers, would, as we will if Biden and his party have their way to wipe out student loans.

Of course, "wipe out" is not the right terminology.

Debts don't get wiped out. They just get transferred to someone else. In the case of government guarantees, that someone else is taxpayers.

The concept of student loans backed by the government is another child of the allegedly compassionate 1960s.

Doesn't it make sense to help the less fortunate obtain funds to pay for college?

But as many theologians and philosophers have noted, the greatest charitable act is to help another individual take control of their own life. Teaching personal responsibility is the most valuable gift that one can provide another.

Our American compassion, our moral compass, has gone awry.

A child growing up in America today looks around and finds himself or herself in a nation where debt is larger than the entire economy, and still growing.

But just as inflation shows that the costs of fiscal irresponsibility cannot be hidden, so the costs of teaching our youth that personal responsibility is irrelevant cannot be hidden. It manifests in the destructive behavior we see now.

The Wall Street Journal reported that one student loan adviser told them, "I'm seeing them say, 'I'm going to take out more loans now and go buy GameStop stock with it because it's going to get forgiven anyway.'"

A new Gallup survey reports "32% of currently enrolled students pursuing a bachelor's degree report they have considered withdrawing from their program for a semester or more in the past six months."

Thirty-six percent attribute this to financial reasons. But 76% attribute to "emotional stress."

Of course, the universities love this. What business wouldn't think the government subsidizing purchase of its product is a great idea?

Per the American Enterprise Institute, from January 2000 to December 2021, college tuition costs increased 175% and college textbook costs increased 150%. Over the same period, the consumer price index for all items increased 65.5%; prices of cars, household furnishings and clothing remained relatively unchanged; and cellphone services were down 40%, computer software down 71% and television sets down 97%.

Per Education Data Initiative, highest default rate—26.33%—is among arts and humanities majors attending nonselective schools. Can anyone really think such loans make sense?

We need to help our youth who want education to get it. But it must be done prudently.

Teaching our youth that they don't need to pay back debts is not a good start.

Misguided efforts by Biden and his party to cancel obligations on student loans should be vigorously opposed.

Congress Ignores Pressing National Business While It Obsesses on Jan. 6

June 8, 2022

As the House Select Committee to Investigate the Jan. 6 Attack on the United States Capitol starts public hearings, we must ask what motivates those on the committee.

Is the sole concern the ideals of the Declaration of Independence and the Constitution of the United States? Or is it to get media to attack and undermine political opponents?

It is indeed possible that infractions of law can be investigated without a carnival platform designed to mobilize media and national attention.

The public material of the committee already reeks of motivations other than seeking truth.

The committee has already announced on its website that the Jan. 6 incident was "one of the darkest days of our democracy."

Really? Against a civil war where some three-quarters of a million Americans were killed, fighting over what American freedom is about, one incident of a few hours, where law enforcement finally prevailed, was one of our "darkest days"?

There are just 24 hours in any day, so time taken on one matter means attention not given to other matters.

If these members of Congress really cared about our principles of freedom and democracy, they wouldn't be ignoring every day other pressing matters in which the freedom of American citizens is blatantly violated.

Take, for example, that as the Jan. 6 investigation

monopolizes media attention, on June 3 the Trustees of Medicare and Social Security issued their annual report.

Both systems are bankrupt and in dismal shape financially.

The cash shortfall of Medicare in 2021 was $409 billion. Projection is that Social Security will be out of adequate cash flow to meet obligations to retirees by 2035—just 13 years from now.

The Trustees estimate that there are only adequate funds in Social Security to meet 80% of benefits in 2035. The payroll tax, now 12.4%, would have to be raised 26% in order to generate sufficient funds to meet those obligations.

In other words, today every working American age 55 and below who plans to collect Social Security benefits at age 67 is paying a payroll tax into a system that cannot provide the benefits promised.

Can you imagine a private insurance company sending a letter to policy holders saying that, in 13 years, they will only be able to meet 80% of the payments promised to policy holders?

The lawsuits would be flying.

Let's forget about the fiscal situation of the system for a minute and whether it is even worth saving this program. How about the issue of freedom that our members of Congress want us to believe they care about so much?

Take a young citizen, age 21, fresh with his or her new degree, entering the work force for the first time. Immediately, 12.4% of their paycheck is deducted into a system they involuntarily enter, in which there are inadequate funds to meet promised benefits.

Shouldn't this new young worker be able to say, “No, thank you, I don't want to participate”?

Even if the system were not broken, and benefits could be met, in our free country, shouldn't everyone be free to manage their own retirement?

According to the Committee to Unleash Prosperity, the average return of Social Security over the last 40 years was 1%. Over the same period, average return on stocks was 6%.

Back to this new young worker, by the calculations of the Committee to Unleash Prosperity, this single worker, if they earned the median national income and were able to invest 10% of their income into a diversified stock and bond portfolio over 40 years, instead of paying the payroll tax, could have annual income at retirement of $55,143 against $19,646 from Social Security.

So, hey, members of the Select Committee. Enough of pretending that you care about American freedom. How about wrapping up the carnival and getting down to the real challenges every American faces today?

US Inflation Starts in Washington, not Moscow

June 15, 2022

President Joe Biden spoke at the Port of Los Angeles the other day and addressed the issue foremost on the minds of Americans today—inflation.

And in the spirit of a tried and true liberal, he blamed everyone in the world for a problem that he is responsible for.

Apparently, our president believes that Vladimir Putin is running America.

"We've never seen anything like Putin's tax on both food and gas. ... Putin's price hike is hitting America hard. ... I'm doing everything in my power to blunt Putin's price hike and bring down the cost of gas and food."

Speaking on CNN, Treasury Secretary Janet Yellen showed she has a little more integrity than her boss by admitting the inflation situation was mismanaged and she was wrong about what was happening.

"I think I was wrong about the path that inflation would take," she said, referring to her observations last year that escalating inflation was a "small risk" and wouldn't "be a problem."

The president does, of course, see that Putin has some accomplices in ravaging Americans with escalating prices.

Among these, per Biden, are the ports, the supply chain, foreign shippers and the oil industry.

"One thing I want to say about the oil companies," said Biden: "they have 9,000 permits to drill. They're not drilling.

...Why aren't they drilling? Because they make more money not producing more oil. The price goes up."

Our president demonstrates that his understanding of economics is less than any college freshman.

Oil markets are global and competitive. No one company, even a huge company like ExxonMobil, controls the market. Even the biggest company is just one participant in a competitive market.

Unless our president wants to argue that American oil producers are a cartel, like OPEC, that controls about 40% of total world oil production, no one company causes the price to move.

Every company is a price taker, not price maker.

Whatever the price is, companies will produce and sell as much as they can to maximize their current revenues. To suggest otherwise is pure economic ignorance.

Unfortunately, the late, great Nobel prize winning economist Milton Friedman, who explained the causes of inflation, has been washed away in today's woke culture.

Friedman's famous observation was that "inflation is always and everywhere a monetary phenomenon, in the sense that it is and can be produced only by a more rapid increase in the quantity of money than in output."

Friedman is unpopular with liberals because once it is understood that inflation is the result of the government printing excessive amounts of money, we understand that inflation can only be caused by government, because only government can print money.

Once it is clear that only government actions, in the way of creating excessive amounts of money, cause inflation, then those in government cannot blame others, as our president is now doing.

Economists Steve Hanke and John Greenwood, looking at the rate at which the Biden government was creating money, wrote in the Wall Street Journal in July 2021, "By the end of the year, the year-over-year inflation rate will be at least 6% and possibly as high as 9%."

Clearly, they were right on target.

Responding to Biden's recent explanations about inflation, Hanke and Greenwood point out, "China, Japan and Switzerland also face elevated oil prices, supply-chain problems and fallout from the war in Ukraine, but their annual inflation rates are 2.1%, 2.5% and 2.5%, respectively. They have avoided the ravages of inflation because their central banks haven't produced excessive quantities of money."

If there is anything we should be grateful for today, given what is happening, it is that Biden and the Democrats in Congress failed in their Build Back Better plan to layer another $5 trillion in new government expenditures into our economy.

Less government spending and more honesty, responsibility and clear thinking is our only path to emerging from today's economic chaos.

Inflation Reduction Act Is the Problem, Not the Solution

Aug. 17, 2022

A central pillar of the just-passed Inflation Reduction Act is $80 billion going to the IRS to hire some 87,000 new agents, doubling the current force, to chase down U.S. taxpayers who allegedly are not meeting their tax obligations.

The rationale is we have a large national budget deficit—that is, government is bringing in less money than it spends—so a larger army of IRS agents chasing down tax deadbeats will help solve our nation's fiscal problems.

But part of this same new law in which U.S. taxpayers are asked to spend $80 billion to hire more IRS agents to shake down their neighbors who are supposedly not paying their fair share, there is $430 billion in new government spending, a large portion of which is earmarked for green energy projects of various shapes and forms.

At the same time that we're expanding our army of tax collectors, we continue to expand government and spending at an even faster pace.

The Congressional Budget Office has just released its latest Long-Term Budget Outlook, and here we get a broader picture of the problem.

According to the report, "From 1972 to 2021, total federal outlays averaged 21% of GDP; over 2022-2052 period, such outlays are projected to average 26% of GDP."

The Congressional Budget Office projects that government will take on average 5% more from our national economy in the next 30 years than it did on average over the last 50 years.

Looking at our GDP in 2022, roughly $25 trillion, at 26% of GDP, government spending will be over a trillion dollars more than it would have been at 21%.

A trillion dollars more in spending on average per year, with another 87,000 IRS agents running after taxpayers to make sure they pay up.

So, the bigger army of tax collectors is about helping raise money to finance ongoing expansion of government and increasing control of government over the lives of private Americans.

Why, as someone whose business is trying to improve the lives of low-income Americans, do I care about this?

Turning pages forward in the CBO report, we get to the really shocking information.

From 1992 to 2021, per CBO, the average growth of the U.S. economy was 2.4% per year. CBO projects that from 2022 to 2052 the average growth of the U.S. economy will be 1.7% per year.

This should shock every American, and it's getting hardly any attention.

The more our national economy is controlled by government and politicians, the more sluggish will be growth of our economy.

It stands to reason. Growth comes from entrepreneurs, work, creativity. More government means less of all these things and slower growth.

Slower growth means lower income and less opportunity.

Anyone who cares about helping those who want to get ahead in America should be cheering for faster growth and less government rather than more government and slower growth.

Hoover Institution economist John Cochrane has pointed out that from 1950 to 2000, the U.S. economy grew at 3.5% per year. Real income per person went from $16,000 in 1950 to $50,000 in 2000. If the economy grew from 1950 to 2000 at 2% instead of 3.5%, notes Cochrane, income in 2000 would have risen to just $23,000 rather than $50,000.

It's why, as someone who cares about helping low-income Americans get ahead and improve their lot, I care about a growing dynamic economy, not a bloated, sclerotic economy controlled by politicians and Washington special interests.

The so-called Inflation Reduction Act takes matters in the exact opposite direction in which we should be going. Pretending to care about the nation's fiscal imbalances while adding $430 billion in new spending, all of it driven and defined by Washington special interests, is the problem, not the solution.

When Will Low-Income Americans Stop Looking to Government?

Sept. 14, 2022

New polling data from Gallup show Americans are not having an easy time through this period of rising prices.

According to Gallup, 56% of Americans say now that rising prices are causing severe or moderate hardship.

Drilling down, we see that the hardship is not shared equally.

Among low-income households, those with income less than $48,000, 74% report they are experiencing hardship. Among middle-income households, with income $48,000 to $89,999, 63% report hardship. And among upper income, $90,000 and above, 40% report experiencing hardship.

But Secretary of the Treasury Janet Yellen showed up at Ford's Rouge Electric Vehicle Center in Dearborn, Michigan, recently with an upbeat economic message reminiscent of the joke, "Who are you going to believe, me or your own eyes?"

Yellen announced that she is "more optimistic about the course of our economy than I have been in quite a while."

The Biden administration hopes to blow enough smoke into the eyes of voters so that reality will not set in until the November elections have passed.

Yellen ought to consider reading the latest long-term budget and economic projections form the nonpartisan Congressional Budget Office.

Per CBO's just-published "The 2022 Long-Term

Budget Outlook," over the next 30 years, the U.S. budget deficit, as a percent of our GDP, will be double what it has averaged over the last half-century, and national debt as a percentage of GDP will reach historically high levels, arriving to a mind-boggling 185% of GDP in 2052.

The result of this ongoing absorption of the U.S. economy into the hands of government and politicians will be, according to CBO, a slowing and sputtering of the U.S. economy.

"From 2022 to 2052, real potential GDP increases an average of 1.7% per year," per the report, compared to an average of 2.4% over the previous 30 years, 1992 to 2021.

However, from 1950 to 2000, the U.S. economy grew at an average annual rate of 3.5%.

So, per the picture CBO paints for us regarding our economic future, we can expect growth to be half what it averaged for the half century following the end of World War II.

What does his mean to the average American?

Per Hoover Institution economist John Cochrane, it means that over the next 50 years household income will be half of what it would have been had the economy grown at the faster historical rate.

This is not a pretty picture for any American.

But for low-income Americans, it is particularly dismal.

The American dream has always been that although you may start with nothing, there is a future for you to build and accumulate wealth.

That dream is being shattered.

And it is being shattered by government and politicians—Democrats who now control our government—

who pretend to be concerned about these same low-income Americans.

More and more government spending, more and more government sucking the oxygen out of our economy by pulling resources away from the private sector and redirecting it toward political control, supposedly to help "have-nots," just destroys opportunity for everyone.

In Gallup polling reported in a survey done by my organization CURE, 70% of Black Americans feel the country is divided into "haves" and "have-nots," and 57% of Blacks feel they are among the "have-nots."

The challenge of all those who see the whole nation sinking under the weight of misguided government, and certainly I am talking about Republicans, is to reach our Black citizens and get them to believe that the path to opportunity, the path to becoming a "have," is a free economy.

If our Black citizens, and all Americans who feel the country is unfair, realize that freedom, and not government, is the path to wealth creation, we can turn a sinking ship around.

Rick Caruso Is the Outsider Los Angeles Needs as Mayor

Oct. 26, 2022

A supporter of my organization sent a video he made driving around in downtown Los Angeles.

Homelessness and crime are rampant. It is shocking to see the social chaos prevailing in one of America's major cities. It is a hard pill to swallow to see the streets of downtown Los Angeles teeming with homelessness.

The crisis is defining the current race for the new mayor of Los Angeles. One candidate, Karen Bass, is the quintessential insider. She is a six-term Democratic congresswoman, former chair of the Congressional Black Caucus and former speaker of California state assembly.

The full gamut of the Democratic establishment has endorsed Bass—including President Joe Biden, Vice President Kamala Harris, Speaker Nancy Pelosi and Hillary Clinton.

Running against Bass is billionaire real estate developer Rick Caruso.

Caruso is pouring tens of millions of his own funds into the race. Latest tally is that he has spent $81 million, compared with Bass's $11 million.

And it is making a difference. Last month, Caruso was 15 points behind. But now polls show him ahead by a few points.

Homelessness is a statewide phenomenon in California, with the state accounting for half of all homelessness in the country. Per the National Alliance to End Homelessness, there are now 161,548 homeless in

California. Number two in the nation is New York with 91,217; and third is Florida with 27,487.

Los Angeles County, with 69,000 homeless, exceeds the third and fourth highest states together, Florida and Texas.

Caruso is an outsider, doer and pragmatist.

He wants to spend $843 million in one year to provide immediately 30,000 shelter beds in existing structures and initiate a longer-term plan of low-cost housing. He says this can be done without raising taxes by cutting waste and using his business experience to get work done efficiently.

Bass would spend a third as much and does not promise to not raise taxes.

Caruso's background touches me somewhat personally.

He was president of the Los Angeles Police Commission 20 years ago after the rioting in Los Angeles in the wake of the Rodney King decision.

Caruso added 800 police officers and cut crime by 30%.

I was operating my first business in Los Angeles then, and it was destroyed in the aftermath of the riots.

Caruso provided practical leadership and guidance then to deal with the chaos in LA, and I believe he can do the same now.

The mess in Los Angeles and the whole state of California reflects Democratic Party establishment politics, to which Karen Bass is deeply connected.

The Congressional Black Caucus, where Bass served as chair, has been going for years making lots of noise and having zero impact on poverty in their own districts.

We don't need any more blame games and crying

about racism.

Recently, the president of the LA City Council resigned after a recording of council deliberations, laced with racial epithets, sparing no ethnicity, surfaced. It showed what dominates city politics.

Democratic Party big-government, ethnic politics explains why homelessness in California increased 42% from 2014 to 2020, while declining 9% in the rest of the country, per the Stanford Institute for Economic Policy Research.

Bass says she will "appoint a homelessness chief and force the city and county to work together and stop their finger pointing."

Caruso says, "The city needs a chief executive ... somebody that can make very smart, tough decisions ... What I am not going to do is form a bunch of committees, like many of these career politicians do, and talk about the issue."

Rick Caruso is the outsider that Los Angeles needs. Someone looking to bring a real personal skill set to solve major problems and not looking for who to blame and which political buddies to enrich. It can be a model for the nation.

Student Loan Forgiveness Meets the Rule of Law

Nov. 16, 2022

President Joe Biden's $400 billion 2022 election bribe—also known as student loan forgiveness—has been now stopped in its tracks on two fronts.

First, in Texas, federal district court Judge Mark Pittman, one of nearly 300 federal judges appointed by former President Donald Trump, ruled the initiative unconstitutional. The judge rejected Biden's claim that the 2003 Heroes Act gives him authority to wipe out these loans. That act, per the judge, was about loan assistance for military personal during war or other emergencies.

The lawsuit was filed by the Job Creators Network Foundation on behalf of two students holding loans that did not qualify for the relief, demonstrating the inequities of the initiative and the failure to provide the usual comment period for citizens to voice concerns.

Now, in response to six states that have sued challenging the legality of this loan forgiveness program, a federal appeals court has issued an injunction blocking the program from moving forward.

The Wall Street Journal has called this loan write-off measure "the largest presidential abuse of power in decades."

I have already written about the folly of this loan forgiveness program.

Private debt markets in our country work extremely well regarding loan management and defaults. The problems arise—excessive defaults—when government gets in the business of providing loans, which are inevitably constructed and targeted with political objectives.

And, these student loan programs simply exacerbate the real problem, which is runaway costs of college education. Over the last 20 years, escalation of the cost of college tuition and textbooks have been more than twice the national average inflation rate.

Universities are essentially being subsidized by government programs designed allegedly to help students get higher education.

But this massive loan forgiveness initiative is also an example of the crass political opportunism that inevitably follows from the accumulation of government power.

Can it possibly be accidental timing that Biden reached out to tens of millions with college loans, offering to wipe these loans out, just prior to elections when the outlook for his party was not looking encouraging and when his own polling has been poor?

A week before the elections, Biden made remarks at the White House saying that our democracy is "at risk ... democracy is on the ballot this year."

Now that the elections produced far better results for Democrats than anyone anticipated, the president called the elections "a good day for democracy."

No one ever accused Biden of being a deep thinker. But it should concern every citizen that his assessment of the state of our democracy follows from the success at the polls of his own party.

In his remarks at the White House, the president stumbled onto the truth.

"We, the people, must decide whether the rule of law will prevail or whether we'll allow the dark forces to thirst—

that thirst for power put ahead of the principles (that) have long guided us."

We saw similar improper and politically motivated behavior by Biden in the recent release of oil from the nation's Strategic Petroleum Reserve. As pointed out by John Hill, who was involved in the legislation that created the reserve, the reserve exists for national security in instances of "severe energy supply disruptions." It's not there to manipulate oil prices when politicians find this expedient.

Fortunately, as evidenced by these court decisions slamming the door on this abuse of power by our president, even conservatives and Republicans who are disappointed by the results of these elections can feel positive that we still have rule of law in our nation.

As Pittman wrote in his opinion, "In this country, we are not ruled by an all-powerful executive with a pen and a phone. Instead, we are ruled by a constitution that provides for three distinct and independent branches of government."

Health Care

In Health Care, We Need Less Government, Not More

Feb. 20, 2019

In a new Gallup poll, 35 percent say government is the worst problem facing the U.S. In the 55 years that Gallup has asked the question—"What do you think is the most important problem facing this country today?"—this is the highest percentage of people who have identified the government as the nation's worst problem.

Given how many Americans see the government as a large problem, you have to wonder about so many Democratic politicians' ambitions to give government increasing power over our lives—particularly in an area as important as health care.

"Medicare-for-all" is the new rage among Democrats, and each of the announced Democrat presidential contenders favors some version of this.

However, as Democrats surge to the left, the enthusiasm of the nation as a whole for government-run health care is more muted. A December Gallup poll shows just 40 percent in favor of a government-run health care system.

Given what we should be looking for in a quality health care system—the best quality health care at the lowest possible prices, making sure that those who are economically challenged get care, too—the answer is less government, not more.

University of Michigan economist and blogger Mark Perry makes a strong case for why we would be better off with open, competitive health care markets.

According to Perry, in the 20 years between 1998 and 2017, the nation's overall consumer price index increased 50.3 percent. Over this same period, the cost of medical services increased by 105.3 percent and hospital services by 189.3 percent.

Perry—and many other economists with a free-market bent—argue that it is lack of competition in health care that drives up prices far more than general price escalation.

Health care is defined as having a "third-party" payer. That is, someone else pays your bill—your employer, your insurance company or the government.

Just think about a typical visit to the doctor. Your health plan gets you in the door, but you have no idea what the doctor is being paid or the cost of anything he or she prescribes you—whether various procedures, tests or drugs. Even the doctor has no idea the costs of what he or she prescribes.

How can a market possibly function this way?

Can you imagine going to the supermarket and seeing the shelves filled but no prices displayed? How could you decide what and how much to buy?

Could you imagine buying a house and having a third party represent you and negotiate what you will pay?

Perry shows, practically, the implications of a third-party payer in terms of costs. He brings the example of the cosmetic surgery market, in which procedures are overwhelmingly elective and individuals pay for them on their own.

Looking at a basket of 20 cosmetic surgery procedures, the average price increase between 1998 and 2017 was 34.2 percent—less than the consumer price index and about one-third the increase of general medical services.

From 1970 to 2017, the portion of U.S. health care expenses made by a third party—insurance or government—went from 65 percent to 89 percent. The portion of expenses made out-of-pocket by consumers went from 35 percent to 11 percent. Over this same period, per capita health care spending increased by at least a factor of 6.

The government is involved in the health care of just about every American. About 130 million Americans get health care through Medicare or Medicaid. Another 156 million get it through their employer; they still have the government involved because employers provide health coverage as a tax-deductible business expense.

The best thing we can do for the country is get health care back to a real market with real transparent costs and competition. For those that need help, provide subsidies, but don't distort prices.

In other words, we need to go in the opposite direction of "Medicare-for-all."

After the Shootings—Look to Culture, Not Politics

Aug. 7, 2019

The nation must now endure another gut-wrenching tragedy, with 31 having been senselessly gunned downed in Texas and Ohio over a weekend.

This following a week where three were gunned down in California.

My appeal is to consider these tragedies a crisis of culture and not to turn them into politics, which is already happening.

I'm thinking about the words of Robert F. Kennedy when he spoke to a crowd in Indianapolis in April 1968, after hearing the news that Dr. Martin Luther King Jr. had been murdered.

"In this difficult day, in this difficult time for the United States, it is perhaps well to ask what kind of a nation we are and what direction we want to move in," said Kennedy. He himself would be assassinated shortly thereafter.

Kennedy appealed to Americans to move away from "polarization" and "hatred" and toward "love and wisdom and compassion."

It is a great temptation to simplify what is complex, and this tends to mean translating everything into politics, looking for some particular individual to blame and looking for some simple policy answer that will allegedly solve the problem.

But these tragedies are not simple and not partisan.

They have occurred too often in our nation and have occurred under Democratic as well as Republican regimes.

There is a sickness in the soul of our nation, and that sickness plays its way through and winds up expressed in deadly, pathological acts of lonely, lost, confused individuals—disproportionately, young males.

We must try to grasp the nature of this pathology and consider how it may be addressed.

If we look, we can see other telling symptoms.

The Centers for Disease Control and Prevention reports that the rate of suicide in the nation is the highest since 1942.

From 1999 to 2017, the suicide rate increased 33 percent, and in 2016, suicide was the second leading cause of death in the age range of 10 to 34.

The rate of suicide among young men is more than three times higher than that of young women.

On the other side of the spectrum, while young Americans are taking their own lives at an increasing rate, fewer are bringing new life into the world.

The CDC reports that in 2018, for the fourth year in a row, the nation's fertility rate—the number of births per 1,000 women ages 15 to 44—dropped and hit a historic low.

And this has occurred coincidentally with a drop in the rate of marriage. The percentage of American adults who are married is one-third less than where is stood half a century ago.

Nicholas Eberstadt of the American Enterprise Institute has written about the huge exit of prime-age males—25 to 54—from the workforce. In 1965, according to Eberstadt, 96.6 percent of prime-age males were working. Now its 88.5 percent, meaning millions of prime-age males have abandoned the workforce.

All this has occurred as Christianity, once a pillar of

American society, has been pushed to the margins.

Per Gallup, in 1974, 65 percent of Americans expressed “a great deal” or “quite a lot” of confidence in the church or organized religion. By 2019, this was down to 36 percent.

Faith builds a sense of belonging to something true and greater than oneself. It provides meaning and an anchor in times of difficulty and uncertainty.

As faith and eternal truths become more marginalized, more young people, particularly young males, become isolated and left with a sense of meaninglessness. They lose the key framework through which one takes personal responsibility for his or her life.

It produces an inclination to look for others to blame for their difficulties, for their personal struggles. Sometimes it becomes violent.

There is a great price to be paid for a culture of meaninglessness.

This is what we should be thinking and talking about, rather than simple political answers and who to blame.

207 Members of Congress Ask Court to Rethink Roe v. Wade

Jan.15, 2020

In March 2020, the Supreme Court will rule on the constitutionality of Louisiana's new abortion law, which requires that physicians doing abortions have admitting privileges at a hospital within 30 miles of the clinic.

Under the leadership of House Minority Whip Steve Scalise, an amicus—"friend of the court"—brief supporting the law was just filed, signed by 207 members of Congress, 39 senators and 168 House members.

A press release from Scalise summarizes the arguments made and lists a number of conservative organizations supporting the brief, one of which is my organization—the Center for Urban Renewal and Education.

What makes this filing particularly interesting is not just the sheer volume of congressional signatories—almost 40% of the Senate and House combined; it's also the fact that it goes further than just arguing support for the constitutionality of the Louisiana law to suggest that the widespread confusion regarding abortion law ties directly to the confusing basic premises under which abortion was found constitutional in the 1973 Roe v. Wade and the 1992 Planned Parenthood v. Casey decisions.

The brief urges the Supreme Court to cast new scrutiny on these two landmark decisions that have defined the abortion legal landscape.

Asking the Supreme Court to reconsider Roe v. Wade is provocative, to say the least. But it is also courageous and on target.

How can we possibly function as a nation when an issue as critical as abortion defies consensus as to its constitutional pedigree as well as its morality?

Can there be any better evidence of this confusion than recalling the famous interchange in August 2008 when Pastor Rick Warren asked then-presidential candidate Barack Obama, "At what point does a baby get human rights, in your view?"

Obama, a Harvard-educated lawyer who would go on to be twice elected president, replied lamely, "answering that question ... is above my pay grade."

Yet despite his candor about his inability to clarify the biological and legal status of the unborn child, he didn't hesitate to be the first sitting American president to address the national meeting of Planned Parenthood, the nation's largest abortion provider, and tell them, "God bless you."

There is a well-known expression from the world of computing that says, "garbage in, garbage out."

Faulty premises will produce faulty results and output.

This is a pretty good summary of what has been happening to American culture since the Roe v. Wade decision.

Once sanctity of life and its legal protections became ambiguous, our entire culture began to unravel.

The percentage of American adults married since Roe v. Wade has dropped by one-third. The percentage of children in households with married parents is down 15%, and the percentage of babies born to unwed mothers up over 300%.

The last decade, according the Census Bureau, is estimated to have the slowest 10-year growth in the U.S.

population since the first census was taken in 1790.

The Census Bureau forecasts that by 2034, for the first time, there will be more Americans over age 65 than under 18.

And, of course, we cannot overlook the damage our national soul has incurred by looking away as 61,628,584 babies have been destroyed in the womb since 1973, as the Guttmacher Institute reports.

In the latest Gallup polling, 49% identified as pro-life and 46% as pro-choice. Fifty percent say abortion is "morally wrong," and 42% say it is "morally acceptable."

For the 47th time, hundreds of thousands will arrive in Washington for the March for Life, noting the anniversary of the Roe v. Wade decision, Jan. 22, 1973.

There is growing appreciation for the notion that what's driving a sense that something is wrong in our nation is ambiguity regarding the sanctity of life.

Let's pray that the court heeds these 207 members of Congress and starts rethinking the Roe v. Wade decision.

Restrict Abortion During COVID-19

April 8, 2020

Here are a few examples of headlines over recent weeks.

"Republicans exploit coronavirus to restrict abortions."—Los Angeles Times

"The Coronavirus Becomes an Excuse to Restrict Abortions"—The New York Times

"Texas women forced to travel 20 times farther for abortion under coronavirus ban."—The Hill

Five states—Texas, Ohio, Alabama, Iowa and Mississippi—that are prohibiting nonessential medical procedures during the novel coronavirus health crisis have included abortion among these nonessential procedures.

These measures have been taken with one objective in mind: saving lives. To suggest otherwise is cynical and obscene.

The logic is straightforward. There is a dire shortage of medical equipment, facilities and personnel. Plus, most states have mandated social distancing to arrest the spread of infection—requirements that would be impossible to adhere to in abortion clinics.

It so happens that halting abortion saves the lives of unborn children. This is always true. But prohibiting needed supplies from being tied up and enforcing distance will also save the lives of Americans under threat of the virus.

Abortion providers in Texas, led by Planned Parenthood, the nation's largest abortion provider, filed suit against the state's decision to restrict abortions under these circumstances. Their claim was upheld in federal district court, and permission for abortions was restored. However, the state appealed the decision, and the appeals court reversed the decision and restored the restriction, pending a hearing on April 13.

New York State Attorney General Letitia James was interviewed on National Public Radio to discuss her efforts to organize opposition to efforts to include abortion as a prohibited, nonessential procedure during this crisis.

Per James, New York and 17 other states have filed an amicus brief to support Texas abortion providers' efforts to restore permissibility of abortion.

James says: "this ban does nothing, nothing to prevent the transmission of the coronavirus. ... Texas is doing nothing more than using this pandemic as an excuse to trespass on the rights of women and to treat them like second-class citizens."

This comes from the attorney general of New York, the state with the nation's highest abortion rate—and the nation's gravest challenges during this COVID-19 crisis.

How is it that the New York attorney general finds time to challenge how Texas is managing its fight against the coronavirus when her own state cannot manage its crisis?

As of this writing, there were 123,018 coronavirus cases in New York, amounting to 37% of all cases in the U.S. In Texas, there are 7,045. New York has 6,324 cases per million people. Texas has 243 per million.

The fatality rate in New York among confirmed cases is 3.38% compared with a fatality rate in Texas of 1.89%.

It should be clear that the attorney general of New York shouldn't be criticizing how those in Texas or any other state are dealing with this crisis given that there is no place more out of control than New York.

In the best of circumstances, crises, personal or national, should be a time of growth and learning. They should bring out the best in us rather than the worst.

I wish Americans would be equally shocked hearing that almost a million unborn children are destroyed in the womb every year as they are shocked hearing an estimated 100,000 to 240,000 will die from the coronavirus scourge.

You would think times like these would inspire humility and reverence for the miracle of life. Challenges like these should make us better Americans and better people.

But, apparently, things have become so coarse that that's not happening in many circles. It certainly doesn't seem to be happening in New York.

Maybe one day we'll grow. Meanwhile, the focus should be on saving lives, born and unborn.

Why We Should Start Going Back to Work

April 22, 2020

At this writing, the number of deaths from COVID-19 in the U.S. is 42,425.

This is just a little higher than the number of deaths in the U.S. each year from auto accidents.

It's no mystery how to reduce those 40,000 auto accident deaths to zero. Simply prohibit driving.

How many Americans would agree to this?

Not many. Most Americans prefer their freedom and the benefits they get from driving, and are prepared to accept the risks associated with driving.

If there were a million traffic-related deaths each year, for sure Americans would become less wedded to their cars and more open to intrusive regulations that would make it much more difficult to drive.

When the news first broke about COVID-19, we were hearing estimates of a death toll of 2 million-plus for the United States. Knowledge of the nature of this threat was very limited.

There was great fear of waves of casualties, and of hospitals without space and equipment to deal with patients.

Under these emergency circumstances, many were open to compromising their freedom and agreeing to lockdown policies.

But the picture has changed dramatically. By the end of March, Dr. Anthony Fauci was estimating 100,000 to 200,000 deaths, and less than two weeks ago, he revised this to 60,000.

A recent opinion piece in the Wall Street Journal reported COVID-19 research results from a Stanford University team. Based on a sampling from Santa Clara County, the team estimates fatality rates of COVID-19 in the range of 0.12% to 0.2%, approximately the range of seasonal flu fatalities and less than a 10th of the initial COVID-19 estimates.

Certainly, this is no final word. But data and what we are observing points very strongly to the severity of this threat being nothing like what we were initially led to believe.

If indeed the risk involved is not all that much higher than the risk of getting into a fatal auto accident or the seasonal flu—which could well be the case now—how many would tolerate what is going on?

We're also seeing that national averages don't tell us much. Regional differences are huge.

Of the 42,425 casualties nationally, 45% are in New York.

Without New York, the national number would be 23,334. So total COVID-19 casualties in 49 of 50 states now total far less than our total annual auto casualties nationwide.

Two conclusions jump out, and they are both consistent with President Donald Trump's latest guidelines.

First, local realities are so disparate that governors and local authorities must lead management of this crisis in their region.

Second, the risks are far less than what was initially thought. We must adjust and prudently start opening our economy.

The price of what we are now doing is astronomical.

Per Hoover Institute economist John Cochrane, "20 million people, more than 1 in 10 US workers, lost their jobs in the first month of this shutdown. That's more than the entire 2008 recession."

"Most guesses say that companies have one to three months of cash on hand, and then fail," he added.

And in the end, the government lending and spending programs designed to get us through this will add, according to Cochrane, $4 trillion of new debt on the American people. That's $12,121 for every man, woman and child in the country.

We never have perfect information. The point in life is always to make intelligent decisions under uncertainty.

Just as one-size-fits-all policy coming out of Washington doesn't work in dealing with poverty, housing or education, it doesn't work in battling this health crisis.

Limit federal bureaucratic control of our lives and engage local government. Focus on individual freedom and personal responsibility. It's what we need now. It's what we have always needed.

Lessons to Learn From COVID-19

April 29, 2020

We're seeing now what efforts against COVID-19 were supposed to produce: a flattening of the growth curve of new fatalities. The growth rate of fatalities is dropping.

We entered the dark tunnel, and now we are on the way out. Rays of light are shining in.

We will survive. But will we learn?

It appears that the initial estimates of the scope of the threat were off by some orders of magnitude. But we started with zero knowledge.

Mistakes are part of living. The problem is when we don't learn.

The country already had huge, pressing problems before COVID-19. The experience with this crisis can and must provide invaluable lessons for coming out a stronger and better nation.

This experience should make it clear that politicians should not be micromanaging our lives.

Can anyone be surprised that when the government dispenses a few trillion dollars in the course of a few weeks, targeting these funds efficiently—the aid being structured properly and funds getting where they need to go—is impossible?

Funds from the aid bills winding up in the hands of big corporations, professional sports teams and rich Ivy League universities while many small businesses that can't meet payroll are being shut out should come as no surprise.

That's not to say we should not shine light where errors have been made, fix those errors and try to get the funds where they are most needed. But we must stay aware about the fact that government aid is by nature grossly inefficient and we shouldn't be doing it unless there is absolutely no choice.

The federal government budget going into this crisis was already approaching $5 trillion, 75% of which is transfer payments—that is, entitlements and social expenditures mostly dealing with welfare and poverty.

So we routinely have annual social spending on the order of what we're spending now to get through this crisis. Do you believe it is any more efficient?

We've also seen in recent months a crisis in the governing structure of the nation.

The founders designed and gave us a very good operating manual for how to run things. It's called the Constitution.

We've witnessed chaos through this crisis between mayors, governors and the federal government regarding who is responsible for doing what. This is the direct result of court decisions over the course of many years obfuscating the clarity of the Constitution as originally drafted regarding the limited powers of the federal government.

The COVID-19 crisis has shined light on a crisis in American government. We should fix it and appreciate the wisdom and efficiencies of the Constitution as drafted and originally understood for defining and limiting power of the federal government.

The crisis should also make us aware of the mistakes we have made in undermining traditional values, which has led to a collapse of the American family.

We now see the vulnerability of our aged.

The collapse of conjugal marriage and the dramatic

drop in births means we are living in a nation growing old, with an increasing number of Americans who will grow old alone.

It's not right. And it's certainly not healthy.

In a recent Pew Research survey, 45% said it "makes no difference" that Americans now live in many different types of family arrangements. Fifty-seven percent say it is "essential" for men to have a career they enjoy, and 46% say that is essential for women. But only 16% say being married is "essential" for men, and 17% say it is for women. And only 16% say having children is "essential" for men, and 22% say it is for women.

Let's pray that COVID-19 will bring forth a new respect for love and marriage in America, and produce new waves of children.

What's Causing America's Baby Bust?

March 10, 2021

When the COVID-19 pandemic started and lockdowns became part of our daily lives, some romantic souls were predicting that this would produce a baby boom.

Now, as the data shows up, we see exactly the opposite.

CBS obtained data from health departments in over two dozen states that shows “a 7% drop in births in December—nine months after the first lockdowns began.”

Research from the Brookings Institution in Washington, D.C., predicts that births may well be down 300,000 to 500,000 in 2021.

The prediction is based on a negative correlation between birth rates and the unemployment rate. Higher unemployment means fewer babies.

Brookings also notes, contrary to what the romantics thought would happen, that surveys of couples, particularly those with young children at home, report declines in sexual activity.

But these COVID-related hits to birth rates really attach to a trend of declining fertility rates in the U.S. that has been going on for years.

In 2020, the U.S. fertility rate stood at 1.78. The fertility rate is the average number of children women have during their reproductive years. A fertility rate of 2.1 is needed to maintain stasis—to have sufficient births to offset deaths so the total population size remains consistent and doesn't shrink.

It's evident that the U.S. is way below this and the rate

keeps dropping. Just a decade ago, in 2010, the fertility rate stood at 2.06.

What's happening? Why aren't Americans making babies?

According to Rep. Alexandria Ocasio-Cortez, it's because the times are so hard and stressful.

"(E)ntire generations are sunk w/inhumane levels of student debt, low incomes, high rent, no guarantee of healthcare & little action on climate change," she tweeted out to explain our baby bust.

Are things really so uniquely hard today compared with times gone by that couples no longer want to bring children into the world?

Are we not procreating because young couples are stressed out that economies are spewing too much carbon into the atmosphere, which will supposedly cause temperatures to rise?

In 1935, at the height of the Great Depression, when the nation's unemployment rate stood at 20%, the fertility rate was 2.17—above the replacement rate and well above today's 1.78.

The U.S. fertility rate in 1900 was almost 4, more than double today's rate. Please don't tell me it was because times were so much more safe and certain over a century ago.

In a 2019 Pew Research survey, 16% said having children is essential for a man to have a fulfilling life. Twenty-two percent said it is essential for a woman to have a fulfilling life.

In the same survey, 57% said that "having a job or a career they enjoy" is essential for a man to have a fulfilling life. Forty-six percent said "having a job or career they enjoy" is essential for a woman to have a fulfilling life.

Regarding being married, 16% said it is essential for a man to have a fulfilling life, and 17% said it is essential for a woman to have one.

This data, I think, sheds light on why Americans are not having children. It's not because times are so hard. Every time is challenging, and Americans are more comfortable and prosperous today than ever in history.

Maybe the Brookings scholars will be right about having 300,000 fewer births in the U.S. in 2021 because of COVID. But consider that in Planned Parenthood's most recent fiscal year, it performed 354,871 abortions.

Having children is about life, and life is about caring for more than just yourself. Calling abortion women's health care and thinking that your job is three times more important than bringing new life into the world is not a sign of a healthy culture with a healthy soul.

If we want insight into our baby bust, this is what we should be thinking about.

Hyde Amendment, Yes. Shalanda Young, No

March 17, 2021

The Office of Management and Budget is the largest office in the executive branch of the federal government.

First and foremost, the OMB prepares the federal budget proposal that the president sends up to Congress. Given we're talking about the allocation of spending for almost $5 trillion of taxpayer funds, this is no small task.

President Biden accepted the withdrawal of his initial nominee for director of this substantial enterprise, Neera Tanden, when the numerous members of Congress she has personally attacked and disparaged over the years via her Twitter account expressed their displeasure.

The talk now is that Shalanda Young, Biden's nominee for deputy director, should be bumped up to the director's job.

But now Young finds herself embroiled in her own controversy.

In written response to questions associated with her confirmation hearings for deputy director, she noted her view that the Hyde Amendment should not be reauthorized, despite having been reauthorized every year since it first became law in 1976.

The amendment, named after its sponsor, Rep. Henry Hyde, was passed three years after the Roe v. Wade decision legalized abortion. It prohibits the use of federal funds for performing abortions, except in cases of danger to the life of the mother, incest and rape.

The amendment was a logical follow-up to Roe v

Wade.

The Supreme Court may have concluded that a woman has the right to destroy the unborn child she is carrying. But that right certainly doesn't extend to the federal government forcing taxpayers to pay for it.

But it turns out that Shalanda Young, who could be representing the president in the allocation and administration of $5 trillion of taxpayer money, doesn't see it that way.

For most of his political career, our Catholic president has supported the Hyde Amendment. But suddenly, in 2019, as he aspired to win his party's presidential nomination, Biden had a change of heart.

"The President has spoken in favor of Congress ending the Hyde Amendment," wrote Young, "as part of his commitment to providing comprehensive health care for all women. Further, eliminating the Hyde Amendment is a matter of economic and racial justice because it most significantly impacts Medicaid recipients, who are low-income."

In polling done by Gallup in 2020, 47% said abortion is morally wrong, and 44% said it is morally acceptable.

Somehow, our potential new director of OMB thinks being a poor black woman means not only having a right to destroy your unborn child but also having a right to use other people's money to pay for it, even though half of them think abortion is morally wrong.

It's also interesting to note that the same Gallup polling shows most of the sympathy for abortion is among high-income Americans, not low-income Americans.

Among those earning less than $40,000 and those earning $40,000 to $99,999, 52% say abortion is morally wrong. Among those earning more than $100,000, 33% say abortion is morally wrong.

If any moral disparity appears to jump out here, it is the apparent disproportional moral tolerance among higher-income Americans of a horrible act that destroys human life and takes place overwhelmingly among lower-income Americans, a disproportionate number of them black.

It is hard not to recall the motivations of eugenicist Planned Parenthood founder Margaret Sanger.

The Charlotte Lozier Institute estimates that the Hyde Amendment saves 60,000 unborn babies each year.

If we are going to talk about women's health, and economic and racial justice, we should talk about helping and encouraging women to take control of and responsibility for their lives. Health is about life, not death.

I suggest that President Biden reach back into his Rolodex and find a new nominee to run the OMB. Someone overseeing the dispersal of $5 trillion of taxpayer funds should have more respect for life and property than does Shalanda Young.

Gov. Hutchinson's Distortion of President Reagan

April 14, 2021

Republican Gov. Asa Hutchinson of Arkansas raised ire from conservatives for vetoing legislation passed by the Arkansas state legislature that would have banned “gender-affirming” medical treatment for transgender minors.

This includes treatment such as hormone therapy, puberty blockers and surgery associated with gender identity.

The legislature then overrode Hutchinson's veto, making Arkansas the nation's first state to ban these procedures.

Of particular interest is Hutchinson's rationalization of his veto; he defined it as a conservative stance and used former President Reagan to justify his thinking.

Hutchinson argued during a TV interview that allowing government to prohibit these procedures pushes up against conservative principles of limiting the role of government.

“I go back to Ronald Reagan, to principles of our party, which believes in a limited role of government,” he said. “Are we as a party abandoning a limited role of government and saying we're going to invoke the government decision-making over and above physicians, over and above health care, over and above parents—and saying, 'You can't do that. You cannot engage in it'?”

Reagan was a conservative president who did indeed want to limit government's control of our private lives. But the word is “limit,” not “erase.”

Let's consider Reagan's words in one of his most famous speeches, known as the "evil empire" speech, which he delivered to the National Association of Evangelicals on March 8, 1983.

In that speech, Reagan called the then-Soviet Union "an evil empire" and cast the struggle between the U.S. and the USSR as a struggle of good against evil. He saw communism as evil because of its explicit godlessness.

However, Reagan also used that speech to make a broader statement regarding the general question of good and evil and his own country.

"I want you to know," he said, "that this administration is motivated by a political philosophy that sees the greatness of America in ... the institutions that foster and nourish values like concern for others and respect for the rule of law under God."

"(T)his puts us in opposition to, or at least out of step with, a prevailing attitude of many who have turned to a modern-day secularism, discarding the tried and time-tested values upon which our very civilization is based," he said.

And here is the crux: "Sometimes their voices are louder than ours, but they are not yet a majority."

That was 1983.

A culture in which the objective reality of male/female, man and woman, is denied—despite the clarity of this reality both in the words of the Bible and the chemical reality of the genetic code—is a godless culture that Reagan would likely call evil today, just as he called the Soviet Union evil then.

"Freedom prospers when religion is vibrant and the rule of law under God acknowledged," Reagan said in his speech.

He quoted William Penn, saying, "If we will not be governed by God, we must be governed by tyrants."

Conservatism should be understood literally. To "conserve" is to save and preserve the core traditional values that enable our freedom.

It is hard to believe that, as Gov. Hutchinson suggests, Reagan's idea of limited government means standing aside as a tyrannical secularism sweeps through our nation and wiping out any remaining remnant of those traditional biblical truths.

All the more so, it is hard to believe that Reagan would see government sitting by passively and uninvolved as those values are imposed on minors, who are not even old enough to vote.

It is far more reasonable to assume that President Reagan would stand by these truths as adamantly and stalwartly with our struggles today as he did in standing up to the Soviet Union in the 1980s.

In the face of Reagan's single-minded and uncompromising stance regarding our core values, the Soviet Union collapsed.

The same battle is being fought now in our nation. We must fight it with the same commitment if we hope to prevail.

Sin of Planned Parenthood Is Abortion, Not Margaret Sanger

April 21, 2021

The president of Planned Parenthood Federation of America, Alexis McGill Johnson, has used The New York Times as a confessional to fess up to the racist history of Planned Parenthood's founder, Margaret Sanger.

"We must reckon with Margaret Sanger's association with white supremacist groups and eugenics," she writes.

Sanger's involvement with the notoriously racist eugenics movement in the 1920s, and her population-control motivations to limit the procreation of "undesirables," is something pro-lifers, particularly black pro-lifers, have been writing about for years.

But Planned Parenthood has always been in denial about these very ugly truths.

Now, apparently, the power and pressure of "wokeness" is even getting the leadership of the nation's largest abortion provider to step forward and unburden themselves from their sins.

But coming to terms with sin means knowing what sin is. And here, unfortunately, Planned Parenthood's president totally misses the point.

The problem today is not what was but what is. The "sin" of Planned Parenthood is its horrible work in leading the nation in the destruction of human life.

Per its annual report, in fiscal year 2019-2020, Planned Parenthood performed 354,871 abortions. This is roughly one-third of all abortions performed in the country.

The recognition we need from Planned Parenthood is

the recognition of the sanctity of life, not public confession of the racist history of its founder.

Regarding racism, according to the Kaiser Family Foundation, 34% of abortions performed in the U.S. in 2018 were on black women. Given that black women constitute 13% of the female population, the incidence of abortion among black women is out of proportion by almost a factor of three.

It is reasonable to assume that this is representative of the disproportionate number of black women on whom Planned Parenthood performs abortions.

As part of Planned Parenthood's great cleansing, Johnson notes that "Planned Parenthood of Greater New York renamed its Manhattan health center in 2020," which apparently bore Sanger's name.

The Wall Street Journal's Jason Riley wrote in 2018, "In New York City, thousands more black babies are aborted than born alive each year, and the abortion rate among black mothers is more than three times higher than it is for white mothers. "

The problem is the wholesale termination of black unborn babies, not the name of the center in Manhattan where Planned Parenthood performs these abortions. New York City is one of the abortion capitals of the nation, and Planned Parenthood wants to take the edge off by renaming its abortion center.

Does Planned Parenthood target black women for abortions? Why is the incidence of abortion so high among black women?

A 2012 study by Protecting Black Life found that 79% of Planned Parenthood abortion facilities were within walking distance of minority neighborhoods.

Abortion rates tend to be higher among unmarried women because of a higher likelihood of unwanted pregnancy. The culture of abortion, aggressively promoted by Planned Parenthood, has disproportionately affected black marriage rates.

In 1970, three years before the Roe v. Wade decision, 76% of white adults age 25 and older were married, compared with 60% of blacks. By 2014, the rate dropped to 60% for whites, but it dropped to 35% for blacks.

Johnson takes one step further into the moral abyss, noting that Planned Parenthood is remiss for having "excluded trans and nonbinary people" from its programs.

She writes that Planned Parenthood pledges "to fight the many types of dehumanization we are seeing right now."

Dehumanization has one cause, of which Planned Parenthood is among the guiltiest in the nation: lack of respect for the sanctity of life.

Confessing what we all know—that Margaret Sanger was a racist—does not solve this problem.

Reverence for the sanctity of marriage and the sanctity of life in the womb solves it.

This is what we are looking for from Planned Parenthood. Nothing less.

End of the Roe v. Wade Era?

Jan. 19, 2022

After a COVID-19 driven timeout last year, March for Life returns this year to Washington, D.C., for the 49th year, noting the anniversary of and support to overturn the Roe v. Wade decision of Jan. 22, 1973. This began the era of legal abortion in the USA.

A high turnout is expected due to last year's hiatus, but even more so, to express optimism that this could well be the last March for Life with Roe v. Wade the law of the land.

The Supreme Court heard last December Dobbs v. Jackson Women's Health Organization, challenging the constitutionality of Mississippi's Gestational Age Act, passed in 2018, posing a frontal assault on Roe v. Wade.

Should the Mississippi law be found constitutional, the Roe v. Wade era, after a half-century, would be over. Given that we now have the most conservative Supreme Court in years, pro-lifers anticipate history in the making.

The Mississippi law alters the viability standard, key to Roe v. Wade, which permits abortion up to the 24th week of pregnancy—the period after which the child is deemed able to survive outside the womb.

The Gestational Age Act moves the focus to when the infant first can feel pain, rather than alleged viability, substantially reducing the time when abortion would be permitted.

Looking back over the last half century that abortion has been part of our national culture, it is difficult to imagine how anyone can see anything but damage that this decision has done to our nation and to our national soul.

The most obvious statistic to consider is the some 63 million children whose lives were taken over those 49 years.

Those whose lives were taken in 1974 would be 48 years old now, at the height of their working careers and, if not for the cultural damage that has been done over these years, may have been well into building their own families.

Surveying our national culture since 1973, I cannot identify a single cultural institution that is better. On the contrary, regarding our core social institutions, everything is uniformly worse.

The American family is in far worse shape today than in 1973.

According to the Census Bureau, in 1968, 85.4% of American children lived with two parents. By 2020, this was down to 70.4%.

Fewer and fewer of our young people are interested in marriage and children.

In 1970, per the Census Bureau, the median age at first marriage for men was almost 24 and for women a little over 20. By 2021, for men this reached almost 31 and for women almost 29.

Fertility rates have dropped dramatically. The fertility rate—the average number of children that a woman brings during her productive years—must be 2.1 to keep a population from shrinking. In 1970, our fertility rate was 2.54. By 2020, it was down to 1.78.

The overall implications are an ageing society. According to the Federal Reserve Bank of St. Louis, in 1970, 10.1 % of Americans were over 65. Today, almost 17% are over 65.

An increasing burden of caring for the elderly falls

each year on a shrinking number of working Americans. Per the Kaiser Family Foundation, those over 65, now 17% of the population, account for over 35% of our health care expenditures.

How can anyone not see all this as flashing danger signs to our national future?

The bottom line is a country with a future is a country that values and respects the sanctity of life.

With all the supposed concerns of woke culture, the truth is that respect between people—whether between races and ethnicities, or between men and women—begins with respect for the sanctity of life.

Let us all pray, as we begin a new year, that this will be the last year that pro-lifers need to march in Washington to protest the Roe v. Wade regime.

Culture

Freedom Starts with Respect for Life

Jan. 16, 2019

Tennessee's new senator, Marsha Blackburn, has just introduced the Title X Abortion Provider Prohibition Act. This coincides with this year's March for Life, noting 46 years since the 1973 Roe v. Wade decision legalizing abortion.

The legislation would end all federal funding to all abortion providers, including Planned Parenthood.

This is the first legislative initiative by Blackburn, elected to the Senate in 2018 after serving eight terms in House of Representatives. Blackburn has been a principled, unwavering pro-life conservative in all her years of public service, and I commend her for this.

It is about time that as a nation we understand the scourge of abortion in the broadest context of how it impacts our nation's health and wealth.

I have spoken and written often about this, comparing our social upheavals of today to those of the 1850s, when slavery was the issue tearing our nation apart.

The 1854 Kansas-Nebraska Act, championed by Senator Stephen Douglas, provided that citizens of these new territories could vote to determine whether slavery would be permitted.

The act was, on the issue of slavery, pro-choice.

Abraham Lincoln touched the heart of the matter in his famous speech, Oct. 16, 1854 in Peoria, Illinois.

"Judge Douglas interrupted me to say," said Lincoln, "that the principle (of) the Nebraska Bill was very old; that it originated when God made man and placed good and evil before him, allowing him to choose for himself, being responsible for the choice he should make."

Lincoln answered that "the facts of this proposition are not true as stated. God did not place good and evil before man, telling him to make his choice. On the contrary, he did tell him there was one tree, of the fruit of which, he should not eat, upon pain of certain death. I should scarcely wish so strong a prohibition against slavery in Nebraska."

Many sided with Stephen Douglas then on the proposition that it made sense that legality of slavery in a given territory be decided by vote, by choice. What American today would agree with this?

On the contrary, who among us did not learn American history without a sense of disbelief that once slavery existed in our nation, founded on the principles of freedom and equality?

On the issue of slavery, Lincoln was pro-life.

He knew that human life is not a creature of political definition, but a divine truth toward which we need to be in deference and awe, as we are in awe of the God that created it.

There is little doubt in my mind that one day Americans will look back on our history with disbelief that it was once legal in America for women to be judge and jury of life itself and to destroy the miracle of life within them.

Meanwhile, we see the warning signs around us of a society falling apart as result of a sickness in the soul.

Family and marriage are collapsing. Birthrates are collapsing.

New Census Bureau data shows U.S. population growth this past year is the lowest in 80 years. They project that in just 17 years, for the first time ever, our population over the age of 65 will exceed our population under 18.

For some reason, we seem to need to plunge into the darkness before we see the light.

But the good news is we have leaders like Martha Blackburn and Americans like the hundreds of thousands who will arrive in Washington for the March of Life.

The incidence of abortion has dropped dramatically since its peak after Roe v .Wade, and it has dropped significantly among young women. Activism by pro-life groups is making a difference.

Slowly, albeit too slowly, awareness is building in America that true freedom starts with respect for the mystery and sanctity of life.

Protect Life Rule Is Good News for America

Feb. 27, 2019

The Trump administration has taken another critically important step in strengthening the moral health of our nation, and hence our future.

The Department of Health and Human Services has issued the Protect Life Rule, stopping the flow of Title X federal funds to family planning clinics that perform abortions or do abortion referrals.

It also requires that clinics receiving Title X funds be "physically and financially" separate from any entity providing abortions.

This puts a stop to organizations like Planned Parenthood, the nation's largest abortion provider, from claiming that, although they perform abortions, Title X funds they receive are used for other purposes.

Estimates are that this rule will reduce federal funding flowing to Planned Parenthood by some $60 million.

The Title X program was enacted in 1970, as part of the Public Health Service Act, to provide family planning assistance, primarily to low-income families.

In 2018, $286,479,000 was appropriated to this program.

Rep. Chris Smith, R-N.J., chairman of the Congressional Pro-Life Caucus, notes that Title X funds were "never" meant to fund abortions services. Given that the program was enacted three years before abortion was legalized nationwide as result of Roe v. Wade, his case is convincing.

A Planned Parenthood spokesperson attacked this rule-making, saying that “the Trump-Pence administration has aggressively targeted the ... rights and bodily autonomy of people of color.”

There was a time in our nation's history when the rights and bodily autonomy of people of color were aggressively violated.

But as vile a sin slavery was, those that committed it did so by choice. Americans who wanted no part of it weren't forced to participate as slave owners.

This isn't the case when taxpayer funds are channeled by the federal government to abortion providers.

According to the most recent Gallup polling, 75 percent of those who attend church weekly and 56 percent of those that attend church monthly are “pro-life.”

Their reverence for the sanctity of life flows directly from their faith.

It is inconceivable that an American citizen who believes and understands that abortion is the destruction of human life should be forced to fund, with their tax dollars, those who perform it.

Although it is currently legal for women to have abortions for whatever reason they want, it is repugnant to think that as a nation we would provide further moral authority for abortion by allowing federal funds to support it.

The loss of reverence for the sanctity of life, and the culture of meaninglessness that it fosters, comes at a great price for our nation's soul.

It's evident in a new survey of American teens, ages 13-17, by Pew Research.

Seventy percent of these young Americans say

anxiety and depression is a "major" problem among their peers. Fifty-one percent say drug addiction is a "major" problem.

Although 95 percent say "having a career or job that they enjoy" is "extremely" or "very" important, only 47 percent say getting married is extremely or very important, and only 39 percent say having children is extremely or very important.

According to research of John D. Mueller of the Ethics and Public Policy Center in Washington, "legal abortion is the main cause of family breakdown, including specifically in the rise of rates of divorce, illegitimacy, and crime."

Thus, this new rule-making strikes at the heart of what is wreaking havoc in urban America. It is sadly ironic that those on the left, who favor abortion and hence the social destruction it cultivates, label the Trump administration racist.

According to Gallup, sentiment is rising against abortion. When Gallup first surveyed the issue in 1995, 56 percent were "pro-choice" and 33 percent "pro-life." Today, it's even at 48 percent for both.

The fight against legal abortion on demand will continue. But for sure, taxpayer funds should not be going to abortion providers, particularly not to corporate giants like Planned Parenthood.

The Suicidal Equality Act of 2019

May 8, 2019

The House Judiciary Committee has voted out the Equality Act of 2019. It now heads for a vote on the House floor with 240 co-sponsors, which means its passage is virtually certain.

The legislation amends all major civil rights law, including the 1964 Civil Rights Act, to include "sexual orientation" and "gender identity" along with race, sex and religion as classes that are protected from discrimination.

There is so much wrong here it is hard to know where to start.

My dictionary defines psychosis as "a severe mental disorder in which thought and emotions are so impaired that contact is lost with external reality."

We now have a majority of members of Congress who are prepared to pass into law that the sex individuals are born with—their chromosomal and physical reality—will take a back seat to how those individuals choose to define their own sexual identity. Henceforth, we'll be done with the idea that there is some objective reality independent of what of any particular individual decides it is.

I once complained that our society was denying morality—right and wrong. Now we're beyond this. We're denying reality in its entirety.

Please, read again the definition of psychosis. We're simply going crazy.

My impulse is to turn to heaven and pray to our God to save us.

But even the reality of our God, to whom the signers

of the Declaration of Independence in 1776 turned for "protection," and to whom they pledged "our Lives, our Fortunes and our sacred Honor," is widely being brought into question.

The situation is dangerous. Hopefully, this disaster will be stopped.

First, let's appreciate that this is oppression dressed up in language of freedom and justice.

Religious freedom goes out the window if this bill becomes law.

It explicitly defines itself as overriding the Religious Freedom Restoration Act that can protect people, such as Christian baker Jack Phillips, from being forced to do commerce that violates their Christian convictions.

There will be no more legal protections for Christians in commerce or in any other circumstance to enable them to avoid complicity with behavior that for them is sin.

A bizarre list of behaviors will become legally protected and enshrined in a new America that will be the total antithesis of the ideals of liberty envisioned by its founders.

I will have to start to worry that my little granddaughter will encounter a man in the restroom who has a right to be there because he thinks he is a woman.

Under the guise of civil rights, our public schools will be forced to teach this sexual nihilism as truth, and teaching the traditional values that have held the American family together will become an actionable offense.

We're talking about civil tyranny, not civil rights.

Civil rights law was designed to protect human dignity by preventing individuals from being reduced to pre-existing realities not connected to their personal choices, such as race. Now with this law, the sexual behavior they choose, and the sex they decide they are, will receive the same protections.

There is a spiritual as well as a legal price that we're already starting to pay for this insanity.

The Centers for Disease Control and Prevention reports the U.S. birthrate is the lowest it has been in 30 years. The general fertility rate, the number of births per 1,000 women ages 15 to 44, dropped 3 percent from 2016 to 2017, to a record low.

The CDC also reports a 33 percent increase in the rate of suicide from 1999 to 2017.

The culture of meaninglessness, driving perverse legislation such as the Equality Act of 2019, will destroy us.

We must vigilantly fight to prevent it from passing into law, as we recall the words of historian Arnold Toynbee: "An autopsy of history would show that all great nations commit suicide."

In Praise of Clarence Thomas

June 5, 2019

Supreme Court Associate Justice Clarence Thomas is, once again, under attack.

And, once again, the attacks are from liberals who cannot tolerate Thomas' consistent, unyielding and faithful commitment to America's founding principles.

The latest concerns Thomas' 20-page opinion offered up in Box v. Planned Parenthood of Indiana and Kentucky, recently considered by the Supreme Court.

Planned Parenthood challenged Indiana law prohibiting abortion for reasons of sex, race or non-life-threatening deformity.

The challenge was upheld in district court and the law overturned. However, the Supreme Court chose not to rule on the matter for procedural reasons, turning it back to be heard on appeal at the district level.

But Justice Thomas used the occasion to write an extended opinion on this important abortion case because the principles involved are too important to ignore for America's present and for our future.

According to the Indiana law as enacted, doctors must inform women that “Indiana does not allow a fetus to be aborted solely because the fetus's race, color, national origin, ancestry, sex, or diagnosis or potential diagnosis of the fetus having Down syndrome or any other disability.”

What liberal would ever tolerate American law protecting this type of discrimination?

Yet these same liberals are adamant that abortion for these same reasons is just fine.

Thomas seized on what is obvious, writing, "Enshrining a constitutional right to an abortion based solely on the race, sex, or disability of an unborn child, as Planned Parenthood advocates, would constitutionalize the views of the 20th- century eugenics movement."

The eugenics movement advocated public policies to manipulate the population to produce what is deemed to be a public that is genetically superior.

In other words, bureaucrats decide the value of human beings—who's worthwhile to have around and who's not.

You would think that such ideas would produce outcries from liberals.

But what is producing outcries from them is that Clarence Thomas suggests that abortion based on these criteria makes abortion a tool for eugenics.

Thomas documents the sympathies of Margaret Sanger, the founder of Planned Parenthood, for the eugenics movement. And although Thomas notes that Sanger's sympathies for abortion were less clear, he points out that the sympathies of later Planned Parenthood President Alan Guttmacher for abortion as a eugenics policy tool were clear.

And he gets to the heart of the matter at the conclusion of his opinion: "Although the court declines to wade into these issues today, we cannot avoid them forever. Having created the constitutional right to abortion, this Court is dutybound to address its scope. ... The constitution itself is silent on abortion."

The nation's founders explained in the preamble to the Constitution that we "do ordain and establish this Constitution" to "secure the blessings of liberty to ourselves and our posterity."

Our Constitution was conceived to protect our liberty, not invent it.

In his dissenting opinion in the Obergefell v. Hodges case in which the Supreme Court legalized same sex marriage, Thomas wrote: "Since well before 1787, liberty has been understood as freedom from government action, not entitlement to government benefits. ... the majority ... rejects the idea—captured in the Declaration of Independence—that human dignity is innate and suggests instead that it comes from the Government."

Liberals cried "foul" when Thomas rightly observed that abortion based on race, sex or disability amounts to giving constitutional protection to the eugenics movement because he struck the highly sensitive note that liberals want to stand in God's place.

Liberals defining life inevitably leads to them deciding who lives and who dies.

America's founders were more humble. They saw the source of our right to life, liberty and property as God.

This strikes at the core of what divides our nation today.

Are we a nation under God, as Clarence Thomas believes, or a nation defined and run by liberals and bureaucrats?

Ilhan Omar's Ideological Attacks on Two Christian Pastors

June 26, 2019

Congressional hearings are a fixture in Washington and are supposedly a tool for investigation by the nation's lawmaking body.

Unfortunately, too often when Democrats are in charge, it's not the case. Rather than hearings being a means for seeking facts and information, they become just a platform for politicking by members of the majority party and a forum for attacking those whose views they don't like.

This distortion of process was in full view at recent House Budget Committee hearings on Poverty in America: Economic Realities of Struggling Families.

Of eight witnesses, six were from the same left-wing organization—the Poor People's Campaign.

The other two were members of the national clergy network of my organization CURE, Center for Urban Renewal and Education: Pastor Latasha Fields, founder of Christian Home Educators' Support System, and Pastor David Mahan, founder of Frontline Youth Communications.

Democrat Congresswoman Ilhan Omar, a member of the committee and one of three Muslims in Congress, showed up at the hearing not looking for facts but with her already established, prefabricated view of the world. Rather than asking questions, she used all her time to pontificate and ridicule CURE's two Christian pastors.

The remarkable stories that these two pastors shared about growing up poor in broken communities and beating the odds through struggle and faith were of zero interest to

Omar. They didn't say what she wanted to hear.

Pastor Mahan summed up his formula for what worked, saying, “Personal responsibility, strong marriages and families, and an active faith in Jesus Christ. ... Government programs will only prove successful to the degree that they supplement these key factors, without supplanting them.”

Pastor Fields talked about her determination as a young woman to not become part of the drugs, crime and despair in the community that surrounded her where she grew up, in Baton Rouge.

She shared the devastation she experienced after becoming pregnant at age 17 and withstanding the pressure from those around her who told her to abort the child.

“I had a big decision to make,” she said. “Do I get rid of my baby and proceed as normal as though nothing happened ...? Or do I live the rest of my life knowing I had killed my baby?”

Mahan and Fields conveyed how they rejected abortion, how they married, struggled, home-schooled their children and are now proud parents of children with university degrees.

Rather than holding up Fields' story of faith and courage as a shining example of what works, Omar mocked her.

“(We) hear someone say, 'It was a choice made—up to me, to have my children and not be like other black people ... We don't get to have those kinds of conversations,” said Omar.

What kind of conversations do we get to have, according to her? “The kind of systematic barriers that exist in prosperity—that's the conversation we should be having,” she said.

The great hymn "Amazing Grace," composed by repentant slave trader John Newton, ends with "I was blind but now I see."

Congresswoman Omar is blinded by hate for the nation to which she had the privilege of immigrating. She is blinded by the distortions of the statist ideology that, despite years of experience and tens of trillions in government expenditures to the contrary, she chooses to believe will improve impoverished lives.

Two courageous Christian pastors presented themselves before the House Budget Committee as living examples that the faith and freedom that made America great is still the formula that works—even in the most difficult and challenging circumstances.

We're now entering election season. Democrats are betting they can still drown out the truth and continue to sell the same failed big-government lies to blacks.

My bet is stories like those of Pastors Fields and Mahan are too powerful, even for the screaming and ranting of Ilhan Omar. Even those who were once blind are coming to see the truth.

Our Changing Values Should Worry Us

Aug. 28, 2019

The late historian and political philosopher Harry V. Jaffa noted the significance that the preamble to our Constitution concludes with the words "secure the Blessings of Liberty to ourselves and our Posterity."

This is how the drafters of our Constitution saw its purpose.

Jaffa continues, saying, "a blessing is what is good in the eyes of God. It is a good whose possession ... belongs properly only to those who deserve it."

In light of this, let's consider a just-released Wall Street Journal/NBC News poll that appeared under the headline "Americans Have Shifted Dramatically on What Values Matter Most."

"Patriotism, religion and having children rate lower among younger generations than they did two decades ago," the headline continues.

Of all surveyed, 61 percent "cited patriotism as very important to them, down 9 percentage points from 1998, while 50% citied religion, down 12 points. Some 43% placed a high value on having children, down 16 points from 1998."

Among those ages 18-38, 42 percent cited patriotism as "very important"; less than one-third cited having children; and 30% cited "religion, belief in God."

The founders of the country saw the nation's existence, its faith and its posterity as a package deal. It all went together.

Now we have a young generation, our future, that dismisses the importance of all the elements of that package. What might this tell us about where we're headed?

The operative questions are: Does the country have a future, a posterity, without children? And will there be children if there is no marriage and family? And will there be marriage and family if there is no religion and God?

Recent statistics provide pretty gloomy answers to these questions.

The Centers for Disease Control and Prevention reported the lowest birth rate in 32 years last year. It was the fourth consecutive year with a decline in the U.S. birth rate.

And the fertility rate, the number of births per 1,000 adult women, has been dropping every year and is well below the replacement rate—the fertility rate needed to keep the population from shrinking.

Regarding marriage, over the last half-century, the percentage of U.S. adults who are married has dropped 31 percent.

According to the Pew Research Center, in 1960, 72 percent of adults in the U.S. were married. By 2016, this was down to 50 percent.

The decline in the percentage of Americans saying religion is “very important” in their life is identical to the decline in the percentage of married Americans.

In 1960, 70 percent said religion was “very important,” and by 2018, this was down to 50 percent, a 20 percent decline.

Although Americans continue to feel free—87 percent, according to Gallup, are satisfied that they can freely live as they choose—a minority now sees this liberty as a blessing, in the sense that Harry Jaffa explains the word in our Constitution. That is, “what is good in the eyes of God.”

As the sense of the importance of faith and religion

diminishes, the values and behaviors that go with them—marriage and children—also diminish.

There are important practical implications on our posterity.

Fewer children means an aging population. More retirees per everyone working means more pressure on the payroll tax, each dollar of which must be distributed to more and more retirees.

The population over the age of 55 accounts for more than half our health care expenditures. As the percentage of the population over 55 increases, our health care expenditure burden will increase proportionately.

And, with the collapse of family, more elderly Americans will be living alone.

If you think this picture is gloomy, the good news is nothing is inevitable. We're still free, and we can change course.

Different discourse in the public square, policies consistent with seeing liberty as a "blessing," can be advanced. But the starting point must be seeing something wrong with the status quo.

Pompeo and Barr

Oct. 23, 2019

Two recent high-profile speeches by Trump administration officials say much—maybe even all we need to know—about the core cultural conflicts in the country and what will define the upcoming election.

One speech, titled "Being a Christian Leader," was delivered by Secretary of State Mike Pompeo to the American Association of Christian Counselors in Nashville, Tennessee. Attorney General William Barr delivered the other speech to the law school and the de Nicola Center for Ethics and Culture at the University of Notre Dame.

Pompeo discussed how, as a young man at West Point, he refocused his Christian faith to the center of his life. He went on to relate how this influences today how he understands America's role in the world and how he does his job as secretary of state.

Barr discussed the aggressive and destructive secularism now sweeping the country. He touched on the key point, made first by then-President George Washington in his 1796 farewell address to the nation, that a free nation must be a self-governing nation and that this only is possible through moral virtue.

Limited government requires a population that rules itself. This requires, as Barr explained, "shared moral values" that "rest on authority independent of men's will—they must flow from a transcendent Supreme Being."

There is no way two high-profile officials from the Trump administration would give public presentations like these without support from the president, particularly in today's highly charged political environment.

Pompeo and Barr communicated a worldview starkly in contrast to what we're hearing from the Democratic presidential hopefuls, most recently at the debate in Westerville, Ohio.

The line is drawn clearly in the sand.

President Trump is running on the premise that America is a free nation Under God.

Democrats see our future in secular humanism.

In the Democrat world, politicians define for us what social justice is, and politicians use the power of government to implement their vision.

Practically, this means massive expansion of government and politicians like Bernie Sanders or Elizabeth Warren, or whomever Democrats wind up choosing, running our lives and deciding who should have what.

At least some Democrats are asking where the tens of trillions of dollars will come from to pay for proposals like "Medicare for All."

But let's look at it a different way.

Who is going to pay for all the government required by the collapse of the American family?

According to the Kaiser Family Foundation, Americans ages 55 and above accounted for 56% of all health care expenditures in 2016.

Our population is now shrinking due to fewer births, a direct result of acceptance of abortion and young people shunning marriage and family.

The result is an aging population. The Census Bureau projects that by 2034, 15 years from now, for the first time ever, there will be more Americans over 65, 77 million, than under 18, 76.5 million.

Fewer and fewer working Americans bearing the health care and retirement burdens of increasing numbers of elderly is not a picture for a healthy future. But it is the future that secular humanism is delivering and will continue to deliver.

The 2016 election was about pushing back from this trend and restoring a free nation Under God.

President Trump is delivering on this with deregulation, tax cuts, more conservative judges at every level of our judiciary, and pro-life, pro-family values.

The American Revolution was about freedom.

Americans don't want a king who thinks he's God running our lives. This includes Democratic secular humanists who want the same kind of power King George in England had, against whom the American colonists rebelled.

George Washington was right in 1796, and President Donald Trump, Secretary of State Pompeo and Attorney General Barr are right in 2019.

A free nation is a self-governing nation, and a self-governing nation lives according to eternal biblical truths.

Democrats Want to Save the Planet, Not Our Babies

Nov. 27, 2019

Students stormed the football field at halftime at the Harvard-Yale game and held things up for about an hour, demanding that the schools divest holdings in fossil fuels investments.

The disruptors were cheered on by presidential candidate Elizabeth Warren while actress Alyssa Milano decried wealthy universities "invested in the destruction of the planet."

When you have important work to do like saving the planet, you certainly have a right—it's assumed by these activists—to violate the time and property of others as you wish.

But these same environmental activists, who feel empowered to interrupt our personal and commercial lives in the name of their planet-saving crusade, conclude just the opposite when it comes to unborn children.

In their view, it is not our right to use the cheapest and most readily available energy and electricity, because they have decided this endangers the planet. But at the same time, they insist it is the right of any woman to destroy the unborn child developing inside of her.

This point of view characterizes the current field of Democratic candidates running for president.

Billionaire and former New York City Mayor Michael Bloomberg has entered the fray, supposedly to provide a more moderate alternative for Democrats.

But Bloomberg is also a climate change activist who

believes destruction of unborn children is just fine. Save the planet while we destroy our children. I guess clear thinking is not a prerequisite for becoming a billionaire.

Bloomberg boasts of having reduced the "carbon footprint" of New York City while he was mayor from 2002 to 2013.

But New York City also has a well-deserved reputation as the nation's abortion capital.

The abortion rate in 2016 in New York City—the number of abortions per 1,000 women ages 15 to 44—was 31.1. In the U.S. in 2014, per the Guttmacher Institute, it was 14.6.

How about black women?

Reported Jason Riley of the Wall Street Journal in 2018: "In New York City, thousands more black babies are aborted than born alive each year, and the abortion rate among black mothers is more than three times higher than it is for white mothers. According to a city Health Department report released in May, between 2012 and 2016 black mothers terminated 136,426 pregnancies and gave birth to 118,127 babies. By contrast, births far surpassed abortions among whites, Asians and Hispanics."

Former President Barack Obama stood out in the Democratic "save our planet, not our babies" school.

He was the first sitting American president to address the national meeting of Planned Parenthood, the nation's largest abortion provider.

And Obama led us into the Paris climate agreement, concluded at the 2015 United Nations Climate Change Conference. The U.S., per this agreement, committed to 26% to 28% carbon emissions reduction below 2005 levels by 2025.

The Heritage Foundation estimated that the agreement would have cost an American family of four 13% to 20% more in annual electricity costs.

In 2017, President Donald Trump pulled the U.S. out of this agreement, saying he was elected to represent "Pittsburgh, not Paris."

One characteristic that distinguishes the "save our babies" crowd from the "save our planet" crowd is humility.

When most of us hear the weather forecast for one week out, we take it with a grain of salt. Who would make huge investments based on accuracy of the weather forecast?

Yet the "save our planet" crowd takes predictions about what will be in 25, 50 or 100 years with grave seriousness and wants to impose huge costs today on working families based on these speculations.

A child in the womb is not speculation. This is life. This is our future. Respecting the sanctity of this life, and the sacred activity and responsibility in producing it, is really the behavior and attitude that will save our planet and our world.

President Trump's Important Step Against Anti-Semitism

Dec. 18, 2019

President Donald Trump has signed an important and timely executive order clarifying that prohibited activities covered by Title VI of the Civil Rights Act of 1964 include anti-Semitism.

Title VI prohibits discrimination based on race, color or national origin in any program or activity where federal funds are provided. Thus, a primary target here is our colleges and universities.

According to the Anti-Defamation League, in 2017, acts of anti-Semitism had increased 57% nationwide over 2016, increased 89% on college campuses and increased 94% at K-12 schools.

We should be as concerned in America about anti-Semitism as we are about racism. But this initiative is getting criticism in some circles.

One allegation is that it will stifle free speech on college campuses, intimidating those who want to criticize Israel. But this confuses the cure with the disease.

Free speech is being stifled now on politicized campuses across the nation.

I have spoken at hundreds of universities over the last 20 years. It has never been more difficult for me to speak to students and share my views as a Christian conservative pro-life black woman without being harassed, sometimes violently. I've had engagements canceled because of political pressure on campus.

Other conservative speakers have similar

experiences. The recently released documentary "No Safe Spaces" focuses on the politicization of our university campuses and the intimidation of free speech.

Too often the same happens to those who go to universities to speak on behalf of Israel. Those who disagree are not interested in civil and enlightened exchange of views. They simply want to shut down, sometimes with violence, those with whom they disagree. They want to shut out supporters of the state of Israel.

According to the nonpartisan Freedom House that issues annual reports on the state of freedom around the world, of 21 countries and territories in the Middle East and North Africa, only two are ranked "free": Israel and Tunisia. And Israel is the most free.

Where are all the protests about the other 19 countries and territories in the region, populated by some 400 million people who are not free?

If anti-Semitism does not explain why the freest country in the Middle East, the only Jewish country in the world, is the only one drawing protests and hostility, what is the explanation?

Another line of misguided criticism of this executive order is the claim that it defines Judaism as a nationality.

Anyone who buys this bogus line, first peddled by The New York Times, should read the order and see that it is not true.

Anti-Semitism is an ancient scourge, which has produced a new strain in our time with the emergence of the state of Israel.

Jewish students at universities may be subject to harassment and discrimination because of the hostile environment to Israel on campuses. It is this problem that this new executive order addresses. It does not define, or redefine, Judaism as a nationality.

The whole point of the civil rights movement, which culminated in the Civil Rights Act of 1964, was the protection of the freedom and dignity of every American.

The evil of all discrimination, be it anti-Semitism or racism, is depriving individuals of their humanity by pretending that they can be defined by what they look like or where they come from.

This points to the sad irony of the identity politics that has gripped and swept the nation and our university campuses. It does exactly what the civil rights movement tried to eliminate: defines individuals by what they look like or where they come from.

President Trump was elected in 2016 because his Make America Great Again message resonated with voters tired of political correctness and identity politics.

Our country is about core principles, universally true for all, that secure and protect individual freedom and dignity.

This is what this new executive order is about.

Elizabeth Warren Anoints Herself God

Jan. 1, 2020

The Pew Research Center reports among its major findings in 2019 a dramatic drop in Americans identifying as Christian.

In 2019, 65% of Americans identified as Christian, down from 77% in 2009. The percentage who identify as religiously unaffiliated—that is, atheist, agnostic or "nothing in particular"—stood at 26% in 2019, compared with 17% a decade ago.

I think this shift reflects less belief in God, rather than what God Americans choose to worship.

Take, for instance, Democratic presidential contender Elizabeth Warren.

There does not appear to be a single aspect of human existence for which she doesn't have her own answer. Warren thinks she's God, and a shockingly high number of Americans seem ready to line up and worship her.

Warren knows what is just and unjust, how much wealth is too much for any particular individual and how much is not enough. And she feels totally empowered to take from one and give to the other to make the world what it is supposed to be.

Needless to say, in her exalted, divine wisdom, she is ready to deliver the last word on sexual identity, marriage, family and, of course, life and death.

I'm focusing on Elizabeth Warren because she is the most unabashedly outspoken and detailed in her views representing the American left. But she is really the American left itself.

At a recent Democratic debate, Warren said: "I believe abortion rights are human rights. I believe they are also economic rights."

I wonder when candidates make these declarations why the moderators never ask, "How do you know that?" It would give Warren the opportunity to clarify by saying, "I know because I am God."

Warren said that abortion is a "hard decision" but "the one entity that should not be in the middle of that decision is the government."

This appears to be the only area in all of American life where Warren does not believe the government should be involved.

The Wall Street Journal recently surveyed "60-some policy papers" from Warren's campaign, which show that no details of the life of every American will escape government dictate.

There is the wealth tax; the "Medicare for All" tax; the corporate surtax; higher capital gains taxes; higher income taxes on "the wealthiest individuals and giant corporations"; the overturning of "right to work laws" to shore up unions; the end of federal funding for charter schools; the vast expansion of government management of our currency, our jobs and our industry; a $3 trillion Green New Deal; the break-up of the big high tech companies, etc., etc.

Let me make a few distinctions between the God of my beautiful leather Bible that I read every day and the self-anointed God Almighty Elizabeth Warren.

The God I worship made man in His image and gave free choice and personal responsibility. My God made man a free, responsible, creative agent.

My God issued a commandment against envy. What

others have is not our business. Our business is conducting our own affairs and building our own life. We must care about those in need, but individuals make this decision, not government or a self-appointed God-politician.

There is also a commandment against theft. In the universe created by my God, there is private property, and there is sin and punishment in stealing what belongs to others.

Politicians who think they are God, mobilizing power by inspiring sinful envy of what others have legally achieved and then using political power to legalize theft to steal the property of some in order to redistribute to others, is not only not Christian but also not American.

In the universe created by my God, life is sacred, as is property. This provides the basis for a free and prosperous country.

As we enter the new year and continue rebuilding our great country, I pray for a rebirth of American Christianity.

Staying Free and Faithful in a Pandemic

March 18, 2020

The coronavirus crisis presents challenges to us as a nation and as individuals. There are principles we should keep in mind.

Let's remember how our nation works. We have a Constitution that assigns limited, defined powers to the federal government and leaves the rest to the states and individuals.

Some governors, like J.B. Pritzker of Illinois, don't seem to understand this. At a time when political leaders should be inspiring confidence, Pritzker is attacking President Donald Trump, accusing the federal government of being "completely unprepared." He wants to lay blame for crowds and delays at O'Hare Airport on the president.

President Trump acted with deliberation, doing his job, shutting down flights from China and then Europe. As Americans massed back to their home country, airports were predictably backed up.

The great Maj. Gen. George S. Patton observed, "A good plan violently executed now is better than a perfect plan executed next week." This exactly captures President Trump's behavior as this crisis began to unfold.

O'Hare Airport is owned and operated by the city of Chicago. Clearly, some functions there, such as customs, are federal functions. But overall operation of the airport is local, and rather than jumping on the president and playing blame games at a difficult time, governors such as Pritzker should step up to do their part.

One thing we know is that this virus is most lethal in

attacking the elderly. The rate of fatality among those ages 70-79 is 21 times that of people under age 60. The fatality rate among those 80 and above is 39 times that of people under 60.

One reason Italy has been hit hard is it has the oldest population in Europe, with 23% over the age of 65.

In the U.S., there are large age variations among the states.

Among the youngest, Utah has a median age of 30.5, and 10% of its population is over 65. Texas has a median age of 34.5, and 13% of its population is over 65. Among the oldest, Maine has a median age of 44.3, and 21% of its population is over 65. Florida has a median age of 41.8, and 21% of its population is over 65.

How can "one size fits all" work with such dramatically different local realities?

The answer is that we should maximize local responsibility and decision-making.

There are two other critically important things to keep in mind.

One: Life is about surprise, the unpredictable. If there is anything predictable, it is that the unpredictable will always be with us.

It's why socialism and illusions about national planning are so bogus and always result in failure. And why freedom is so critical and important.

Only through freedom is responsibility focused where it needs to be: on individuals. And freedom delivers maximum flexibility and creativity to deal with life's inherent surprises.

Two: Faith is critical. It is faith that keeps us human. It is faith that binds together free, unique individuals into one great whole cloth.

This health crisis is precipitating an economic crisis. With all eyes turning toward Washington, our business leaders must step up and take responsibility.

I've been writing for years about my belief in free economy and the importance of earning a profit.

With almost 50% of our youth now expressing misguided enthusiasm for socialism, it is critical that business leaders behave thoughtfully and humanely in this crisis. The future of our free, capitalist system rides on it.

Clearly, there is a place for government in keeping the economy moving and helping individuals in distress. But business leaders should not just look to government.

In areas such as sick leave, business leaders should pick up the brunt.

They should not forget that the same God that made employers made workers.

Faith will play a key role in helping our nation through this crisis and emerge better for it.

Free People Take Responsibility and Solve Problems

April 1, 2020

Several months ago, before anyone imagined the current crisis, I read a book called “Man's Search for Meaning” by Viktor Frankl.

Frankl was a Jewish Viennese psychiatrist who was captured by the Nazis during World War II and managed to survive four concentration camps including the infamous Auschwitz and Dachau.

He went through the ordeal observing human behavior, and the result was his formulation of a system of therapy he called logotherapy.

Frankl found that those who were most successful, surviving under the most challenging circumstances, were those who retained a sense of meaning in their lives. That is, the real challenge that every person faces is not what's happening outside of themselves but what's happening inside.

In Frankl's own words: “Everything can be taken from a man but one thing: the last of human freedoms—to choose one's attitude in any given set of circumstances, to choose one's own way.”

He continued: “Freedom is but the negative aspect of the whole phenomenon whose positive aspect is responsibleness. In fact, freedom is in danger of degenerating into mere arbitrariness unless it is lived in terms of responsibleness.”

With all our talk about freedom, somehow its essence has gotten lost: human beings taking responsibility for their own life and the world around them. Human beings are causes, not results. They are free agents, not victims.

I can't think of a more important message as we face these great challenges today as a nation and as individuals.

The whole idea of America was, and hopefully still is, freedom, which means America must be about individuals taking responsibility.

The country now faces two huge areas of uncertainty and lack of clarity.

One is regarding the nature of the health threat we are dealing with. I am still reading different opinions from knowledgeable sources about how lethal this virus is and the best way to stop it without totally shutting down and destroying our economy.

Second, we're suffering great absence of clarity in government regarding who is responsible for what.

Times of uncertainty are times, in the spirit of Viktor Frankl, for individuals to step up and take responsibility.

But, unfortunately, we're getting the opposite.

It's obscene that House Speaker Nancy Pelosi, who held up the emergency stimulus bill to insert left-wing nonsense, accused President Donald Trump of fiddling while "people are dying."

Michigan Gov. Gretchen Whitmer complained to the press, "We're not getting what we need from the federal government."

But this isn't new. Back in February, Whitmer delivered the Democrats' response to President Trump's State of the Union address and went on for her full 10 minutes about the federal government not doing enough.

She touted her efforts to expand health coverage under the Affordable Care Act, meaning more bureaucratization of our hospitals and health care delivery, and creation of government health care incapable of flexibility to changing market realities, let alone dealing with a crisis.

New York Mayor Bill de Blasio is taking deserved heat for his delayed action in response to the crisis in his city. Weeks ago, he was on television talking about how this crisis could only be addressed by the federal government.

This is all the result of generations degrading the clear constitutional lines between the federal government and the states, resulting in massive growth of the welfare state.

But while Democratic governors and mayors and Speaker Pelosi use valuable time looking for who to blame, America's private business is already churning to develop better and faster testing procedures, and soon we'll see a drug to eradicate COVID-19.

Small and large businesses are deploying resources in new and creative ways that will pay great dividends when we emerge from this crisis.

Challenges are met by free, responsible people stepping into the void: exactly what Viktor Frankl was talking about.

Church Attendance Essential to America's Greatness

May 27, 2020

President Donald Trump stepped up to declare houses of worship "essential places that provide essential services" to the American people.

"The governors need to do the right thing and allow these very important, essential places of faith to open right now for this weekend," he said.

The president raised eyebrows by declaring that he will "override" governors if they don't do it.

Where's the president's authority to override governors on this matter?

I'm not a constitutional attorney, but I do have common sense.

The president takes an oath of office during which he swears to "preserve, protect and defend the Constitution of the United States."

The First Amendment of our Constitution protects the right to "free exercise" of religion.

Is it complicated during a difficult time like this when governors have a responsibility to manage the health and welfare of the citizens of their state? Of course it is.

But difficult times mean difficulty applying principles, not erasing those principles.

Is it reasonable for President Trump to categorize religious services as "essential"?

I have been writing for weeks that the COVID-19 crisis is highlighting the same conflicts we've been dealing with as a nation all along.

My guess is California Gov. Gavin Newsom, who, as mayor of San Francisco, paved the way for the legalization of same-sex marriage, does not at all believe houses of worship provide essential services.

I don't question that he understands that religious freedom is protected by our Constitution. But I certainly doubt he believes in his heart that church attendance is "essential," and he probably thinks going to the mall or the beach is more essential.

We're dealing with a core conflict in America today. How vitally important is religion?

In the 1830s, French nobleman Alexis de Tocqueville traveled across the still-youthful America to try to understand what was happening and what was driving the remarkable success of the young nation.

He recorded his thoughts in "Democracy in America," which many believe to be the greatest book ever written about our nation.

Here's what he wrote: "I sought for the greatness and genius of America in her commodious harbors and her ample rivers ... and it was not there ... in her rich mines and her vast world commerce ... and it was not there ... in her democratic Congress and her matchless Constitution ... and it was not there. Not until I went into the churches of America and heard her pulpits aflame with righteousness did I understand the secret of her genius and her power. America is great because she is good, and if America ever ceases to be good, she will cease to be great."

According to a 2018 Gallup survey, 51% of Americans said religion was "very important" in their life. But when Gallup first asked the question, in 1952, 117 years after Tocqueville published his book, 75% said it was "very important."

Although the sense of the importance of religion is still quite strong in America, it has weakened. With that weakening, we're seeing a weakening of behaviors that keep a nation strong: record lows in the rate of marriage and the number of children born.

Also, according to a Kaiser Family Foundation poll, 45% say that the coronavirus crisis has had a negative impact on their mental health. This could be tied to a weakening of faith.

Leadership is about staking out principles and standing by them. President Trump ran for president to "Make America Great Again." He is exercising leadership by declaring religion and church attendance essential to American greatness.

The president is right to defend the constitutional protection of religious practice and to identify the freedom to worship as essential.

Hopefully, governors will listen.

Equality Act Slams the Door on Religious Freedom

June 23, 2021

The Supreme Court's recent decision, Fulton v. Philadelphia, is justifiably getting mixed reviews.

Catholic Social Services sued the city of Philadelphia, through the Philadelphia Archdiocese, for canceling its 50-year contract with the Catholic social services agency because it refuses to certify same-sex couples as foster families for the purpose of foster care.

The Supreme Court ruled in favor of CSS, finding that Philadelphia violated its First Amendment protections

The criticism is that the decision was narrow and technical, skirting the core question of how we understand religious liberty today, when it is under assault almost everywhere.

According to existing precedent, First Amendment protections do not apply against measures that are "generally applicable" and not targeted specifically to religion. When some general measure incidentally impacts a particular religion or religious practice, religious protection can be impinged.

In the case of Philadelphia, the local law provides discretion to city officials to make exceptions to the nondiscrimination provisions of its law. The Court used this to argue that the law is not "generally applicable," and therefore First Amendment protection of CSS was violated.

Justice Samuel Alito, writing on his own behalf and on behalf of Justices Clarence Thomas and Neil Gorsuch, although agreeing with the Court's decision that CSS First

Amendment rights were violated, disagreed with the narrow interpretation.

As Alito pointed out, the city could remove the latitude for exceptions in its law, and suddenly Catholic Social Services' First Amendment protection is gone.

It is a tragedy that something so fundamental as religious freedom is now buried in the weeds of legal hair-splitting.

There could be no better example of what this is all about than Sharonell Fulton, who was the lead plaintiff in this case against Philadelphia.

Fulton is a Black foster mother, who has fostered over 40 children in her home over the last 30 years.

LGBTQ activists like to portray Christians as hateful and discriminatory. But listen to Fulton:

"Children need to be accepted and loved. They have to feel that somebody cares ... I've had gay couples stop me in the supermarket ... And I told them, 'Listen, this is not personal. I'm standing with the church because this is what I believe.'"

The Catholic Church has been reaching out to orphans in Philadelphia for over 200 years. This is motivated by one thing: love.

Why do we need Harvard-trained lawyers to justify something so obvious, that the essence of American religious freedom is Catholics raising children, or providing foster care, according to their biblical values?

They are not forcing their values, or asking government to force their values, on anyone.

The preamble of our Constitution explains that its mission is "to secure the blessings of liberty to ourselves and our Posterity."

When did this get lost?

Now that same-sex marriage is law of the land, the option of foster care in the home of same-sex couples should be examined.

But they should not be free to shut down organizations insisting on biblical values.

Now congressional Democrats are trying to pass the Equality Act that would do just that.

In 1993, the Religious Freedom Restoration Act was passed to restore some protections to religious freedom. If some government measure impinges on religious freedom, it must be demonstrably essential.

But the Equality Act would make the Religious Freedom Restoration Act null and void.

Lost would be the protections that saved Little Sisters of the Poor from being forced to provide abortifacients in their health care plan, as the Affordable Care Act required. Or protections from forcing a doctor or nurse to provide abortions services against their religious convictions. Or bakers, photographers or wedding planners forced to provides services for same-sex weddings against their religious convictions.

The Equality Act is not about equality. It is about forcing the LGBTQ agenda on all Americans.

America is supposed to be about freedom. Remember?

Time To Overturn Roe v. Wade

Aug. 4, 2021

In May, the Supreme Court put abortion on the docket for its upcoming session by agreeing to hear Dobbs v. Jackson Women's Health Organization.

The high court's decision to hear this case registered on the seismometer of every American that carefully follows the abortion issue. It means that Roe v. Wade, which has defined abortion reality in the country since 1973, is open to review and could be overturned.

The Mississippi law in question, which bans abortion after 15 weeks of pregnancy, was struck down by an appeals court in 2019. The state then appealed to the Supreme Court.

Last week, Mississippi's attorney general submitted its brief to the Supreme Court.

A central point of contention will be the issue of viability. Viability—the point at which the unborn child can survive outside of the womb—has been the legal criterion for drawing the line beyond which a woman's alleged right to destroy the child within her is no longer assumed.

Given that viability is assumed to occur at 24 weeks, the 15-week provision of the Mississippi law upends this standard.

The Mississippi attorney general questions the relevance of the viability standard, challenging particularly that there is any basis for it in the Constitution.

But we must dig deep here, because we're not just dealing with the question of viability of the unborn child. We are dealing with questions about the viability of our society and our country.

Can we really function as a society and as a nation while turning away from the most central issue that any society faces—awe of the mystery of life?

There might indeed be a point in time when an unborn child can be removed from its mother and physically survive. But although there may be a point where that child might not need its mother to survive, it still needs others. Someone must take care of that child, meaning someone must care about that child's life. If not, that child will die.

So, the legal idea of viability that has been sustaining the Roe v. Wade world really has no meaning.

In 2014, the Vatican hosted an international colloquium on "The Complementarity of Man and Woman."

Rabbi Lord Jonathan Sacks, the former chief rabbi of the U.K., gave an address about marriage. He spoke of "the idea of the love that brings new life into the world." Sacks observed that "life begins when male and female meet and embrace."

It is hard to believe that in our nation today, when there is so much outrage about racism, many of those who see racism as a problem do not see indifference to the sanctity of life as a problem.

But if all life is not sacred, if every human being is not a unique creation in the image of God, what is wrong with being a racist?

Why would slavery be a problem if every human being is not a divine creation?

It is no accident that following the Roe v. Wade decision in 1973, we have seen a collapse of the American family and now the general collapse of birth itself.

The Wall Street Journal reported last week: "In half of

all states last year, more people died than were born, up from five states in 2019. Early estimates show the total U.S. population grew 0.35% for the year ended July 1, 2020, the lowest ever documented, and growth is expected to remain near flat this year."

A society without family and children, with increasing drug overdoses and suicides, with reports of far too great a frequency of individuals pointlessly murdering people they don't know, is a society whose soul is in bad shape.

Restoring sanctity of life in the womb is a good place to start turning things around.

My prayer is that the U.S. Supreme Court will agree.

It's Time for National Soul-Searching

Aug. 25, 2021

After the attacks on our nation on Sept. 11, 2001, President George W. Bush took to the airways to address the American people.

Speaking to a nation in shock, he cast what had occurred in the framework of good and evil.

"Today, our nation saw evil," the president said.

And he offered up solace in Psalm 23, "Even though I walk through the valley of the shadow of death, I fear no evil for you are with me."

Several days later, a number of evangelical pastors, including Pat Robertson and Jerry Falwell Sr., picked up on the theme of good and evil, reward and punishment, and suggested we must look inside of our nation as well as outside. We must check ourselves.

Pat Robertson issued a press release, as was reported in The New York Times, saying, "In a country rampant with materialism, internet pornography and lack of prayer, 'God Almighty is lifting his protection from us.'"

These pastors got major pushback in the country for suggesting that this horrible occasion provided good reason for self-examination, and Bush, himself a born-again Christian, disavowed the pastors.

The White House issued a statement saying: "The president believes that terrorists are responsible for these acts. ... He does not share those views, and believes that those remarks are inappropriate."

Of course, no pastor questioned who actually committed the acts of terror. They suggested that, along with the actions we take against the terrorists, we must also check our own moral state of affairs to try to understand why such a horrible act of violence could have been successfully carried out on our own soil.

We might recall that the pilots who flew those planes, transforming commercial airliners into lethal weapons, trained in our country.

And while these preparations in our own backyard for what occurred on Sept. 11, 2001, were taking place, the president of the United States, Bill Clinton, was preoccupied committing adultery in the Oval Office.

Now here we are, 20 years later, having spent more than $2 trillion in our operations in Afghanistan, with a loss of some 2,400 American lives. The Taliban, against whom we launched hostilities in 2001, is back in power. By some estimates, their control in Afghanistan is broader than it was in 2001.

Maybe today, as the United States withdraws from Afghanistan in despair, shame and confusion, and as we note 20 years since the loss of 2,977 American lives to terror in our homeland, there will be greater appreciation for doing some national soul-searching.

We needn't just turn back to the admonitions of a few evangelical pastors 20 years ago. We can turn back 225 years to 1796, to the counsel provided to a young, new nation by its first president, George Washington in his farewell address.

Washington reminded his countrymen that theirs is a country rooted in eternal truths and warned about detaching from those truths and allowing the nation to deteriorate into raw politics.

"Of all the dispositions and habits which lead to

political prosperity, religion and morality are indispensable supports. ... Let it simply be asked: Where is the security for property, for reputation, for life, if the sense of religious obligation desert the oaths which are the instruments of investigation in courts of justice? And let us with caution indulge the supposition that morality can be maintained without religion. Whatever may be conceded to the influence of refined education ... reason and experience both forbid us to expect that national morality can prevail in exclusion of religious principle.

"It is substantially true that virtue or morality is a necessary spring of popular government."

Over the last 20 years, as a nation, we have moved further from these truths. Under President Joe Biden's leadership, we have politics, secularism and moral relativism on steroids.

Let's understand that we will have no clarity abroad until we get our house in order at home.

Abortion Is About Our Core National Values

Dec. 1, 2021

The Supreme Court will hear this week Dobbs v. Jackson Women's Health Organization.

At issue is the law in Mississippi that bans abortion after 15 weeks of pregnancy.

A decision finding the Mississippi law constitutional will fundamentally change the abortion regime in our country, defined by Roe v. Wade since 1973.

Roe said the mother has a right to abort her child as long as that unborn child cannot survive—is viable—outside the womb. Generally accepted is 22-24 weeks as the time when viability occurs.

Mississippi's abortion law says that the defining issue should not be viability but when the child first feels pain. Their claim is that this occurs at 15 weeks.

Surveys show the nation evenly split in attitudes toward abortion.

Per the most recent poll from Gallup, 47% say abortion is morally acceptable and 46% say it is morally wrong.

Forty-nine percent self-identify as "pro-choice" and 47% as "pro-life."

However, if we break down the averages into components, we see a deeply polarized nation.

Sixty-four percent of Democrats say abortion is morally acceptable, and 70% self-identify as pro-choice.

Only 26% of Republicans say abortion is morally acceptable, and 74% self-identify as "pro-life."

Abortion is really a bellwether issue that shows the profound split in the nation regarding worldview.

Are we a nation of moral absolutes, that sees our culture grounded in traditional, biblically sourced standards of good and evil, right and wrong? Or are we a nation defined by secular humanism and moral relativism, where the center of the world is not God but man?

We have moved dramatically in the latter direction over the last half-century, and the results are out there to evaluate.

Since the Roe v. Wade decision in 1973, the percentage of American adults who have never been married has quadrupled, as has the percentage of babies born to unwed mothers.

We are moving to becoming a childless nation.

In a recent Pew Research survey, 44% of nonparents, ages 18-49, say it is unlikely that they will have children. Among parents ages 18-49, 74% say it is unlikely they will have more children.

U.S. fertility rates have dropped every year for the last six years and now are at a historic low of 1.64, well below the 2.1 necessary to keep the population at a steady state.

Are women "empowered" by being free of responsibility for bringing into the world the child in their womb?

Per blogger Mark Perry, for the last 12 years, women have earned the majority of doctoral degrees in the country. In 2020, 53.1% of doctoral degrees awarded went to women. Of master's degrees awarded, more than 60% went to women.

Is using abortion as birth control necessary for women to achieve?

There is a certain irony among liberals, whom we can credit for today's politically correct, woke culture.

We don't want dehumanizing racial stereotypes, but the same people obsessed with racial categories are not at all bothered by a culture in which men and women use each other as sexual objects and women can be free to destroy a child that might result from a sexual encounter if its birth could lead to responsibilities that might disturb her career.

To get back to the Dobbs decision and Roe v. Wade and the issue of viability.

In my view, these games with language really point to the victory thus far of secular humanism.

The true issue is if life is sacred. If the answer is yes, it is sacred in and out of the womb.

If we conclude it is not, we are on the road to becoming a nation without children, where the only love is self-love and, I am sorry to say, without a future.

I say no thanks to this and hope the Supreme Court will make the right decision and allow Mississippians to protect sacred life.

More Government, Less Religion—the Progressive Doctrine

Dec. 29, 2021

One great mystery is the persistent refusal of those on the left to abandon what is clearly not true.

That is, that the means for reducing the burden of poverty is more government spending.

It all really started in the 1960s under President Lyndon B. Johnson. He declared in his State of the Union address in January 1964 an "unconditional war on poverty in America." Despite tens of trillions of spending since then, poverty remains, and so does the conviction of progressives that it can be wiped out with government spending.

Worth recalling is that the avalanche of government spending launched in the 1960s was followed in the 1970s by runaway inflation.

We now face the latest round of this misguided idea with the expansion of the Child Tax Credit in the Build Back Better Act—now derailed thanks to Sen. Joe Manchin.

Fellow Democrats are now all over the beleaguered senator for allegedly not caring about child poverty.

Build Back Better would have increased the credit from $2,000 per child to $3,000, or $3,600 for children under 6.

In a particularly destructive move, they detached any work requirement from receiving the Child Tax Credit.

A team of University of Chicago economists estimates providing a new generous Child Tax Credit, with no work requirement, would result in 1.5 million parents leaving the workforce.

More government, less work. This is somehow the answer that Democratic Party leadership is serving up to us for how to build a better future for our nation.

Where does the passion of Democrats really lie—in improving lives of Americans or in dramatically expanding government?

Equally revealing is what does not interest progressives at all.

A little more than a decade ago, Ron Haskins and Isabel Sawhill at the Brookings Institution publicized what they called the "success sequence."

The success sequence consists of three steps in behavior to avoid poverty. Complete at least a high school education, work full time, and wait until age 21 before getting married and then having children.

According to testimony of Haskins in the U.S. Senate in 2012, those following the "success sequence" have a 2% chance of being in poverty and a 75% chance of reaching the middle class.

But the success sequence doesn't much interest progressives because the focus is about individuals taking personal responsibility for their lives in a free country. The "personal responsibility" part and the "free country" part have little standing in the Democratic Party.

Also of little interest to our progressive friends is that larding down our economy with massive amounts of government retards economic growth. Why would anyone think slow economic growth is good for the poor, let alone any American?

As Americans allow themselves to be convinced that government is the answer to their lives, they become more likely to abandon faith and religion, which provide the light and principles for individuals to take control of their own lives.

New data from the Pew Research Center shows the toll that secularization is taking on our country.

According to Pew, 63% of Americans in 2021 identify as Christians, compared with 78% in 2007. In 2021, 29% indicated they have no religion, compared with 16% in 2007. Whereas in 2007, 56% said religion was "very important" in their lives, in 2021 this was down to 41%.

Perhaps as we close out 2021, we should again recall the words of America's first president, George Washington, in his farewell address.

"Of all the dispositions and habits which lead to political prosperity, religion and morality are indispensable supports. ... And let us with caution indulge the supposition that morality can be maintained without religion. Whatever may be conceded to the influence of refined education on minds of peculiar structure, reason and experience both forbid us to expect that national morality can prevail in exclusion of religious principle."

Faith and Freedom Go Together

June 22, 2022

Per a new report from Gallup, the percentage of Americans now saying they believe in God is the lowest since they first started doing the survey.

In 2022, 81% of Americans say they believe in God.

When Gallup first asked this question in 1944, 96% said they believed, and in the early 1950s, it was up to 98%. It remained over 90% until 2013, when it dipped down to 87%.

The current 81% is a 6-point drop from the last time Gallup asked the question in 2017.

Digging down into the data, we get a mixed message about what it tells us about the future.

On the one hand, the age group with the lowest percentage saying they believe in God is the youngest—18 to 29. Only 68% say they believe. Given that these young people reflect our future, we must assume that, with no change in their views, the country will continue its purge of religion from our lives.

On the other hand, the ethnic cross section with the highest percentage saying they believe is what Gallup defines as "people of color." I assume this means Blacks and Hispanics. This group registers 88% belief, 9 points higher than "white," who register 79%.

Given that that the demographic "people of color" is growing faster than "white," and becoming each year a larger percentage of our population, this could point to a strengthening of faith, on average, in our population as we move into the future.

Why should we care about this?

From a practical point of view, faith translates into behavior, and as faith diminishes, the incidence of behaviors that once were viewed as morally unacceptable increases.

In 2001, the percentage of Americans saying the following behaviors are morally acceptable was as follows: birth to unwed mother 45%; gay/lesbian relations 40%; abortion 42%. In 2003, polygamy was deemed morally acceptable by 7%; in 2011, pornography was deemed morally acceptable by 30%; and in 2013, teenage sex was deemed morally acceptable by 32%.

Here are the percentages of Americans saying in 2022 these same behaviors are morally acceptable: birth to unwed mother 70%; gay/lesbian relations 71%; pornography 41%; abortion 52%; teenage sex 45%; polygamy 23%.

Again, we can ask, "So, what?".

The vision of the founders of the country was freedom. The point was to keep government intrusion at a minimum and permit individual freedom at a maximum.

The preamble to the U.S. Constitution notes that it was put forth "to secure the blessings of liberty to ourselves and our posterity." The Constitution was designed to limit government power to very specific defined areas that were deemed essential and appropriate for government.

For this to work, we must assume we have a population of free individuals who manage their own personal affairs in a responsible way.

It is worth recalling, once again, George Washington's famous observation in his farewell address, which first appeared in print Sept. 19, 1796:

"Of all the dispositions and habits which lead to

political prosperity, religion and morality are indispensable support ... reason and experience both forbid us to expect that national morality can prevail in exclusion of religious principle."

Clearly, we have departed in a major way from this.

Supreme Court decisions over the years have reinterpreted the Constitution to grant far more authority to the federal government than the founders had in mind.

And along with this, as we see in Gallup polling, we see major deterioration in faith and significantly higher acceptance of many behaviors that were once deemed morally unacceptable.

Hence, we find where we stand today.

Again, per Gallup, only 16% are satisfied with the way things are going in the country.

Government is in our lives in a major way, with trillion-dollar deficits and debt the size of our entire economy. And now inflation, which reflects all this.

Is there a way out without restoration of religious principle and personal responsibility, as George Washington warned?

I think not.

Court Restores Culture of Life

June 29, 2022

The cries from the left predicting the end of the world in the wake of the Supreme Court's decision to overturn Roe v. Wade is a familiar sound.

We heard the same after the historic reform in welfare in 1996 when Aid to Families with Dependent Children, which effectively subsidized low-income women to have children out of marriage, was replaced with Temporary Assistance for Needy Families—which introduced the idea of workfare.

The reform, the left screamed, would throw low-income women mercilessly to the streets. But the result was quite the opposite. We had a dramatic decrease in welfare cases and increase in work among low-income women.

Human beings respond to incentives and to the realities around them.

When those incentives inspire responsibility, productivity and creativity, this is what we get. When incentives inspire irresponsibility and dependence, this is what we get.

What we call morality, the morality rooted in biblical truths that still influence and guide large parts of the American population and that served as a guide to many more in our past, provides the rules and framework that sustain life and living.

Everyone that knows me knows how I celebrate this court decision that overturns that decision in 1973 that opened the door to the destruction of 60 million-plus pregnancies.

That decision introduced a culture of death to our nation.

When I say a culture of death, I don't only mean the widespread physical destruction of infants in the womb, which is what the decision brought about.

A culture of death means introduction of behaviors that threaten the future of our communities, of our nation.

When we lose appreciation for the sanctity of life, along with this we lose the sense of sanctity of behavior that brings life to the world. Marriage and sex become no longer responsible expressions of love and creation but expressions of egoism and self-gratification of the moment.

Sadly, and predictably, following the Roe v. Wade decision in 1973, we saw collapse of the institution of marriage and of childbearing.

The fertility rate in the United States today is at a historic low and well below the rate necessary for the population to replace itself.

This is what I call a culture of death.

An aging nation, where the number of souls departing exceeds the number of new souls being brought forth, is not a nation with a future.

Particularly troubling is the disproportionate extent to which the culture of death has rooted itself in Black communities.

About one-third of the nation's abortions are performed on Black women.

In 1960, the percentage of Black adults and white adults, age 25 and above, who had never been married was almost identical—around 10%. By 2012, among whites this increased to 16%, but among Blacks to 36%.

Black poverty is largely centered in Black households

headed by single women.

Sadly, the Congressional Black Caucus wants to perpetuate the culture of death. They decry the court's decision to overturn Roe v. Wade.

But the Supreme Court decision to overturn Roe v. Wade is not a ban on abortion. It is a rejection of the bogus decision that claimed the U.S. Constitution grants abortion rights.

Those on the left, who regularly express their concerns about our democracy, now have things the way they want it.

The future of abortion lies in democracy. Each state will decide if they want a culture of death.

My prediction is Americans will choose life. And Black Americans will choose life.

The result will be a rebirth of the American family, children and future.

Yes, I am rejoicing that so many will be called "Mom" this time next year and am praying that God will shower their offspring with a double portion of His blessings.

There is great reason today to celebrate in America.

Abortion, Democracy and History

July 27, 2022

When Abraham Lincoln gave his famous address in Peoria, Illinois in 1854, slavery was the issue tearing apart the country, and Congress had just passed the Kansas-Nebraska Act championed by Sen. Stephen Douglas.

A central issue was whether slavery would be permitted in new territories entering the union.

Douglas' answer to the question was politics. Lincoln's answer was morality and the Bible.

Douglas' answer to slavery in new states, the Kansas-Nebraska Act, was democracy. Citizens would vote to permit or not permit slavery in their state.

Lincoln opposed the expansion of what he saw as the inherently evil institution of slavery.

In his Peoria speech, Lincoln stated, "Judge Douglas interrupted me to say that the principle of the Nebraska bill was very old: that it originated when God made man and placed good and evil before him, allowing him to choose for himself, being responsible for the choice he should make."

Lincoln's answer was, "God did not place good and evil before man, telling him to make his choice. On the contrary, he did tell him there was one tree, of the fruit of which he should not eat, on pain of certain death."

Lincoln argued, essentially, that at the heart of political freedom stands man's free choice and that the choices man makes have profound importance and consequences.

Douglas argued that the most important thing is that we can choose. Lincoln argued that the most important thing is what we choose.

Now here we are, almost 170 years after Lincoln and Douglas faced off in Peoria, and the nation is at a similar crossroads in another issue of grave moral consequence—our responsibilities to the unborn.

Justice Samuel Alito, in his opinion in the Dobbs decision that overturned Roe v. Wade, argued from a legal, constitutional perspective. His conclusion, contrary to the court's conclusion in Roe v. Wade, was the U.S. Constitution does not contain a right for a woman to abort her child.

However, the practical, moral result of this decision is that Alito put the nation on the moral footing where Lincoln argued regarding slavery.

The moral consequence of Roe v. Wade was to institutionalize Douglas' argument that our ultimate American value is choice—not what we choose.

The moral consequence of the Dobbs decision is to secure the notion that where, in the preamble of the U.S. Constitution, it says its aim is to "secure the blessings of liberty," that what the Constitution protects is our responsibility to make the right choices. Choice is not the ultimate end, but what we choose.

But it's not over. Now we have clarification that it is not moral relativism that our Constitution secures, but deeper truths of right and wrong.

Now that we know what the Constitution does not do, we will find out what our 50 states will choose to do, meaning where the consciences are of the individual citizens in those states, who will determine these outcomes.

We are in a place eerily similar to what Douglas wanted regarding slavery. Now states will choose yes or no on abortion.

In other words, will states decide that the ultimate value is the ability to choose, or is the ultimate value what choices are made?

Is our ultimate value that a woman have the option to destroy her unborn child, or is our ultimate value sanctity of life?

These are the questions before us and that will define who we are as a nation and as a people.

Although in the 1850s the country was deeply divided on the issue of slavery, one would be hard-pressed today to find anyone who would agree with Douglas that democracy and the vote should decide whether slavery would be permitted.

I predict that history will take the same course regarding our increasing awareness regarding the sanctity of life and our responsibility to protect the unborn. But clearly, we are in for the long haul.

Religious Freedom Means Nothing If Religion Means Nothing

Sept. 21, 2022

In August of 1790, President George Washington visited Rhode Island, which a few months earlier had ratified the U.S. Constitution.

Among those who welcomed the new president was the Hebrew Congregation of Rhode Island, founded in 1763. Now known as the Touro Synagogue, it is the oldest standing synagogue in the nation.

The synagogue's representative wrote to the president, expressing gratitude that Jews in Rhode Island, in the newly formed United States of America, lived, in contrast to their co-religionists in other parts of the world, with "invaluable rights as free citizens."

Washington wrote to the congregation, "May the Children of the stock of Abraham, who dwell in this land, continue to merit and enjoy the good will of the other Inhabitants; while every one shall sit in safety under his own vine and figtree, and there shall be none to make him afraid."

A little more than a year later, the guarantee of religious freedom would be formally enshrined in the Constitution with the ratification of the Bill of Rights, including the First Amendment saying, "Congress shall make no law respecting an establishment of religion, or prohibiting the free exercise thereof."

Now, in a sad stroke of irony, the religious freedom of observant Jews is being threatened not by "other inhabitants" but by their own co-religionists.

Yeshiva University, the nation's only orthodox Jewish university, has been sued by Yeshiva University gay students for refusing to sanction an LGBTQ club.

A New York State court ruled in favor of the students, and now Yeshiva University has been dealt another setback by the Supreme Court. The Supremes, to whom Yeshiva University appealed, refused to block the state court decision requiring that the university allow the LGBTQ club to operate.

The position of Yeshiva University is clear. The Torah—the five books of Moses—explicitly prohibits homosexual behavior. To officially accept the LGBTQ club as part of the university would be to negate and undermine the very mission and identity of the university.

Religious freedom is an integral part of American identity.

Historically, religious persecution came from those of other religions.

But today we have a new phenomenon.

The threat to religion is not coming from those who worship other gods. The threat is coming from those who worship no god and refuse to accept Christians and Jews to practice their religion as taught in their scripture.

An interview with one of the gay students makes clear what is happening. She challenges that Judaism actually prohibits homosexuality.

But the prohibition in the Torah is absolutely clear and explicit.

To accept her and her argument is to ask that Yeshiva University negate its very existence.

How did Yeshiva University get to this situation? As I googled for background information on this story, it became clear that the issue with gays on the campus at Yeshiva University has been going on for years.

The LGBTQ club that now seeks official sanction has been operating informally.

Can it be that Yeshiva University has been not clear and aggressive enough on where they stand on this issue, and this lack of clarity has led to this destructive situation?

I think it is time for religious organizations to stop being intimidated by threats from those whose real agenda is to destroy what they stand for.

Certainly, America must stand strong as a free society. Anyone should be able to live as they choose.

But Americans of faith should be proud and clear about the precepts of their religion and aggressively push back against those who use the headline of tolerance as a pretext to undermine and destroy the precepts of scripture.

Let's wake up that religious freedom means nothing if religion means nothing.

We are already seeing our nation implode as our sacred principles so essential to life go out the window. Those who still live by these principles should stand strong and unbending toward those who want to destroy them.

Marriage Is a Truth That Cannot Be Redefined

Dec. 7, 2022

The Respect for Marriage Act, codifying same-sex marriage as federal law, already decided as such by the Supreme Court in the Obergefell decision in 2015, has now passed the Senate. If it passes in the House, President Joe Biden will sign it into law.

Let's take a moment and consider what is going on.

Some view acceptance of same sex marriage as a bold new step to a freer and more just society. But, despite Gallup now showing 71% in favor of same-sex marriage, 58% of those who attend church weekly are opposed.

Only 17%, per Gallup, now say that they are satisfied with the direction of the country. According to the General Social Survey, the percentage of Americans, since 2000, saying they are "not too happy" has increased from 10% to 24%, and those saying they are "very happy" has decreased from 34% to 19%.

Clearly, many Americans sense there is something very wrong going on in our country.

May I propose that the eternal truths we receive through religion, now so widely rejected, are there because we need them?

Is freedom really about ideologues having license to rewrite our language and redefine our sacred institutions?

Some have found it politically expedient to use the once prohibition on interracial marriage as a rationale for showing the alleged unfairness of a prohibition on same-sex marriage.

But the bans on interracial marriage had nothing to do with our understanding of marriage.

The ban on interracial marriage, which the Supreme Court found unconstitutional in 1967, stemmed from the ban on interracial marriage in Virginia going back to 1924. That legislation was called The Racial Integrity Act. It was about racial purity. It had nothing to do with the definition of marriage.

In 1924, few did not accept that marriage was the sacred bond between a man and woman. The racists were concerned about a man and woman of different races entering into that sacred bond.

But somehow race gets dragged into every perverse ideological battle that happens in our country.

In 1857, the Supreme Court ruled that African Americans were not human beings. In the Dred Scott decision, the court ruled that people of African descent "are not included, and were not intended to be included, under the word 'citizens' in the Constitution, and can therefore claim none of the rights and privileges" accorded to citizens.

The meaning of "citizen" was reinvented to serve a political and ideological agenda.

With the passage of the 14th Amendment, the American people restored the truth and integrity of the word "citizen"—"All persons born and naturalized in the United States and subject to the jurisdiction thereof"—and obliterated a corrupt, ideological ruling of the Supreme Court.

The Obergefell decision did to the word "marriage" what the Dred Scott decision did to the word "citizen."

It took a civil war to bring forth the 14th Amendment. What will it take to restore how, as a society, we understand what it means to be married?

Per recent data from the Census Bureau, in 2022, 34% of those over age 15 had never been married, compared to 23% in 1950.

In a 2020 Pew survey, 16% said it was “essential” for a man to marry and 17% said it was essential for a woman.

French nobleman Alexis de Tocqueville wrote in his classic study, “Democracy in America, “One cannot say that in the United States religion exerts an influence on the laws ... but it directs mores, and it is in regulating the family that it works to regulate the state. ... Of the world's countries, America is surely the one where the bond of marriage is most respected.”

That was in 1835. In 2022, know that those who love our country and understand what made and makes it great are in for the long haul. An America without truth is an America without a future.

How Do We Get Our Nation Back on Track?

Dec. 21, 2022

Some thoughts about our country as Christmas and the new year approach.

In his Farewell Address to the nation in 1796, America's departing first president, George Washington, observed: "It is substantially true that virtue or morality is a necessary spring to popular government."

And what is the basis upon which we define morality?

Washington answers, "reason and experience both forbid us to expect that national morality can prevail in exclusion of religious principle."

Per our first president, for a democracy to function properly, it must be guided by moral principles. And the guidelines and rules by which we define what is moral are framed by principles of the Bible.

This is not exactly what we have going on today.

Rather than our democracy following prior moral principles, our moral principles now are defined by our democracy. What we deem to be moral—good and evil, right and wrong—now arrives to us not from heaven but from Hollywood.

Consider how, over the last 20 years, our idea of what is morally acceptable has changed.

Twenty-two years ago, in 2001, per Gallup polling, the following percentages of Americans viewed these activities as "morally acceptable": gay/lesbian relations: 40%; birth to unwed mother: 45%; polygamy: 7%; suicide: 13%; pornography: 30%.

In the latest survey in 2022, following are the percentages calling these same activities "morally acceptable": gay/lesbian relations: 71%; birth to unwed mother: 70%; polygamy: 23%; suicide: 22%; pornography: 41%.

What exactly happened over 22 years that, on average, the percentage saying each morally sensitive area is morally acceptable has more than doubled?

One thing that has happened is that the percentage of Americans that think the Bible is relevant to their life has dramatically dropped.

Per Gallup, the percentage saying that religion is "very important" in their life has dropped from 70% in 1965 to 49% in 2021.

The percentage saying they attended church in the last seven days has dropped from 49% in 1960 to 29% in 2021.

Certainly contributing to this is a long series of court decisions in which interpretations of the First Amendment have been more about purging religion from our public spaces than about protecting religious liberty.

The 1962 decision banning prayer in public schools was just the opening salvo producing our reality today in which traditional values and morality are gone from the instruction our children receive in public schools. Those values have been replaced by the secular humanism of the far left.

It is very popular to think about public policy in terms of the social agenda and the economic agenda, as if these are two separate worlds. But they're not. As religion declines, government grows.

Perhaps George Washington's point that a moral and

virtuous culture enables popular government can be best understood in that a free society cannot function when individuals cannot govern themselves through personal responsibility.

Tens of trillions have been spent on anti-poverty programs with practically zero impact. Substantial research shows that what really combats recurring poverty is the so-called "success sequence." Those who finish high school, do not have children before marriage and work overwhelmingly move out of poverty.

Government and politics have become our new religion, despite their dismal track record of success in improving the human condition.

The Penn Wharton Budget model, an economic research group at the University of Pennsylvania Wharton School of Business, projects now that by 2050, our national debt will be 225% of our GDP.

A national culture increasingly rooted in falsehoods is spending itself into oblivion and bankruptcy.

How about we Americans who still pray direct our prayers that in the upcoming year we see a revival of truth in our nation? Let's pray that all our citizens see that the only path to freedom is each embracing eternal truths that enable all of us to successfully govern our own lives.

Politics

Response to the State of the Union

Feb. 6, 2019

My fellow Americans.

Given that the Democratic Party chose to select a recently defeated political candidate to give a response to the president's State of the Union address because she is black and a woman, I feel I should also step up and give my response.

Although I have not recently lost a governor's contest, I am black and I am a woman.

Democrats want Americans, particularly minority Americans, to believe that a left-wing agenda is what they need and what will define America's future.

I am here to say today that the agenda of the left is the problem, not the solution.

For too many years the left—and I am talking here about those with a hard-core secular humanist and socialist agenda—have been dominating discourse in our minority communities.

America's future is in the values that defined it from the beginning.

Christianity, capitalism and the Constitution.

When I say Christianity, I do not mean to deny the bedrock of religious freedom. I mean to say that theses values must be predominant and define our nation and our culture.

There is no freedom without family, and there is no family without faith. It's as simple as that. Should every American be free to choose—yes.

But recognize that in 2018, growth of the American

population was the lowest it's been in 80 years. The Census Bureau projects that in 16 years there will be more Americans over 65 than under 18. Without children, our future is in danger.

Our future is about life, not the 61 million abortions since Roe v. Wade.

The effect of the left's agenda on our black communities has been devastating. Single-parent homes and out-of-wedlock births have tripled since the 1960s. What kind of future can we expect for our black children when they so often come from low-income single-parent households?

We must restore the integrity of family in all American communities. This can only happen with a revival of faith. For sure this will not happen with the sick message from the left of moral relativism and nihilism.

Capitalism is also the bedrock of our future.

Freedom is about individuals taking responsibility for their lives. It is about building, creating, working, saving and owning. This is capitalism.

It is not a culture of victimhood, of blaming everyone else for your challenges and your problems.

No. We don't want that. We want freedom. This is where our future is.

Personal empowerment comes with personal responsibility.

America is about YOU, not politicians.

And the Constitution is the handbook that our founders provided us to keep government limited and keep politicians out of our lives.

Let's honor it and not try to destroy it like the left wants to do.

America is in a fiscal and moral crisis.

We have budget deficits and national debt like this nation has never experienced before.

This bankruptcy is the product of a half-century of increasingly adopting welfare state policies. We can turn it around.

This president, who the left is attacking as a racist and a dictator, has gotten America growing faster than it has in years, with black and Latino unemployment rates the lowest they have been in history.

He is digging us out of the hole that the left wants to get us back in.

I am one black woman who believes in America and loves this country, who believes that our future lies in Christianity, capitalism and the Constitution.

And I am here to tell you that tens of millions of Americans of all backgrounds are with me—and are with President Trump.

Let's stand up and fight, fight those that hate our nation and what it stands for.

Let's win back our nation, our freedom and our God for our future, for our children. God Bless America.

Russiagate: Deceit, Fake News From Democrats

March 27, 2019

So now special counsel Robert Mueller has issued his report, and it turns out after two years of investigation, at an estimated cost of $40 million, that "Russiagate" was fake news.

Much to the dismay of Democrats, Mueller found no collusion between the Trump presidential campaign and the Russians to influence the 2016 election.

Who are the winners here?

Of course, the American people—and, of course, President Donald Trump and the Republican Party.

And, we might say, also House Speaker Nancy Pelosi.

At the age of 79, with 32 years in the House of Representatives, Pelosi has a well-honed nose for sniffing out which political road to take.

She told The Washington Post earlier this month: "I'm going to give you some news right now, because I haven't said this to any press person before. ... Impeachment is so divisive to the country that unless there's something so compelling and overwhelming and bipartisan, I don't think we should go down that path, because it divides the country. And he's just not worth it."

Either the speaker's time-tested political sniffer is so fine-tuned that she smelled the fake news driving the Russia conspiracy investigation or she knew that driving the whole thing were dirty tricks that originated in her own party and that Mueller would not and could not cover this up.

This is the big and troubling story left in the wake of

the Mueller investigation.

How is it that the FBI, including former Director James Comey, was scammed by the so-called Steele dossier, which was financed through the back door by the Clinton campaign and the Democratic National Committee and created the story of the alleged collusion between the Trump campaign and the Russians?

How could the supposed elite of our intelligence community be so deceived?

Or maybe, even more troubling, they weren't deceived and were party to the scam.

Enough to give any upstanding American goose bumps.

But unlike their wise old leader, many Democrats are not giving up.

House Judiciary Committee Chairman Jerrold Nadler said weeks ago on ABC's "This Week" that he didn't care what the Mueller report would conclude, noting, "It's very clear that the president obstructed justice."

So why did taxpayers have to shell out tens of millions for this special counsel if Democrats really didn't care what the investigation would conclude?

And how could the president obstruct justice if no crime was committed to begin with?

The answer, of course, is that discovering what is true is something that is of zero interest to Democrats.

They have only one agenda: damaging this president and making it as difficult as possible for him to advance a conservative program.

So despite the conclusions of the Mueller report, there will be document requests and subpoenas pouring forth from Nadler's committee under the claim of suspected obstruction of justice from the White House.

There are many things Democrats do not do well. But the thing they do least well is lose.

For liberals, there is no truth; there is no fair and square. There is only politics.

Hillary Clinton's latest explanation of her loss in 2016 is voter registration shenanigans in Alabama, Georgia and Wisconsin.

Stacey Abrams still refuses to concede that she was defeated in the gubernatorial race in Georgia, persisting that voter suppression engineered by Republicans caused her loss.

We had to suffer recounts in 2018 in Florida in the senatorial and gubernatorial races because losing Democrats refused to concede. This was reminiscent of the "hanging chad' recount in Florida in the 2000 presidential election, when Al Gore refused to concede.

The idea that Russians somehow manipulated the outcome of the 2016 presidential election, with or without collusion from the Trump campaign, is absurd.

The American system works, and we have a president who is fixing this country. These are the truths that Democrats find most difficult to swallow.

Biden Launches Presidential Campaign With Lies

May 1, 2019

We can all agree with Joe Biden that "we are in a battle for the soul of this nation."

Biden's video announcing his presidential candidacy provides the best raw material we could ask for regarding how he sees this battle.

In this opening salvo of his campaign, Biden serves up as his centerpiece transparent lies and distortions about President Trump's remarks following the violence in Charlottesville, Virginia, in August 2017.

In other words, Biden makes a pretty good case why President Trump will be reelected.

A major factor that drove many working-class Americans into the Republican column in 2016 was that so many were sick and tired of what they know in their heart to be true being pushed to the sidelines and displaced by intolerant left-wing political correctness and distortions.

Really, folks, does any sane person really believe that Donald Trump thinks neo-Nazis are "very fine people"? And that even if he has such a sick and distorted side, he would blatantly say it for public consumption at a press conference?

Does anyone really think that if Donald Trump were sympathetic to neo-Nazis and white supremacists, he would have appointed Nikki Haley, the daughter of Indian immigrants and former governor of South Carolina who signed legislation to remove the Confederate flag from the state's capitol grounds, to be America's ambassador to the

United Nations?

Anyone reading the readily available transcripts of President Trump's remarks on Charlottesville will see, if they care about the truth—a big assumption these days—that "very fine people" on both sides referred to the demonstration regarding taking down the statue of Robert E. Lee in Charlottesville.

I, myself, favor local government voting to remove flags, statues and memorabilia celebrating the Confederacy. Such celebrations cause great anguish to African Americans who have a history of deep pain associated with that time of great injustice.

Nevertheless, I believe in free speech, and I believe in the right to assembly and peaceful demonstration—even if I find what is being expressed repugnant.

America's left wants us to believe—and it gets great help from a sympathetic left-wing media—that all of America's intolerance comes from the right.

So, in fact, President Trump made a world-class effort in his remarks about the incident in Charlottesville to be fair, balanced and faithful to the facts. And he was.

His condemnation of neo-Nazis and white supremacists was unequivocal.

But the left could not handle that there might have been peaceful Americans who showed up to protest removal of the Robert E. Lee statue.

Nor could it tolerate that the president would note that there was unacceptable violent behavior on the other side—those favoring removing the statue—which there was.

I can speak from personal experience of the intolerance of the left.

I speak on university campuses across the country

and know firsthand what it means for the left to try to shut you down, sometimes violently.

I also have experience saying something on national television opposing abortion or same-sex marriage and then needing to send my staff home because of violent threats that shut down my office.

Far less convenient for Biden would have been quoting accurately Trump's initial remarks on Charlottesville: “Above all else, we must remember this truth: No matter our color, creed, religion or political party, we are all Americans first. We love our country. We love our God. And we love our flag. ... we must love each other, respect each other and cherish our history and our future together. ... We have to respect each other. Ideally, we have to love each other.”

The partisan left will be pleased with Biden's lies. But decent Americans of all ethnicities understand that President Trump is restoring America's freedom, tolerance, prosperity—and soul.

Kamala Harris' Hypocrisy on Guns

Aug. 14, 2019

Kamala Harris weighs in on guns on her campaign website with the headline "Taking executive action if Republicans continue to cower to the NRA."

Sure, the National Rifle Association, with a reported 5 million members nationwide, is an influential policy group.

But is it really running the Republican Party on gun policy?

How about if I propose a counter-headline?

"Taking action against a culture of death if Democrats continue to cower to Planned Parenthood"?

My guess is if I ask which organization has more political sway, the NRA or Planned Parenthood, many would say the NRA—probably because of our left-wing media.

But pull up OpenSecrets, the website of the Center for Responsive Politics, which tracks money in U.S. politics.

What you will find is that in 2018, the NRA made political contributions of $873,071. Planned Parenthood made political contributions totaling $7,183,139, more than eight times greater than those of the NRA, 99.5 percent of which went to Democratic candidates or to organizations supporting them.

The Center for Responsive Politics ranks Planned Parenthood No. 54 out of 19,225 making political contributions, and the NRA No. 543.

Is it relevant to bring Planned Parenthood into this discussion about guns? Yes.

As I have been arguing all along, we cannot get to an appropriate approach for dealing with guns without considering the culture that produces deranged, detached, violent loners.

Sen. Harris reports on her campaign site, "In 2017, nearly 40,000 people were killed by guns in America."

But also in 2017, 332,757 children were destroyed in the womb at Planned Parenthood abortion clinics.

Want to tell me that this third of a million babies who were destroyed, whose heartbeats could have been discernable at six weeks, and who could have felt pain at 20 weeks, were not alive?

For sure the perpetrators of death, most recently in Texas and Ohio, did not see those they murdered as living, breathing human beings created in the image of God.

Yet Harris declares: "We are living through an all-out assault being waged on women's health and reproductive rights. ... States have mandated that women submit to invasive ultrasounds ... and placed onerous and medically unnecessary restrictions on health clinics. ... Their sole purpose is limiting access to abortion."

No. Their sole purpose is protecting innocent unborn life.

Regarding guns, Harris says, "Fine, if you want to go hunting, but we need reasonable gun safety laws." And she says that, as president, she would deal with this through executive order if Congress would not pass legislation within 100 days.

But the Second Amendment, as Sen. Harris should know, is not primarily about going hunting.

According to the Pew Research Center, more than 40 percent of Americans live in a gun-owning household, and the major reason for gun ownership, per 67 percent of respondents, is protection. Only 38 percent say it is hunting.

One of the plaintiffs in the landmark 2008 District of Columbia v. Heller case, in which the Supreme Court confirmed the right of individuals to own and bear arms, independent of service in a militia, was a black woman. Shelly Parker, from the District of Columbia, wanted to have a gun for protection in her crime-ridden neighborhood where she was threatened by local drug dealers. DC prohibited her from having a gun.

Our Declaration of Independence declares our God-given right to life and liberty. Our Constitution protects these rights.

Kamala Harris wants to use it to violate both.

If we want to solve our gun problem, we need to solve our leadership problem.

Kamala Harris may be drawing large crowds in Iowa, provoking some to think she might be filling Barack Obama's shoes.

But let's recall that President Obama was the first sitting U.S. president to address the national meeting of Planned Parenthood, and he concluded his remarks to the nation's largest abortion provider saying, “God bless you.”

Harris needs to be asked about this hypocrisy. Are we fighting for life and liberty, or not?

Israel Right to Shut out Tlaib and Omar

Aug. 21, 2019

It perplexes me why anyone would question the perfectly logical move by Israel to deny Reps. Rashida Tlaib and Ilhan Omar entry to the country.

Who invites guests whose motive is to destroy their host?

We certainly don't do it in the USA. No one, elected official or not, is permitted entry into the USA whose agenda is the destruction of our country.

Both Tlaib and Omar are aggressive supporters of the BDS movement—boycott, divest, sanction—whose objective is economic strangulation of Israel. They are voices of unremitting hostility toward Israel's existence.

Let's get some perspective.

According to Tlaib, the BDS movement is a freedom movement. She tweeted that she is "tired of folks discrediting a form of speech that is centered on equality and freedom."

But Tlaib's agenda is not freedom. It's about eliminating Israel.

Freedom House is a nonpartisan organization in Washington, D.C., that issues an annual report ranking nations around the world according to freedom—measuring political rights and civil liberties in each country.

Freedom House ranks countries in three categories, "free," "partly free" and "not free."

In the region that Freedom House calls Middle East and North Africa, there are 21 countries and territories, and only two are ranked free, Israel and Tunisia, with Israel receiving the highest total freedom score in the region.

The total population of the region is 420 million, and of the 420 million, 5% are free, including Israel's tiny population of 8.9 million.

So freedom is the exception rather than the rule in the Middle East, and Israel is the shining light. Yet Israel is the only country in the region that seems to bother Rashida Tlaib and Ilhan Omar.

Have we heard a word from them about the 95 percent—nearly 400 million—in the region who are not free? Of course not.

They do not lose sleep because there is not enough freedom in the world. They lose sleep because Israel exists.

There's more.

Although the West Bank, where Tlaib's grandmother lives, and Gaza are not sovereign countries, Freedom House identifies them as territories and includes them in its freedom rankings.

Both are ranked "not free" and have rock-bottom scores.

This is not because of Israel. Palestinians have autonomy in their internal affairs.

Why doesn't Tlaib speak to the fact that where Palestinians do have control over their own affairs, they choose to live under a corrupt, un-free regime?

In 2005, Israel unilaterally pulled out of Gaza, and Palestinians assumed full control.

What did they do? Rather than starting to build, they announced, "Today Gaza, tomorrow Jerusalem," and started firing rockets into Israel.

Meanwhile, as part of the operation, Israel uprooted 8,500 Israeli settlers who were living there. Despite protesting being evacuated from their homes, these Israelis accepted the fact, and some moved eastward into the desert, which, in short order, they irrigated and made bloom—characteristic of the history of Israel.

Within five years, they were exporting $50 million per year of organic vegetables.

According to the Pew Research Center, there are 49 Muslim-majority countries in the world. Two, per Freedom House, are free. But what bothers Tlaib and Omar is the world's single Jewish country, Israel, which is free.

You would think they would admire and want to help others emulate the social and economic miracle that Israelis have created in their young country. Instead they spread hate and blame.

A former prime minister of Israel, Golda Meir, famously said, "Peace will come when the Arabs will love their children more than they hate us."

This was true when she said it 62 years ago, and unfortunately, Rashida Tlaib and Ilhan Omar continue this destructive legacy today.

Both Prime Minister Netanyahu and President Trump are right to marginalize these negative personalities who work so hard to push the world in the wrong direction.

Noisy Presidential Politics Is a Good Sign

Sept. 18, 2019

Wall Street Journal columnist Peggy Noonan bewails, in her column this week, that "the sane center is getting ignored" in the current round of presidential politics.

"When we talk about politics," she writes, "no one speaks of the center, which is vast and has something neither way-left nor way-right has, and that is a motivating love for America itself ... As a group they are virtually ignored, and yet they are the center of everything."

I am tempted to say that Peggy Noonan is locked in a time warp, stuck in an American reality that may have once been. But I doubt that America was ever defined by some plain vanilla moderate center that she longs for.

Noonan wrote speeches for President Reagan, who emerged big time on the national scene with a speech he gave at the 1964 Republican convention called "A Time for Choosing." That speech's message was the exact opposite of idealizing some moderate political center. Reagan conveyed that our nation is about ideals, about right and wrong, and the willingness to fight and sacrifice for these ideals.

The same time as that Republican convention, Rev. Billy Graham spoke to 29,000 in Columbus, Ohio. "The country is disturbed," he said. Young people "are desperately wanting someone to tell them this is right and that is wrong."

I am on and off airplanes all the time, in constant motion around this great nation. I talk to fellow Americans constantly—at work in a variety of communities, in hotels, in airports.

Americans are, in general, not happy with the state of affairs. It has been over 15 years since more than 50% of Americans told Gallup that they are satisfied with the way things are going in the nation.

If the political stage is polarized, it is because the nation is polarized—not because politicians are ignoring some "vast" political silent majority in the center.

Several years ago, Pew Research Center reported just how increasingly polarized Americans have become.

The gap in opinion between Republicans and Democrats regarding government activism in welfare was 47 points in 2017 compared with a difference of 20 points in 1994.

The gap in opinion between Republicans and Democrats about the problem of discrimination was 50 points in 2017 compared with a difference of 13 points in 1994.

The gap in opinion between Republicans and Democrats on the immigration issue was 42 points in 2017 compared with 2 points in 1994.

Overall, on 10 different political issues that Pew tracked from 1994 to 2017, the average gap between Republicans and Democrats increased from 15 points in 1994 to 36 points in 2017.

There is no vast political "center" that is being ignored.

Americans are deeply divided about what the country is about and is going to be.

For sure, the status quo is not an option. Fiscally, there has been dramatic expansion of government over the years, with it entering into practically every aspect of the lives of private Americans. Socially, there has been vast deterioration of the traditional values that preserved the

American family and our respect for the sanctity of life.

We may recall Abraham Lincoln's prophesy that "A house divided against itself cannot stand."

Lincoln was talking then about slavery. Today, we have a house deeply divided—a major part now defined by socialism and secular humanism, and the remainder true to the vision of the founders, a free nation under God.

As Lincoln said back in 1858, we can't stay divided. We'll become "all one ... or all the other."

It's the theme of my new book, "Necessary Noise: How Donald Trump Inflames the Culture War and Why This Is Good News For America" (Center Street).

Today's "noise" emanates from the eye of the political storm searching "who we are now, who we should be, and this clarity matters."

This is what is playing out now before us and will continue through November 2020.

What Democrats Today Really Want

Oct. 9, 2019

Daniel Patrick Moynihan was an American public servant with characteristics all too rare today—integrity, intelligence, wisdom.

Moynihan was a Democrat who would find a hard time being at home in today's Democratic Party.

He was a policy adviser in Democratic—Kennedy—and Republican—Nixon—administrations and went on to serve four terms as a Democratic senator of New York.

Here are two of Moynihan's many famous observations that are particularly relevant in today's chaotic times:

"The central conservative truth is that it is culture, not politics, that determines the success of a society. The central liberal truth is that politics can change culture and save it from itself."

"Everyone is entitled to his own opinion but not his own facts."

As a policy adviser in the early '60s, he opposed and prophetically warned about the mistake made in the welfare law that required no working man present at home in order for the household to receive welfare.

His concerns proved well founded. Black families were devastated. But the thinking that went into welfare touched the whole country. Marriage and family in America since the 1960s has collapsed.

One-third less American adults are married today than were in the 1960s. The percentage of babies born to unwed mothers has gone from less than 10% to over 40%.

A critical moment in the slippery slope of cultural collapse was the legalization of abortion on demand in 1973, opening the door to 60 million-plus unborn children destroyed in the womb.

It is the cultural war that fractures our country today: whether we are a nation of culture, facts and a Constitution that draws the line where government stops and individual freedom begins; or whether America is just about politics, where political power brokers write the script of our lives.

It is now one year since the confirmation hearings of Supreme Court Associate Justice Brett Kavanaugh. We saw what it means when a country detaches from reality and any sense that there is something called a fact.

In such a world, any individual with an unsubstantiated charge who appeals to someone with political power can wind up sitting as a witness in a Senate hearing and hurl charges that can destroy the reputation of a fine man.

In such a world, little boys and girls can arrive at school and claim their sexual identity is different from the biological reality that defined them at birth.

And the idea that there is law that precedes politics is out the window. Ambitious politicians can claim they know what is just and use their power to expropriate wealth and property from whom they choose and redistribute to whom they choose.

This is what divides America today, not what happened in a conversation between President Trump and the president of Ukraine. It is not President Trump whom Democrats want to impeach but 63 million Americans who voted for him.

President Trump managed to do what two previous

Republican candidates failed to do: win back the White House for the GOP and for Americans who want a nation where culture and the Judeo-Christian ethos matters, where facts and law and a constitution exist. It is all this that enables our freedom.

And it is our freedom that is threatened by the left-wing power brokers and fiction writers.

Even some in the president's own party are missing the point—like Sen. Romney, whose bruised ego from his own political failures is more important to him than the great issues at stake in the culture war. Romney has violated President Reagan's 11th commandment—thou shalt not speak ill of a fellow Republican.

With 150-plus conservative court appointments and an unemployment rate the lowest in half a century, conservatives, under President Trump's leadership, are winning back our country. This is what Democrats hate and want to destroy.

Al-Baghdadi Is Dead. Let's Pray for Our Dog

Oct. 30, 2019

The Washington Post obituary read, “Abu Bakr al-Baghdadi, austere religious scholar at helm of Islamic State, dies at 48.”

“(A)ustere religious scholar”? How about terrorist?!

After Twitter world went berserk, The Post obituary reappeared with a new headline: “Abu Bakr al-Baghdadi, extremist leader of Islamic State, dies at 48.”

At a time when we should all share President Trump's exuberance about catching and destroying a terrorist, mass murderer and rapist—a threat to our nation and all the civilized world—The Washington Post accused the president of “creating spectacle” around this great achievement.

Once again we are made aware of the enormous chasm that exists in America between the right and the left.

For those who see good and evil in the world, the defeat of evil is cause for celebration.

But for those on the left, who reject the moral clarity of our Judeo-Christian ethos, we live in an ambiguous murk of moral relativism, and any claim to moral clarity is itself the problem, not the solution, even when it comes to the apprehension and destruction of a notorious terrorist/murderer.

The Washington Post, the nation's capital's megaphone for the American left, criticized the president for not being “more measured” in his tone, as was then-President Obama, per The Post, after the elimination of Osama bin Laden.

We might recall that Obama's two terms were bookended by two notable and revealing stands in international affairs.

Obama's first major international appearance was in June 2009, when he traveled to Cairo, Egypt, to give a speech to the Muslim world with the objective of apologizing to them for the behavior of his country.

"9/11 was an enormous trauma to our country," he said. "The fear and anger that it provoked was understandable, but in some cases, it led us to act contrary to our ideals."

Nowhere did the American president convey to his worldwide Muslim audience that there is anything unique in American principles—principles that created our strong and prosperous nation—or anything worth paying attention to and emulating.

In December 2016, at the conclusion of Obama's second term, his administration abandoned our friend and ally Israel by abstaining from a vote in the U.N. Security Council, allowing passage of a resolution condemning Israel for its settlement activity.

One Israeli minister said that the U.S. "abandoned Israel, its only ally in the Middle East," while the Palestinian Authority called it "a victory."

Anyone who loves our country and loves what it stands for will be as exuberant as President Trump was in his announcement of the death of this evil man from ISIS.

Was the president being political? Of course. Politics is the means through which we as a nation define and choose sides.

You're either going to be on the side of a free nation Under God, identifying with the sanctity of life, liberty and property, or not.

President Trump and American conservatives are. The Washington Post and America's left are not.

This is where we are today.

Sen. Lindsey Graham summed it up well in his remarks at the White House.

He described the operation saying, "(T)he best of America confronted the worst of mankind, and the good guys won."

We need to make another distinction between President Trump and his predecessor. A mission such as this requires intense focus and coordination. President Trump did this, despite daily scrutiny by a hostile press and being under constant siege by Democrats in Congress looking for an excuse to impeach him.

Sen. Graham was right to call this "a game changer." Putting fear in the hearts of terrorists is the only way, and President Trump is doing it.

Many were killed on their side. On our side, only one military dog sustained serious injury.

Let's follow Graham's advice here also: Let's pray for the dog.

Necessary Noise

Nov. 13, 2019

American voters are motivated by a fever pitch.

That's the message from last week's elections.

The headlines were the Democratic sweep of the state legislature in Virginia that put the entire state government under Democrat control for the first time in 25 years and the defeat of incumbent Republican Gov. Matt Bevin in Kentucky.

An important part of the story is that voter turnout was off the charts.

In Kentucky, an estimated 43% of eligible voters turned out compared with 31% for the last gubernatorial election, in 2015.

Voter turnout in Virginia was the highest it has been for a state legislature-only election in at least the last 40-some years.

There's a lot of noise in the political and cultural arenas in America today, and it's exactly what I talk about in my new book, released this week, "Necessary Noise: How Donald Trump Inflames the Cultural War and Why This is Good News for America."

A new Gallup poll measuring voter enthusiasm reports that 64% are "more enthusiastic" compared with previous elections, a percentage "among the highest Gallup has measured across presidential election years."

It's actually the highest ever measured because previous levels in this range were reported one to five months before upcoming election. Voter enthusiasm at this accelerated level one year before an election is unprecedented.

Also unprecedented is that high voter enthusiasm is bipartisan.

As Gallup reports, usually enthusiasm is notably higher among the opposition party.

But this time, it's not the case.

Reported enthusiasm is 66% among Republicans and 65% among Democrats.

It's not a surprise to me. It's why I wrote "Necessary Noise."

The noise that is ramping up voter heartbeats is the sound of American democracy at work. It's a consciousness-raising noise that is waking up Americans to the fact that muddling through the mediocre middle is no longer an option. And the man responsible for generating this noise is President Donald Trump.

Donald Trump is the great disruptor.

Political candidates always run on an agenda of change.

But Donald Trump understood that given what is happening in America today, the agenda must be disruption, not change.

Change does not take place at the roots. The change conventional politicians offer up amounts to rearranging deck chairs. Disruption reaches down deep and severs at the root the status quo kept in place by special interests and habit of thought.

America needs this kind of disruption today because we have drifted too far from our founding, too far from what the nation is supposed to be about.

An America that grew and thrived because it was "biblical and free" is transforming into a nation that is "secular and statist."

There is no better way to know what Americans are thinking and feeling than to travel and talk to people.

This is what I have been doing for 25 years. It's why I know that the people who voted in 2016 for the disruptor Trump are those who have had enough with where we've been going. They are the people of America's heartland, and I have been listening to them.

Now, as result of disruption, the pretentions of the mediocre middle are gone. Because of Trump the disruptor, Americans will have a clear choice to make.

Move to the right, or move to the left.

Part of the drama of the effectiveness of Donald Trump is that his own background and personal history provide an unlikely resume for the role he now plays. It's why so many still have a hard time with him.

As I point out in "Necessary Noise," the process of disruption produces the noise we need, whether it's draining the swamp of interests in Washington; taking on the politics of political correctness, gender and race; or restoring a society of ownership and property.

The only thing I can predict for sure is that come November 2020, Americans will have a clear choice, and for this we should thank Donald Trump.

President Trump's Timely Move Against Evil

Jan. 8, 2020

The muted reaction of leading Democratic politicians to the elimination of Iranian Maj. Gen. Qasem Soleimani reinforces my sense of what divides our country and differentiates the two parties.

One part of America still believes that there is good and evil, and one part doesn't.

The American left, whose political home is the Democratic Party, lives in a world where good and evil don't exist. Everything is about politics including redemption itself.

Only someone who does not believe there is good and evil experiences no joy when evil is defeated.

The destruction of Soleimani, whose life's work was carrying out the will of a despicable regime, is cause for celebration. As commander of the Quds Force, his hands dripped with the blood of hundreds of Americans, and hundreds of thousands of others throughout the Middle East, particularly in Syria.

According to authoritative reports, the Iranian ideological imperialism extends to managing terrorist forces in Lebanon, Iraq, Afghanistan, Pakistan and Yemen. And much of their activity focuses on threatening the existence of Israel.

This network of terror has spread to our own hemisphere in South America.

In 1994, a bomb was detonated at the AMIA Jewish community center in Buenos Aires, Argentina, killing 85 and injuring 300. In 2006, Argentinian special prosecutor Alberto

Nisman indicted eight former Iranian officials accused of being responsible for the operation, and the following year, Interpol issued "red notices" for the arrest of six of them.

The Wall Street Journal has reported Iranian activities in Venezuela, Bolivia, Nicaragua, Brazil, Peru and Chile. According to Joseph Humire, executive director of the Center for a Secure Free Society in Washington, D.C., "Latin America is arguably Iran's top foreign policy priority outside of the Middle East."

The evil Iranian regime is a clear and threatening global danger, and Soleimani was its most powerful general. How can there not be unreserved joy at his elimination?

But Senate Minority Leader Chuck Schumer, House Speaker Nancy Pelosi and others of their party are not joyful. As was the case when ISIS leader Abu Bakr al-Baghdadi was eliminated, instead of celebrating, they are attacking President Donald Trump.

No one wants war. And no one believes that the United States should expend its resources being the world's policeman.

But refusal to recognize the threat of aggressive evil is irresponsible and dangerous.

In March 1983, then-President Ronald Reagan addressed the National Association of Evangelicals and delivered the famous address in which he called the Soviet Union "an evil empire."

Reagan unleashed his passion, noting the standing threat from the Soviet communists, arguing for aggressive confrontation.

"There is sin and evil in the world," said the president, "and we are enjoined by scripture and the Lord Jesus to oppose it with all our might."

"(I)f history teaches anything," he continued, "it teaches: Simple-minded appeasement or wishful thinking about our adversaries is folly. It means the betrayal of our past, the squandering of our freedom."

Reagan stood tough, and not many years later, the unthinkable happened. The Soviet Union collapsed.

Some of the foolishness we are hearing from the left cynically suggests that this operation was a diversionary tactic by President Trump to take attention from the impeachment proceedings.

Let's recall what he said three years ago in his inaugural address: "We will reinforce old alliances and form new ones—and unite the civilized world against radical Islamic terrorism, which we will eradicate completely from the face of the Earth."

President Trump is focused and consistent with his agenda—rebuilding a strong, creative and safe America.

Despite Iran being among the most oil-rich nations in the world, the average per capita income of its citizens is a paltry $5,400. Rather than investing to develop the potential of their own country, they squander their wealth to terrorize the world. No one suffers more than Iran's own citizens.

We should celebrate this blow to the regime in Iran and this timely, courageous act of President Trump.

It Doesn't Matter Which Democrat Wins

Feb. 5, 2020

There is poetic justice in the chaos we've witnessed in Iowa.

First, the Des Moines Register pulled its definitive poll, to which everyone turns as the final word before the caucuses, because of "irregularities."

Then results of the caucuses themselves were hung out to dry because of "inconsistencies."

No one ever said that making political sausage is pretty.

But it is for this very reason that we should want to minimize the extent to which political sausage-making impacts our lives. But if those who are running for the presidency in the Democratic Party get their way, we can only expect more and more of it.

We too often make the mistake of thinking that democracy and freedom are the same thing. This is a big mistake.

Democracy is about the process by which we elect government. Freedom is about how big that government is and how much of our lives it controls.

Democrats will talk to us forever about the former but could care less about the latter.

The rhetoric from all these Democrats boils down to how they claim they're going to make our lives better by increasing government/political power over every decision we make.

More government power over health care, education, housing and business. More power in the hands of politicians in general to determine what is fair and not fair.

In the end, private citizens will cower in the corner waiting for marching orders about what they're allowed to do.

History tells us, as did the founders of our country, that the path to corruption is giving politicians more power.

It's why they wrote in our Declaration of Independence that our freedom comes from God. Government's job, they wrote, is to protect it.

Those who think the main issue facing us is how we elect politicians, rather than the power that we give to politicians, need to look at what has happened in Iowa.

What divides America today are those who aspire to American ideals of individual freedom and those who want to crush it and turn our lives over to a governing political class.

The growth in government over the last half-century has been about the growth in political power. In 1970, 35% of the federal budget consisted of so-called transfer payments, that is, government taking money from taxpayers and recycling to others by way of government programs. Today it's 70%.

And with all the talk about democracy, it's done in a most undemocratic way. Instead of raising taxes so voters know what's happening, the government just borrows the money. It's like turning your credit card over to your neighbor.

Now we've got a federal government debt load the size of our whole economy. Scholars from Stanford University's Hoover Institution estimated recently that the national debt will soon amount to a quarter million dollars per every American family of four.

Unfortunately, after the civil rights movement, African Americans largely bought the lie that government would make their lives freer and fairer.

Government took over large portions of their lives—housing, education, health care, welfare. The main thing that happened by turning government into a deity is that the real values that free us were pushed aside. Black marriage and families were decimated.

And today, black poverty, and the gap between black household income and wealth and the national averages, are not much different from half a century ago.

It's why I called one of my books "Uncle Sam's Plantation."

The truth is it doesn't matter which Democrat wins in Iowa or elsewhere. They all have the same misguided answers for America. Follow me onto the government plantation.

The secret of American success, of all human success, is people free in body and spirit, taking responsibility for their lives.

All of American history is about fighting for freedom. This is what the 2020 election is about.

President Trump's Masada Moment

Jan. 13, 2021

There seems to be only one area of common ground in our country today: agreement that something is wrong.

But regarding what that "something" is, and what we need to do, there is profound disagreement throughout the nation.

The violence in which the sacred ground of our nation's Capitol building was violated by unruly hooligans, resulting in the death of five, is a low point in our history.

Clearly, something is wrong. But we won't be able to fix it until we define it correctly.

Those on the right are entirely correct that the tone of violence, chaos and nihilism was set by the left.

Our cities and institutions have been vandalized and looted with impunity by the Black Lives Matter and antifa movements over the last several years, receiving support and endorsement by Democratic Party leaders and, sadly, many business leaders.

After a violent mob pulled down a statue of Christopher Columbus in Baltimore, a journalist asked House Speaker Nancy Pelosi, "Shouldn't that be done by a commission or the city council, not a mob in the middle of the night throwing it into the harbor?" Pelosi's response: "People will do what they do."

The speaker tore up, for all to see on international television, the president's State of the Union address after he finished discharging that constitutionally directed duty.

I, of course, could go on.

The point is that the answer to horrible behavior is

not horrible behavior.

It's the absolute secularization of the nation, the purge of the Almighty from our public life, the crowning politicians king of the universe, that is destroying us.

Our democratic republic, our freedom, is vital. But with no absolutes, it deteriorates to chaos.

It is why President Lincoln refused to let the issue of the spread of slavery be submitted to democracy. There must be absolutes that precede politics.

It is the Ten Commandments where we learn that murder and theft are forbidden. When life and property are turned over to politics, the result is the chaos we now see.

The nation's high court, in many bad decisions over the last century, has undermined our Constitution as a limiting factor on federal government power. But the critical moment of detaching the nation as a free nation under God occurred in 1973, in the Roe v. Wade decision that legalized abortion. The federal government took charge of defining life and giving women license to destroy it.

Then, in 2015, in the Obergefell v. Hodges decision, government seized the authority to define, or redefine, the sacred institution of marriage.

President Trump had a successful presidency in his effort to "Make America Great Again."

A powerful economy was restored and has sustained us through the COVID-19 crisis. Our courts are now filled with principled, conservative judges. The United States led the way to recognize Jerusalem as the capital of Israel, and a new, unbelievable peace has been achieved in the Middle East.

But America cannot be great if America, as Alexis de Tocqueville said, is not good.

President Trump now has an opportunity to sign off on a powerful note that will totally change the tenor that Democrats want to set.

He cannot control Democrats' ability to politicize events and impeach him. But, if they do it, he can take control by resigning.

He can take the high, high ground, in contrast to their low, low ground. He can take responsibility for the horror that just occurred at the Capitol, because it occurred on his watch. And he can use the opportunity to declare that America must be a free nation under God, and that this is the great challenge that faces us going forward.

He can turn the reins of leadership, in these waning days, to Vice President Mike Pence, an upright Christian man and American patriot who could speak truth to the nation as the unruly Democratic mob takes charge and begins its long campaign to drag our nation into the abyss.

Freedom of Speech Slipping Away

Jan. 20, 2021

As the new Biden-Harris administration assumes power, the most basic American freedom of speech and expression is under unprecedented threat.

For the first time ever, I am concerned about my freedom to do my work, to run a policy institute addressing issues of culture, race and poverty from a conservative perspective.

Technology—the internet—which was largely nonexistent just 25 years ago, now plays a huge role in our lives as a tool of communication.

In a survey just published by the Pew Research Center, 86% say they "often" or "sometimes" get their news from a digital device—smartphone, tablet or computer. This compared with 68% who say they "often" or "sometimes" get their news from television, 50% who get it from radio and 32% who get it from print publications.

According to Statista.com, the United States has 223 million Facebook users, almost the size of the entire U.S. population over age 18. Per Pew, 22% of U.S. adults use Twitter.

These developments have put enormous power at the disposal of technology firms over what we see and read.

Power alone doesn't worry me. Exclusive power, power to control, does.

The decision by Twitter to kick the president of the United States off of Twitter, disconnecting him from the 89 million who follow him, is mind-boggling.

President Trump has noted, with total legitimacy, that

he turned to social media as his platform of preference to communicate with the country because of widespread bias in the mainstream media.

What gives the technology companies so much discretion over communication, the oxygen of our free country?

This comes from a provision of the 1996 Communications Decency Act that was passed to set the ground rules for the powerful new technologies that were emerging. Technology companies are protected from liability for the content they carry: The liability exists with whomever provided that content. But they were also given discretion over what they choose to carry.

The discretion part comes from logic that the operators of these platforms should be able to refuse truly inflammatory, dangerous content. But what about content that is normally protected by the First Amendment?

Jack Dorsey, CEO of Twitter, appointed himself judge and jury, deciding that President Trump incited the assault on the Capitol building and banning the president from Twitter for life.

We know that President Trump's own words were that the demonstration on Capitol Hill should be "peaceful." The point is, if Donald Trump broke the law, this should be determined through legal channels, not by the subjective decision of a businessperson with a net worth of some $12 billion accrued because of American freedom.

I produce a weekly television talk show, "CURE America with Star Parker." The show was booted off Vimeo because the far-left Southern Poverty Law Center identifies one of our Christian advertisers as a hate group and one pastor said that homosexuality is a sin.

Now quoting the Bible, expressing views of a believing Christian, is out of bounds—banned from the nation's major media platforms?

We must recognize that our nation's most precious commodity, our freedom to speak, to act and to assemble, is seriously being threatened.

Because those controlling these technology companies disproportionately have political sympathies to the left, it is the freedom of conservatives that is most seriously under siege.

Fortunately, many are now concerned.

The argument is made that First Amendment speech protections only pertain to government action, not private companies. But technology has enabled a concentration of private power not previously imagined.

The Communications Decency Act could be amended such that speech on technology platforms receives the same protections as all speech protected by the First Amendment.

Another possibility would be to amend the Civil Rights Act to include those with religious conviction based on teachings of Judaism and Christianity as a protected class.

Conservatives must push for new law and new platforms.

Biden's Anti-Unity Agenda

Jan 27, 2021

President Joe Biden focused on the theme of unity in his inaugural address.

"Today, on this January day, my whole soul is in this: bringing America together, uniting our people and uniting our nation," he said.

It sounds so nice. But only a career politician can be this disingenuous and speak the words as if he were so, so sincere.

If Biden's top priority were really unity, would he really have allowed a trial of former President Donald Trump to move forward in the Senate? Or immediately signed 30 executive orders in his first three days in the Oval Office, many of which focused on undoing and dismantling Trump's policies?

Such actions immediately alienate the 74 million Americans who voted for Donald Trump.

Appreciating that if you want to know what someone is about, pay attention to what they do, not what they say, it is obvious that Biden's concern is advancing the left-wing agenda of his party, not unity.

On the other hand, there probably wouldn't be much difference with a Republican president. Republicans would be pushing for the president to advance their agenda. The game is to defeat the opposition, not unity.

So, what about unity? Is unity something we should care about?

After all, this is the United States of America, so named by the founders in 1776.

Eleven years later, in 1787, the Constitution was adopted, the preamble of which explains its purpose to "form a more perfect Union."

The glue holding together what the founders called the United States is adherence to the principles upon which the country was founded. We can read them clearly in the Declaration of Independence: "(A)ll men are created equal ... they are endowed by their Creator with certain unalienable Rights, that among these are Life, Liberty and the pursuit of Happiness. ... That to secure these rights, Governments are instituted among Men."

The country is about individual freedom and the purpose of government to protect that freedom. The Constitution was designed to define more clearly legitimate tasks of the federal government, and to keep government within those boundaries. This is what makes us the United States.

Unity broke down and led to civil war because one of the core principles—protecting the rights of all men—was violated by the presence of slavery.

When we all accept the core principles that enable us to be free and the limited role of the federal government as defined in the Constitution, we function successfully as a unified country, and we grow and prosper.

It means each of us respects the uniqueness and freedom of each of our neighbors.

Reading through Joe Biden's laundry list of what he calls unity, we see a list of everything that pulls us apart: "We can right wrongs. We can put people to work in good jobs. We can teach our children in safe schools. ... We can reward work, rebuild the middle class ... We can deliver racial justice. We can make America, once again, the leading force for good in the world."

I would never rely on Joe Biden to define for me right and wrong, to decide how to create "good jobs" or "rebuild the middle class."

Joe Biden's idea of unity is more government and more politics. This means forcing all Americans to buy into his values—something that will never happen—and the idea that government can micromanage our lives.

This is exactly where things have been going, and this is why it's all breaking down.

For perspective: Combined federal, state and local government spending as a percent of gross domestic product—our entire economy—in 2020 was 39.8%. A mind-boggling 40% of our entire economy in 2020 was controlled by government. In 2000, it was 26%. In 1950, 17.7%, and in 1900, 6.8%.

We should indeed strive for unity—unity around the principles upon which the nation was founded.

A New GOP Future—Beyond President Trump

Feb. 3, 2021

The Congressional Budget Office now projects that economic recovery in 2021 will be faster than it predicted last July. It projects that the economy will be back to its pre-pandemic levels by mid-2021. This very good news reflects the fact that the economic turndown was not as severe as the CBO had expected, and that the recovery was stronger than expected.

Former President Donald Trump, recently rejected for reelection by American voters, can take full credit for this.

These are the dividends of the strong economy that the Trump administration put in place through well-directed tax cuts and deregulation.

Let's again recall that last September, 55% of Americans told Gallup that they were "better off now" than they were four years ago. This is the highest percentage since Gallup first asked the question in 1984.

Most astounding is that this question was asked in the midst of the COVID-19 crisis. Yet, most still saw themselves better off than four years earlier.

Across the board, the Trump presidency was transformational and indeed went a long way to "make America great again."

Among many important accomplishments, Trump departed leaving an economy much stronger than the one he inherited, likewise with our court system and the support received by the pro-life movement to end abortion.

It is also essential to note how he remarkably

achieved peace accords in the Middle East that no one ever dreamed possible.

That there are peace accords between Israel and a lineup of Arab and Muslim countries—the most recent announcement coming from Kosovo, a majority-Muslim Balkan nation, which has announced its intent to open an embassy in Jerusalem—is mind-boggling.

We might say that just as Donald Trump defied convention in getting elected to the presidency, he defied convention in failing to get reelected.

Despite tangible and meaningful achievements, Trump departed with an approval rating of 34% and was the first president in history to not crack a 50% approval rating for the duration of his presidency.

I will leave it to others to speculate why President Trump failed to connect with sufficient numbers of American voters, despite a presidency of remarkable achievement.

One obvious answer is a decidedly left-leaning and hostile media.

Certainly, President Trump must take some credit for this failure with voters because of his personal style, which, to say the least, is not always the most endearing to those who are not already on board with him.

The extraordinarily strong Republican showing in House elections, with Republicans picking up 13 seats, enforces the sense that the repudiation of Donald Trump in the presidential election was not a repudiation of his policies and accomplishments but rather a personal repudiation.

The question is: What now for the Republican Party? How does the party pick up the pieces, regroup, refocus and advance forward once again?

I would suggest more focus on what, rather than who.

Republicans need to get the discussion back on agenda and away from personalities.

President Trump was taking America in the right direction. That direction, refocusing on the core principles that indeed made American great to begin with, is certainly the place to start: limited government, capitalism, sanctity of life, faithfulness to our Constitution and the rule of law.

As our national debt spins out of control, and as our new government, which thinks it can print and borrow money to no end, clamps down on business and individual freedom, America will again start down the wrong path that President Trump worked hard to get us off of.

As Republicans regroup, I think of the words often attributed to General MacArthur: "We are not retreating. We are advancing in another direction."

Republicans Must Unify Against the Left

Feb. 17, 2021

Former President Donald Trump captured the core of the problem in his official statement following his acquittal in the Senate impeachment trial: "It is a sad commentary on our times that one political party in America is given a free pass to denigrate the rule of law, defame law enforcement, cheer mobs, excuse rioters, and transform justice into a tool of political vengeance, and persecute, blacklist, cancel and suppress all people and viewpoints with whom or which they disagree."

This is the state of affairs today.

House Speaker Nancy Pelosi, salivating over the one article of impeachment hastily passed by her House against Trump, used national time and resources to do this for one reason and one reason only: to personally damage Trump and create division in the Republican Party.

It was clear that there was no way Donald Trump would be convicted in the Senate. But politics was the point, not the Constitution.

Now that President Trump has been acquitted, the left-wing media is stepping up to do its part to fan the flames and assure that no burning ember that could potentially damage Republicans is wasted.

Longtime Fox News token lefty Juan Williams wrote a piece for The Hill newspaper under the guise of truly caring about the health of the Republican Party, offering his heartfelt advice to Republicans to purge the "kooks" in favor of the conservatives. Or, as he says, to choose "reality" over delusion.

Williams, saying he's got Rep. Liz Cheney's "back," defends her against the pursuit of Republican "kooks" who condemn her for voting to impeach Trump.

For years, the media has portrayed the Democratic Party—the party of abortion on demand, same-sex bathrooms and every failed socialist idea known to mankind—as the party of sobriety and sanity, in contrast to Republican wackos.

Former U.N. Ambassador and South Carolina Gov. Nikki Haley availed herself to an interview with Politico, which did the expected hatchet job on her.

This was one of these so-called interviews where not the full transcript was published but rather only snippets, interlaced with comments and editorializing by the interviewing journalist.

The headline practically all of the media have run about the interview includes Haley saying that Trump "let us down."

This extraordinary woman of accomplishment comes off in this feature as lost and confused.

Let's face it. President Trump's challenge of governing in the face of "fake news" and media dominated by liberals was real.

Maybe it's wrong for someone, certainly the president of the United States, to become angry and combative.

But consider that Trump spent the first half of his presidency fending off fabricated charges of abuse of power and conspiracy to influence the 2016 election, which led to his first impeachment and acquittal. And it turned out that the basis of it all was a dossier whipped up by someone in the employ of the Democratic Party and used as legitimate intelligence by the FBI. And all the perpetrators of this horrible, corrupt scheme are off scot-free.

I appeal to Republicans to not let the smoke bellowing forth daily from the Democratic Party/left-wing mainstream media complex blindside them.

Our nation is limping, deeply wounded and dangerously close to fiscal and moral bankruptcy.

There is a reason why Americans picked a man with no prior political experience as their president in 2016. "Make America Great Again" was about the critical and noble crusade to restore "one Nation under God, indivisible, with liberty and justice for all."

Compared to this vital and noble mission, current injuries and differences in the party are but superficial wounds.

Republicans must unify to continue working to restore American greatness and keep focus on the real enemy: A corrupt, deeply confused and dangerous left-wing regime now holds the reins of power in our nation.

Trump Gets It Right at CPAC

March 3, 2021

Donald Trump showed up at CPAC, the Conservative Political Action Conference, and reminded everyone why, with all his provocations, so many are still on board with him.

Our country IS in trouble—big trouble.

No parent reading this would not be up in arms if his or her children were threatened.

Well, all Americans, including our children, are being threatened—threatened by the militant left now holding the reins of power. It's why passions are running high.

Trump wasted no time getting to the heart of the matter.

"(W)e're in the middle of a historic struggle for America's future, America's culture and America's institutions, borders and most cherished principles," he said. "Our security, our prosperity and our very identity as Americans is at stake, like perhaps at no other time."

The reason Trump stirs up so many is because he is right.

And it's the reason why those on the left hate him so much. He's got their number; he fearlessly calls them out; and he speaks directly into their insidious distortions and lies targeted to crush the core institutions that hold our country together.

Last year, I wrote about Black Lives Matter intimidating billboard company Clear Channel Outdoor to take down a billboard my organization posted in a poor Milwaukee neighborhood to encourage work, marriage and education as the path out of poverty.

BLM, whose business is about blaming everyone else, would have none of this personal-responsibility message about dealing with poverty. And Clear Channel Outdoor immediately caved.

It's what's happening across the country, and we're losing our nation.

Our largest corporations are selling out to "woke" politics and undermining the very values of capitalism that built every one of those firms.

The Wall Street Journal points out that in the $1.9 trillion spending bill that Democrats now want enacted, COVID-19-related provisions tally up to some $825 billion. The rest, another trillion-plus, is simply expenditures for Democratic pet programs along for the ride.

Last year, government spending at the federal, state and local levels came to 43.3% of the U.S. economy. Almost $1 out of every $2 produced by the nation's economy went to government.

Now Democrats want to add another $1.9 trillion on top of it.

It is clear that Democrats are not letting this crisis go to waste and want to use it as an opportunity to advance their agenda of socialism, secularism and left-wing totalitarianism.

Here's Trump again: "The future of the Republican Party is as a party that defends the social, economic and cultural interests and values of working American families of every race, color and creed."

"Trumpism," he said, "means low taxes and eliminating job-killing regulations."

"We are committed to defending innocent life, and to

upholding the Judeo-Christian values of our founders and of our founding," he said.

Democrats and the left have succeeded in redirecting attention from the accomplishments of Trump's four years as president—55% of Americans polled told Gallup last September that they were "better off now" than they were four years earlier—to one unfortunate incident on Jan. 6.

But what some rowdies who got out of hand did to bricks and mortar for a few hours Democrats and the left have been doing to our whole country for years.

The Equality Act that Democrats now push denies the insurmountable reality of every man's and every woman's sexual identity coded by God and nature into their DNA and their soul.

One needn't agree with Donald Trump 100% of the time or be happy all the time with the way in which he delivers his message. But at a time when America as a free nation under God is under siege, when a nation like Iran appears to be developing nuclear weapons, when China is shutting down the bastion of democracy in Hong Kong, we need strong, tough leaders.

Donald Trump is strong, tough and right.

Biden, Not Trump, Driving Border Crisis

March 24, 2021

Secretary of Homeland Security Alejandro Mayorkas summed up our border crisis in a statement he released March 16: "We are on pace to encounter more individuals on the southwest border than we have in the last 20 years."

According to The Wall Street Journal, Border Patrol agents made about 75,000 arrests of migrants crossing illegally in January.

And, the Journal reports, "the government is seeing more children arriving each day than ever before, with an average of 523 children taken into custody by Border Patrol agents each day over the last three weeks ..."

The basic factors driving those from the Northern Triangle of Central America—Honduras, Guatemala and El Salvador—to want to come to the USA is no mystery.

Per capita income in the U.S., per the World Bank, is $65,298. In Honduras, it's $2,575. It's $4,620 in Guatemala and $4,187 in El Salvador.

The already-horrendous economic conditions in these countries were further exacerbated over the last year by the COVID-19 pandemic and by hurricanes.

However, the conditions that motivate people to consider entering the United States illegally and that motivate them to actually try it are different. They try to do it when they think they can succeed.

And for this reason, those wanting to do it followed our November presidential election carefully.

The New York Times quoted one such asylum seeker from Bolivia. "He's our only hope," she said of President

Biden. "With Trump there was no hope. ... Everything was going backward, backward, backward."

Not surprisingly, Mayorkas put the blame on former President Donald Trump.

A ramped-up wave of migrants trying to enter illegally is Trump's fault, per Mayorkas, not because he secured our borders but because he cut foreign aid to these Central American countries.

The root cause of the problem "is the poverty, violence, the persecution of people ... of the Northern Triangle," said Mayorkas. "And why we are seeing the surge now is in part because the funds that were dedicated to those three countries, to address the root causes, was discontinued under the Trump administration ..."

Spoken like a true liberal.

The Trump administration announced a $560 million cut in foreign aid for these three Northern Triangle countries.

The waste and inefficiency of foreign aid money is legend and well documented.

The root cause of poverty, violence and persecution in these countries is corrupt, mismanaged governments, not the absence of U.S. taxpayer dollars.

Transparency International publishes annually its Corruption Perceptions Index, rating countries worldwide based on perceived corruption. Out of 180 nations rated, with 180 being the worst, El Salvador ranks 104, Guatemala 149 and Honduras 157.

In addition to our border problem, American taxpayers should be worried that those running our government now think sending hundreds of millions of U.S. taxpayer funds to the most corrupt countries in the world will solve their poverty problems.

But personal responsibility has never been a big point on the liberal agenda.

We might note that becoming an American immigrant once meant embracing the values of freedom and personal responsibility.

Today it means arriving to a culture dominated by critical race theory, where outcomes are government-mandated racial and ethnic head counting rather than work and personal initiative.

The fact that skin color and ethnicity may grant these potential immigrants from Central America special standing in the U.S. may give them further motivation to enter illegally.

Revealingly, Hispanic voters aren't buying it. In a recent interview in New York Magazine, Democratic Party analyst David Shor discussed the 2020 election.

"Hispanic support" for Democrats "dropped by 8 to 9 percent," noted Shor.

Hispanics are voting more like "white conservatives," he says.

Big government and open borders are not selling well with Hispanic voters.

They don't want the USA, the country they came to for opportunity, to become like the country they left.

Police Reform and Personal Responsibility

April 28, 2021

It is indeed rare, if not unprecedented, to see a highly diverse group of organizations such as the conservative Alliance Defending Freedom, the liberal American Civil Liberties Union, the libertarian Cato Institute and the Reason Foundation on the same page as the NAACP Legal Defense and Education Fund on the same issue.

But it is happening as the U.S. Senate takes up police reform. The issue is a legal doctrine known as qualified immunity.

These diverse organizations all agree that qualified immunity is bad law and should end.

The discussion is particularly high-powered today because it stands at the center of police reform that many see is needed in the wake of incidents such as the murder of George Floyd by former police officer Derek Chauvin.

The nation's first major civil rights law, the Civil Rights Act of 1871, passed shortly after the Civil War, contains a provision known as Section 1983 that protects citizens from violation of their civil rights by government officials. It says that a government official who violates a citizen's civil rights is liable and can be sued by the injured party.

Thus stood the law, until a series of Supreme Court decisions from 1967 to 1982 reinterpreted its application.

A new standard, qualified immunity, was added saying that it must be shown that rights were violated per "clearly established law." That is, there must be a previous case in which rights were violated the exact same way.

So, if a citizen's rights are violated but there is no previous case in which rights were violated in exactly that way, there is no protection. The government official is immune from liability.

Although the law applies to violation of a citizen's civil rights by any government official, the hot button today is violations by police.

The qualified immunity doctrine makes establishing liability next to impossible, thus removing a serious deterrent against police violating civil rights in their law enforcement activities.

Police leadership and unions argue that qualified immunity is essential for them to do their job. This is a tough and dangerous business, they say, and split-second law enforcement decisions must be made, often under great uncertainty, sometimes with life-and-death implications.

But police officers being able to make deadly decisions, with no sense of personal responsibility and costs, leads to some of the horrors that we are seeing today.

Derek Chauvin had 18 complaints against him before he committed his final deadly act against George Floyd. Had the incident, in all its gory and tragic details, not been captured on video by a young onlooker, the legal outcome likely would have been much different.

Personal responsibility must be the hallmark in a free country, whether we're talking about obeying the law or enforcing it. When right and wrong become ambiguous, when personal responsibility becomes ambiguous, we see the chaos we are witnessing today.

Police officers perform a vital function in our society. But what does law enforcement mean when law has no meaning? And law has no meaning if officers have free license to violate citizens' civil rights.

A creative solution has been proposed by the Cato Institute: Require police officers to carry liability insurance, like other professionals do. This would provide them the coverage they need. And those who are flagrant violators, like Derek Chauvin, would be priced out of the market.

The only stalwart on the Supreme Court questioning the status quo on qualified immunity has been Clarence Thomas.

Thomas is an originalist—read the law as written—and opposed to judicial activism. He has written that qualified immunity is “the sort of 'freewheeling policy choice(s)' that we have previously disclaimed the power to make.”

Thomas has urged the court to take on and review this issue. “I continue to have strong doubts about our ... qualified immunity doctrine,” he wrote last year.

Policing should be a local issue, not a national one. But civil rights is a national issue, and qualified immunity should be reformed.

A Test for the Nation in Virginia Governor's Race

May 26, 2021

Americans may not have to wait until 2022 to sense the potential for Republicans to move the nation back in a conservative direction.

The race for governor in Virginia, one of just two major elections taking place this year, could be a barometer of national sentiment.

Republicans have just nominated a dream-team ticket, combining talent and achievement with all the diversity demands of today's political marketplace.

The nominee is investor/businessman Glenn Youngkin, who campaigned for his party's nomination as a "conservative, Christian outsider." Youngkin is a wealthy man who was co-CEO of the highly respected investment firm The Carlyle Group.

On the ticket for lieutenant governor is former Marine Winsome Sears, a conservative black woman and immigrant from Jamaica.

Running for attorney general is Jason S. Miyares, a member of the state legislature and son of a Cuban immigrant.

This conservative ticket—pro-Second Amendment gun rights, pro-family, pro-life, promoting growth through lower taxes and less regulation—advertises the truth those on the left wish to muzzle: that the conservative values that built America are not "white values" but universally true American values.

The state of Virginia is an appropriate laboratory for

this test because Virginia is a poster child for the maladies of our nation.

Virginia was for years a solid red state. Virginians voted for Republicans in every presidential election from 1952 through 2004, with the exception of 1964. It has picked Democrats in every election since—2008, 2012, 2016 and 2020.

What's happening?

The population growth of the state has been in northern Virginia, which is basically a suburb of Washington, D.C. From 2010 to 2019, according to University of Virginia research, northern Virginia accounted for 66.5% of the state's population growth.

Per Washington Post reporting of a 2017 study from Old Dominion University: "Virginia's fortunes are more tied to the federal budget than those of perhaps any other state. Almost 30 percent of Virginia's gross domestic product—its total output of goods and services—is directly related to federal spending."

Given that government is increasingly the meal ticket for northern Virginians, it should be no surprise that Democrats—the party of big government—are increasingly becoming the party of Virginia.

In 2020, Joe Biden won 51.3% of the vote nationwide, and Donald Trump won 46.8%. In Virginia, Biden got 54.1% and Trump 44%.

Even among white voters nationwide, Biden got 41% and Trump 58%. But in Virginia, Biden won 45% of white voters and Trump won 53%.

In northern Virginia's Fairfax County, with a median household income of $124,831, 70.4% of the vote went for Biden and 28.2% for Trump.

As more Virginians benefit from the largesse of profligate government, they increasingly turn to Democrats, who promote this government meal ticket while advancing policies that are destroying our country.

The inflation that many have been worried about, due to excessive government spending producing record deficits and debt, is beginning to show itself in the marketplace.

Recent Census Bureau reports showing historically low birth rates mean there is an aging population—a direct result of the collapse of family and an increase in pro-abortion attitudes and policies.

What is happening in Virginia points to the same trend nationally: more citizens getting government money and thus getting behind policies that are destroying our country.

Leadership can turn things around.

This dream-team Republican ticket in Virginia must run on principles and patriotism and against the moral and fiscal profligacy that is taking us down the path to moral and fiscal bankruptcy.

Virginia's Hispanic population has grown substantially in recent years and is now an electoral force. Hispanics are the nation's youngest demographic. They should be particularly sensitive to policies that jeopardize our future.

Sanctity of life, sanctity of family, and sanctity of ownership and markets is what Virginia and America needs for a future. For this, America needs Republicans.

Will Republicans Step Up to Challenge on Values?

June 16, 2021

For sure, Democrats rejoiced as they watched Republicans painfully twist in the wind at the beginning of LGBTQ Pride Month, trying to figure out how to position their party on this issue.

Republican National Committee Chairwoman Ronna McDaniel got flak from the right and from the left, as she essentially waved a white flag, declaring Republican Party neutrality on a key issue of our cultural conflicts.

"We will continue to grow our big tent by supporting measures that promote fairness and balance protections for LGBTQ Americans and those with deeply held religious beliefs," she tweeted.

But McDaniel's invitation to relegate these life-defining issues to the sidelines and enter a Republican big tent wasn't received with great enthusiasm.

In America's raging culture war, there is little doubt who is winning.

In 1996, according to Gallup, just 16% of Republicans said same-sex marriage should be legal. In 2021, this was up to 55%.

Across the board, what are generally thought of as traditional values have collapsed.

Twenty years ago, 40% of Americans said gay/lesbian relations were morally acceptable. In Gallup's most recent polling, it was 69%. Similarly, over this period, Americans saying out-of-marriage childbirth is morally acceptable went from 45% to 67%, sex between unmarried adults 53% to

73%, and divorce from 59% to 79%.

In 2006, 49% said that it is "very important" that couples with children legally marry. In 2020, this was down to 29%.

The point is that Republican pretense about neutrality on so-called social issues—marriage, family, sexual identity—is self-delusion.

Those pushing the LGBTQ agenda, the anti-Christian, the anti-traditional values agenda, are totally clear with themselves that this is not about peaceful coexistence, mutual acceptance or religious liberty.

They are in an all-out cultural war to eradicate all influence of biblical values in our culture.

And why should they back off? As the data above shows, they are winning. So, why not continue this successful war until no further burning embers of orthodoxy are left in America's public places.

At this writing, the Department of Education is being sued by LGBTQ activists, challenging the Title IX exemption for Christian schools to maintain biblical standards in the behavior they require at their schools. Although Attorney General Merrick Garland has indicated the Department of Justice will defend these protections for religious schools, as the LGBTQ assault aggressively persists, the language coming from the DOJ regarding how intensely they will defend these protections is becoming attenuated.

A Republican state committeewoman in Massachusetts, Deborah Martell, has been condemned by fellow Republicans, including McDaniel, for saying she was "sickened" by learning that a gay Congressional candidate adopted children with his husband. Martell is under pressure to resign, which she says she refuses to do.

Alaska Airlines is being called out by the ACLU, and threatened with a lawsuit, as result of a complaint from one its flight attendants that its uniforms do not accommodate nonbinary attendants—those who do not identify as male or female.

So, where does this go without an opposition party?

Values matter because they translate into behavior.

If the Republican Party becomes a big tent of moral relativism, who will fight for transmission of the values that sustain life and freedom?

In the early 18th century, French nobleman Alexis de Tocqueville traveled around the United States, trying to grasp the secret of the great success of the new, young country. In his classic book "Democracy in America," he observed as follows:

"America is, however, still the place in the world where the Christian religion has most preserved genuine power over souls. ... one cannot say that in the United States religion exerts an influence on laws or on the details of political opinions, but it directs mores, and it is in regulating the family that it works to regulate the state."

We know quite well what the Democratic Party is about. The question is whether the Republican Party will provide the country a choice, championing the Christian values that de Tocqueville identified as the "secret sauce" of America's success.

The Costs of Biden's Big Government

July 27, 2021

It is one of the unfortunate ironies coming out of the Biden administration that, with all the obsession about so-called equity, policies they are putting forth will only hurt the very low-income Americans they pretend to want to help.

The Biden administration is growing government at a record pace.

If what they want is opportunity for every American, government policy should aim to encourage economic growth. Bigger, more intrusive government achieves the opposite. It stifles economic growth.

The Biden administration submitted its first 10-year budget to Congress last month.

The budget projects average annual economic growth for 2023 through 2031, after they're done with all the stimulus spending in 2021-22, of 1.9%.

What does 1.9% growth mean?

Economist John Cochrane, of Stanford University's Hoover Institution, notes that from 1950 to 2000, the U.S. economy grew at 3.5% per year. Average real income over that period grew from $16,000 per person to $50,000.

Suppose instead of 3.5%, growth over that period of time was 2%, asks Cochrane.

With average growth of 2% instead of 3.5%, a $16,000 income would have grown over the 50 years to $23,000 rather than $50,000.

In recent years, since 2000, average growth has been more sclerotic, in the range of 2%.

What's the problem? Too much growth of

government, says Cochrane.

There are different indices that measure government intrusiveness. Cochrane points to the Doing Business report from the World Bank, which measures the difficulty in starting and running a business.

Other more general measures of economic freedom—one from the Fraser Institute in Vancouver, Canada, another from the Heritage Foundation in Washington, D.C.—look at size of government, regulation and taxation.

They all point in the same direction. More government means lower incomes and slower growth.

Per Glenn Hubbard, who headed the Council of Economic Advisers under President George W. Bush, the average percent of the U.S. economy that government was taking in those 50 years after World War II, when growth was averaging 3.5%, was around 20%.

The average percent of the economy that government will take over the next 10 years, per Biden's budget, is 24.5%. At least Biden's economists are being honest to project anemic economic growth that will accompany this huge growth in government.

One of the major spending initiatives in Biden's plans is what they are calling the American Families Plan, with a price tag of $1.8 trillion.

At a time when we have historic drops in our fertility rates and marriage rates, somehow the Biden administration thinks, contrary to experience, massive new government spending and entitlement programs will be a boost to the American family.

Hoover Institution's John Cogan and Daniel Heil call this massive expansion of government entitlements "the largest expansion since Lyndon B. Johnson's Great Society."

"For the first time in U.S. history," they note, "except possibly for the pandemic years 2020 and 2021, for which we don't yet have data—more than half of working-age households would be on the entitlement rolls."

With all our division and disagreements today, there is no disagreement about the shame that the vile institution of slavery was once present and legal in America. We all agree it is a blot.

We all also agree that racism is deplorable.

But the reason slavery and racism are terrible things is that every human being must live with dignity and in freedom.

How can we arrive to the conclusion that the remedy and antidote to slavery and racism is putting all Americans on the government plantation?

Not only is it immoral, but it doesn't work. Government is supposed to be about protecting, not confiscating, our life, liberty and property.

If we want every child in America, of every background, to realize his or her potential, let's strive for their dignity by making sure they grow up in a free country.

Debacle in Afghanistan Symptom of Confusion at Home

Aug. 18, 2021

President Joe Biden was right in his speech to the nation about our withdrawal from Afghanistan, that a long legacy of American involvement there preceded him.

But across the board, in domestic as well as foreign policy, any new president inherits realities that precede him. The issue confronting every president is what principles and policies will he put in place to deal with these existing realities that will define his administration.

Most clear now is that America's withdrawal from Afghanistan is surrounded by a perception of confusion, weakness and humiliation.

For anyone who believes that our nation should be a beacon of strength for freedom in the world, that beacon has been deeply tarnished.

According to The Jerusalem Post, these are the nations that will most benefit from this moment: Qatar, Russia, China, Pakistan, Turkey and Iran. According to the Post, "Most of these countries have hosted the Taliban or tacitly backed them."

In other words, this round has been won by forces in the world for whom freedom is not a value.

Biden in his remarks said, "We went to Afghanistan almost 20 years ago with clear goals: get those who attacked us on Sept. 11, 2001, and make sure al-Qaida could not use Afghanistan as a base from which to attack us again."

This is inaccurate. Months after the attack on Sept. 11, 2001, President George W. Bush defined a two-pronged strategy of retaliation in his State of the Union address. One, "Shut down terrorist camps, disrupt terrorist plans and bring terrorists to justice." This was accomplished in our successful military incursion in Afghanistan.

But second, "We must prevent the terrorists and regimes who seek chemical, biological or nuclear weapons from threatening the United States and the world."

Bush rightly noted that Afghanistan could not and cannot be viewed in isolation from forces in the world that hate us and hate our ideals. This humiliation of our nation in the current withdrawal from Afghanistan strengthens those forces.

Although Biden decided to continue the process of withdrawing from Afghanistan, he reversed President Donald Trump's withdrawal from the deal with Iran, and Biden's deal strengthens rather than weakens Iran and creates a path leading to nuclear capability of this dangerous and threatening nation.

But most critical is to appreciate that we cannot succeed in defending our nation abroad if we are not clear at home who we are.

President Ronald Reagan observed, "While America's military strength is important ... I've always maintained that the struggle now going on for the world will never be decided by bombs or rockets, by armies or military might. The real crisis we face today is a spiritual one; at root, it is a test of moral will and faith."

Our enemies, per Reagan, "must be made to understand: We will never compromise our principles and standards. We will never give away our freedom. We will never abandon our belief in God."

It is here that Biden's credibility is so deeply in

question.

Under the leadership of this administration, the values that Americans have always known that protect individual freedom and protect God-fearing Americans—certainly those that understand this as Christianity—are on historically shaky ground.

Cancel culture and wokeness limit our ability to speak and run our private lives and businesses freely. The values that have sustained marriage and family and protect the unborn have been dangerously weakened.

Government expansion and incursion into private life is unprecedented. Per the Hoover Institution's John Cogan, if Biden plans find their way into law, "for the first time in history, more than half of all Americans would be on the federal dole."

How can we expect leadership in Afghanistan or anywhere else abroad for these American values, when we don't see it at home?

Is the Left Losing Its Grip on California?

Sept. 8, 2021

The Democratic Party is rolling out its left-wing big guns to go to California to support Gov. Gavin Newsom in the recall election scheduled for Sept. 14.

In California, the bluest of blue states, where, in 2020, challenger Joe Biden defeated incumbent President Donald Trump by a margin of almost 2-1, the polls are within the margin of error showing Newsom holding on in the recall.

Why are Vice President Kamala Harris and Sens. Elizabeth Warren and Amy Klobuchar putting it on the line to campaign for Newsom?

They know that what is going on in California is a laboratory for what is going on in the nation and in the Democratic Party.

The beginning of Newsom's fall from grace was discovery of his dining at a party at a fancy French restaurant in California wine country, where dinners start at $450 per person, keeping no COVID-19 restrictions while he had his whole state on strict lockdown.

This was more than an embarrassing moment for the governor. And it was more than a graphic picture of political hypocrisy and double standards. It was a portrayal of very different takes on how America works that is now being driven home by radio talk show host Larry Elder, who is leading the pack of candidates challenging Newsom.

Elder is Black, from humble origins in Los Angeles. After finishing high school in LA's inner city, he moved on to the Ivy League, getting a bachelor's degree at Brown University and then a law degree at the University of

Michigan. He then found his voice talking about ideas on talk radio.

Elder's background and experience gave him a hard gut-feel of what is crucial for getting ahead in America: freedom.

He developed a deep understanding that a free economy is what drives growth, and creates jobs and opportunity for those trying to get ahead.

He also understands that nowhere is freedom more important than in education and nowhere is competition more badly needed than in Los Angeles' substandard, union-controlled public school system.

Newsom represents a Democratic Party that delivers a different picture of reality. It is controlled by progressives, many of whom are wealthy, and the nitty gritty that drives economic growth really doesn't interest them.

They are more interested in their own feel-good progressive values.

Newsom's own career has been driven by support from wealthy California liberals such as Getty Oil Co. scion Gordon Getty, who employed Newsom's father.

House Speaker Nancy Pelosi and California Sen. Dianne Feinstein, both from Newsom's northern California, are listed in the top 10 wealthiest members of Congress. In a Center for Responsive Politics report in 2018, Pelosi showed a net worth of $114.7 million and Feinstein $87.5 million.

California is an ethnic minority majority state. In the 2020 presidential election, 49% of California voters were white, compared with 67% nationwide.

It could be that California's ethnic minority voters are waking up to the truth that the America that Elder is talking about—lower taxes and regulations, free markets, education competition—is what they need, rather than the left-wing progressivism of rich white liberals.

The U.S. Supreme Court pushed back against Newsom's move to use COVID-19 as an excuse to shut down churches while giving more latitude to restaurants and hair salons to operate freely. He clamped down on public schools while sending his own kids to operating private schools.

According to the most recent report from the Bureau of Labor Statistics, California is tied with New York and New Mexico with the second highest unemployment rate in the country—7.6%. Only Nevada is higher at 7.7%.

According to United Van Lines' annual report on household movements out of and into states, in 2020 California was fourth highest in the country in out migration.

In elections last November, Republicans won back four of eight seats they lost in 2018.

Maybe change is coming to the bluest of blue states.

Clarence Thomas and the Declaration of Independence

Sept. 22, 2021

Last week, Supreme Court Associate Justice Clarence Thomas arrived at the University of Notre Dame to speak about the Declaration of Independence.

Speaking invitations like this that Thomas accepts are few and far between.

Anyone who cares about our country and listens to this address will wish that he would agree to speak more.

His presentation was a brilliant and profound articulation of what America is about at its core.

It is what every American needs to hear in these troublesome and divisive times.

Thomas tells his own story and how his life's journey led him to understand what America is about.

He grew up poor near Savannah, Georgia, raised by his grandparents, under the tutelage of his grandfather, a devout Catholic and American patriot.

Thomas' grandfather understood that the injustices of the country were not about flaws in the country but about flaws in human beings in living up to ideals handed down to them. What needed to be fixed were the people—not the nation.

This insight strikes at the heart of the divisions going on today that are so bitterly dividing us.

But Thomas left his grandfather's house and went to college in the midst of the civil rights movement. Dr. Martin Luther King Jr. was assassinated, and Thomas became filled with bitterness and the sense that America is an irredeemably flawed, racist nation, which is so much in the spirit of the times today.

In his own words, "What had given my life meaning and sense of belonging, that this country was my home, was jettisoned as old-fashioned and antiquated. ... It was easy and convenient to fill that void with victimhood. ... So much of my time focused intently on our racial differences and grievances, much like today."

"As I matured," Thomas continued, "I began to see that the theories of my young adulthood were destructive and self-defeating...I had rejected my country, my birthright as a citizen, and I had nothing to show for it."

"The wholesomeness of my childhood had been replaced with an emptiness, cynicism, and despair. I was faced with the simple fact that there was no greater truth than what my Nuns and grandparents had taught me. We are all children of God and rightful heirs to our nation's legacy of equality. We had to live up to the obligations of the equal citizenship to which we were entitled by birth."

As he continued work in the federal government, Thomas became "deeply interested in the Declaration of Independence."

"The Declaration captured what I had been taught to venerate as a child but had cynically rejected as a young man. All men are created equal, endowed by their Creator with certain inalienable rights."

"As I had rediscovered the God-given principles of the Declaration and our founding, I eventually returned to the church, which had been teaching the same truths for millennia."

Despite the strident voices dividing us today, Thomas observes "there are many more of us, I think, who feel

America is not so broken, as it is adrift at sea."

"For whatever it is worth, the Declaration of Independence has weathered every storm for 245 years. It birthed a great nation. It abolished the sin of slavery. ... While we have failed the ideals of the Declaration time and again, I know of no time when the ideals have failed us."

The Declaration of Independence "establishes a moral ideal that we as citizens are duty-bound to uphold and sustain. We may fall short, but our imperfection does not relieve us of our obligation."

Thomas' message about the Declaration may be summarized: There are eternal truths; they are true for all of humanity; and it is the personal responsibility of each individual to live up to them.

Thomas' detractors are those who reject these premises. This defines the culture war that so deeply and dangerously divides America today.

2022 Looking Good for Republicans

Oct. 6, 2021

Going back to the first term of President Franklin D. Roosevelt in 1933, the party of first-term presidents gained seats in House midterm congressional elections only twice.

Karl Rove reminded readers a few months ago in his Wall Street Journal column that, since World War II, the average loss of House seats of the party of each first-term president in congressional midterms is 28.

The largest loss was 63 in the first midterm elections in Barack Obama's first term. This was after Democrats rammed through the Affordable Care Act without a single Republican vote.

Given that Republicans need to pick up only five seats in 2022 to regain control of the House, Democrats who retain any sense of reality are concerned by the political atmospherics being created by their $3.5 trillion welfare state/Green New Deal spending blowout.

But the very idea that there is something called "reality" is now politically incorrect in today's woke-dominated Democratic Party.

The sway of Democrat "moderates"—that is, those who have not detached entirely from reality, such as Sens. Joe Manchin and Kyrsten Sinema and Rep. Josh Gottheimer—is in question now that the on-again, off-again vote on the trillion-dollar infrastructure bill, independent of the $3.5 trillion welfare state blowout, is now off-again.

The infrastructure bill, $1 trillion of spending on public works projects like roads, bridges and trains, is something of more conventional pedigree in Washington, which we normally expect from our elected officials.

The strategy of crazy left-wing House Democrats, pushing the $3.5 trillion welfare state/Green New Deal spending, has been to link this to their support of the $1 trillion infrastructure bill. If you want roads and bridges, sign off on the $3.5 trillion socialist dream.

It had appeared that sobriety would have its day in Washington as the Senate passed, with Democrat and Republican votes, the infrastructure bill, with understanding that the House would vote on it and Speaker Nancy Pelosi pushing back on the far left's condition of linking this to the welfare state trillions.

But lo and behold, the speaker backed off on scheduling the vote, and we're back to the "roads and bridges on condition of the socialist dream" deal.

One notable factor pushing things in this direction was a visit by President Joe Biden to Capitol Hill, indicating his support of the House far-lefties to link infrastructure to socialism.

This could well do for the president's ratings on domestic policy what his horribly botched exit from Afghanistan did for his ratings on foreign policy.

Let's recall that initially the Democratic presidential nomination was heading to the far-left Sens. Bernie Sanders/Elizabeth Warren wing of the party.

Things turned around for Biden when House Majority Whip James Clyburn endorsed him, delivering for him the South Carolina primary.

Clyburn's endorsement was essentially an "establishment" endorsement of the Democratic Party. Clyburn cautioned against the far-left campaign rhetoric on issues like defunding the police.

Now Biden has put his presidential seal on that far-left wing of the party, and this will cost him.

New Gallup polling shows record-low trust in government.

Trust in federal government handling of international problems now stands at 39%, compared with an average from 1997-2021 of 59%. Trust in federal government handling of domestic problems stands at 39%, compared with an average of 53% from 1997-2021.

Earlier this year, Gallup polling showed satisfaction with the country plunging to 39%, compared with 53% in 2020. Satisfaction with overall quality of life was 67%, down from 84% in 2020; with opportunity to get ahead with hard work at 58%, down from 72%; with size and power of government at 31%, down from 38%; with our system of government and how well it works at 27%, down from 43%; and the moral and ethical climate at 18%, down from 32%.

Given how Democrats are running our government, 2022 should be a big year for Republicans.

House Progressives Detach From Reality

Nov. 3, 2021

Rep. Cori Bush, a Democrat left-wing "squad" member in the House, attacked Democrat Sen. Joe Manchin for his opposition to the multitrillion-dollar Build Back Better Act.

Manchin is "anti-Black, anti-child, anti-woman and anti-immigrant," according to Bush because of his opposition to this megaspending welfare bill.

If Bush wants to identify politicians hurting Blacks, children, women and immigrants, she needn't go further than to look in the mirror.

Bush represents Missouri's 1st Congressional district, which includes a big chunk of St. Louis.

The district is 49% Black. According to Census Reporter, median household income in the district is $50,163, compared with a U.S. average of $65,712; the poverty rate is 16.4%, compared with a national average of 12.3%; and 41% of households are headed by a married couple, compared with a 60% nationwide average.

Only someone who thinks history is irrelevant would believe that plunging low-income Americans deeper into government dependency will free them from the cycle of poverty and underachievement.

The Build Back Better Act, with child care subsidies that progressives like Bush are touting as critical for women and low-income families, is effectively a rebirth of the old welfare program, Aid to Families With Dependent Children, that devastated Black families by penalizing marriage and work to qualify for welfare.

According to University of Chicago economist Casey

Mulligan, the child care subsidies are structured such that single parenthood will be rewarded and marriage punished.

Per Mulligan, a single mother earning 75% of median income in her state would pay nothing for child care. But a married couple each earning 75% of median income would pay full price.

Further, that "full price" will cost more than today because the bill regulates how much child care providers must be paid—"equivalent to wages for elementary educators with similar credentials and experience."

Mulligan estimates this would increase the cost of child care providers by some 151%.

He also notes that various subsidies in the bill for Medicaid and "affordable housing" will discourage work because subsidies disappear as earned income increases.

Mulligan summarizes saying the result of all this will be "more kids will come home from a regulated child-care facility to an unmarried parent who is out of work."

The Commerce Department just reported horrible third-quarter results for the American economy, showing growth at a sclerotic 2%.

We're now seeing inflation at higher rates than we've seen in years.

Larding down with trillions in ill-conceived welfare spending while holding hostage legitimate work of government—the trillion-dollar infrastructure bill—is not what we need now, and even Democratic voters nationwide are seeing this.

President Joe Biden's approval ratings are crashing. But so are those of Congress in polling among Democratic voters.

Chuck Todd got to the heart of the matter in last

Sunday's "Meet the Press," asking his panel, "Is the elected Democrats in Congress farther to the left than the rank-and-file Democratic voter?"

Despite mixed replies from his panel, the answer is clearly yes.

In February, Democrats polled by Gallup gave Congress a 61% approval rating. In the latest results in October, this was down to 33%. And, of course, Biden's approval is now 15 points lower than where he stood at the beginning of the year.

Biden is showing himself to be a very weak leader.

The very narrow margin of Democrat control in the House is giving disproportionate power to the progressive caucus. They are causing this havoc.

Their president should be getting them in line. But instead, he is kowtowing to progressive demands that most Americans, Republicans and Democrats alike, understand will just hurt the country.

There should have been a separate vote on the trillion-dollar infrastructure bill already. It is a weak president who has allowed some 100 progressives in Congress to hold it hostage.

I wrote a few weeks ago that 2022 is looking good for Republicans. That's still my message.

The Political Center Is Gone

Nov. 10, 2021

In a new USA Today/Suffolk University poll, President Joe Biden's approval is down to 38%. Which looks pretty good compared to Vice President Kamala Harris, whose approval now stands at 28%.

Democrats have just been reprimanded by voters, with the upset victory of Republican candidate and political novice Glenn Youngkin in the governor's race in Virginia, an almost upset victory in New Jersey by Republican gubernatorial candidate Jack Ciattarelli, who came within 2% of the vote of winning, and revolts in school board elections nationwide, pushing back against critical race theory and COVID-19 government interventions.

It's not rocket science that Biden and his party have lost touch with the voters who elected them. Large percentages of these Democrats did not vote for Rep. Alexandria Ocasio-Cortez and the "squad." And they are unhappy with Biden's capitulation to the far-left elements of his party.

Respected Democrat strategist Mark Penn has a piece in The New York Times urging Biden to shake off these progressives and reconnect with the moderates in his party. This is what Bill Clinton did, he reminds readers, to save his presidency in the mid-1990s.

Former Louisiana Republican Gov. Bobby Jindal offers up a similar message in a Wall Street Journal op-ed. Both parties, after victories, tend to relinquish too much influence to the "extreme" elements in their party, he says. Statesmanship, the message goes, means understanding the need to move to the middle.

But there are problems with this sage advice. One, voters themselves are moving away from the middle. And, two, the reality of culture and politics of the country is things keep moving left. The only difference between when Republicans are in control and when Democrats are in control is how fast it happens.

Yes, it's true that Bill Clinton saved his presidency by turning to the middle. But then, in 1994, according to Gallup, 25% of Democrats self-identified as liberal, 25% conservative and 48% as moderate. Today, per Gallup, the percentage of Democrats identifying as liberal has doubled to 51%; the percentage identifying as conservative is half what it was in 1994—12%—and the percentage of moderates has dropped from 48% to 35%.

At the same time, Republicans have become more conservative than they were in 1994.

In 1994, 58% of Republicans identified as conservative. Today, it's 75%.

Statesmanship and compromise are only realistic when most voters, of both parties, are generally on the same page regarding our core values. But what happens when the common ground of core values is lost?

I started writing several years ago, noting the similarities of what is happening today in our country to where things stood in the 1850s when the institution of slavery was tearing at the soul of the nation.

Where is compromise about whether slavery should be accepted or not in a country that is supposed to be about freedom? Some insisted yes, some insisted no, and everything exploded into a civil war.

What is happening today is similar.

In a Pew Research survey from last November, 80% of Biden voters and 77% of Trump voters agreed with this statement about voters from the other party: "Not only do we have different priorities when it comes to politics, but we fundamentally disagree about core American values."

Culturally, there is no more room for compromise about differences of opinion regarding those accepting and those rejecting biblical, traditional values regarding marriage, family and sex than there was about slavery.

Fiscally, government involvement in the lives of Americans is off the charts. In 2020, government spending at federal, state and local levels was already at 43% of our GDP. With the Democrats' spending blowout, government will be headed toward taking half our economy.

The challenge today is not to find a middle that doesn't exist. The challenge today is for Americans to choose who they are and what kind of country they want—free or not.

America Should Be Shining the Light of Liberty, Not Government

Dec. 8, 2021

The Biden administration is hosting, in upcoming days, a "Summit for Democracy," in which 110 nations worldwide have been invited to participate in this global virtual event.

The U.S. State Department notes that the purpose is "setting forth an affirmative agenda for democratic renewal and to tackle the greatest threats faced by democracies through collective action."

The Biden administration lists on the White House website as among its priorities "Restoring America's Global Standing."

This summit will accomplish exactly the opposite.

The nations of the world will see on display that those at the helm of leadership in America have barely a clue what their own country is about. And then want to impose their fractured understanding of America's mission on the rest of the world.

The State Department brings the phrase from the preamble to the U.S. Constitution, "to form a more perfect union," in noting the aims of the summit.

But the nations of the world are not part of a union, as are our states, bound by a constitution.

They are autonomous nations, each marching to its own drummer, trying to live and, hopefully, thrive together on one planet.

The State Department could have picked a much more relevant phrase from the constitution's preamble, to "secure the blessings of liberty."

Liberty is the point. And I am sure it is no accident that the Biden administration chooses to focus on democracy and not liberty.

To appreciate the basic difference, we can turn to our Declaration of Independence that says that, among our God-given inalienable rights, are "life, liberty, and the pursuit of happiness." Then, continues the Declaration, "That to secure these rights, governments are instituted among men."

The principles of liberty, on which our great nation was founded, precede government. Men form government to protect their liberty, not to bestow it or deny it.

But liberals love control. They don't love liberty. So, they want to grow government to impose their values, their worldview, on citizens.

The State Department states that the themes of the summit are "1) defending against authoritarianism, 2) fighting corruption and 3) promoting respect for human rights."

If authoritarianism is about government imposing itself on individuals, what else can we call it when government takes over an increasingly large percentage of our economic activity.

In 2000, the U.S. government consumed, per the Cato Institute, 17.7% of our GDP—our national economy. In 2020, this was up to 32%. With the passage of the additional trillions that Democrats are now trying to move into law, the percent of our economic lives taken over by government will ratchet up another several percent points. Coupled with state and local government spending, Americans are now turning over almost half their economic sovereignty to government.

The fact that the politicians who are enacting these vast government programs were democratically elected simply says that Americans are choosing authoritarianism; they are voluntarily giving up their liberty.

The Wall Street Journal notes, for example, that the Build Back Better Act just passed in the House contains $555 billion in "grants, credits and deductions" for green energy projects.

In order to qualify for these funds, firms must pay "prevailing wages." Meaning union wages. Nonunion and small contractors will be shut out.

Of course, the reason that this can even happen in a nation founded on the principles of human liberty is because, over many years, our courts and unelected judges have undermined and changed understanding of our Constitution that was originally written "to secure the blessings of liberty."

Now, of course, government looms large everywhere. Employers are told who they can hire and how they must speak and relate to their employees.

No, I am sorry, Mr. Biden. America should be promoting liberty, not government. Our confusion and duplicity will be there for all the world to see.

Nikki Haley's Christmas Present to America

Dec. 15, 2021

Nikki Haley, former U.S. Ambassador to the United Nations, has served up a kind of Christmas present to the nation in the form of a new comprehensive policy book, issued by her organization Stand for America, serving up conservative solutions for our nation's many challenges—domestic and foreign.

Conservatives get a bad rap that they just say "no." That they're against everything but never clear what they are for.

Haley is one conservative that cannot be accused of not having a broad vision and not being forthcoming in sharing it.

It's all here in "American Strength: Conservative Solutions Worth Fighting For."

Latest Gallup polling shows just 24% of Americans are satisfied with how things are going in their country.

Recent polling from Pew Research shows only 24% of Americans say they trust their government to do the right thing "always" or "most of the time."

The only thing Americans seem to agree on these days is dissatisfaction with their government and the state of affairs in their country.

Trust in government has not exceeded 30% since 2007. The last time it exceeded 50% was in October 2001, after the nation unified behind President George W. Bush's effort to respond to the horrible terrorist attack on our nation on Sept. 11, 2001.

Per Pew, data reporting trust in government started in 1958, when the National Election Study first began asking the question. Those years from the late 1950s to the early 1970s were the last time, except for that brief moment in October 2001, 50% or more of Americans surveyed said they trust their government to do the right thing. Subsequently, it all went downhill.

What characterizes the years from the late '60s/early '70s up until the present is vast expansion of government power and intrusion into the lives of citizens. In other words, the more government goes where it doesn't belong, the more confidence and trust that citizens feel in their government deteriorate.

Only when we were attacked, when government was the focus of what is clearly its job—national defense—did trust get back above 50%.

The flow of information from the economic and cultural fronts in the nation radiates troubling news.

Inflation is surging for the first time in over 30 years. National debt is growing to dangerous levels, equal to the size of our whole national economy with projections from the Congressional Budget Office that it will get much worse.

Our entitlement programs—Social Security and Medicare—have severe projected financing problems that make it impossible to continue without major reform.

Culturally, family and marriage are collapsing. Birthrates are at historic lows, and surveys show Americans of ages where families are formed indicate low interest in having children.

America needs conservative leadership to get us back on track with policies driven by traditional American values of limited government.

"American Strength: Conservative Solutions Worth Fighting For" serves up the blueprint.

I was honored to write the chapter on Overcoming Poverty and Building Long-Term Wealth.

But I am in distinguished company with leaders such as Ken Langone, founder of The Home Depot; Sens. Tim Scott and Pat Toomey; former House Speaker Newt Gingrich; Pastor John Hagee; Dennis Prager; and others, covering the full gamut of domestic and foreign policy.

The USA is badly in need of a 21st-century conservative makeover.

Nikki Haley and Stand for America serve up the vision and the plan.

Thank You, Sen. Manchin

Dec. 22, 2021

The saying, "One man with courage makes a majority" has been attributed by historians to different sources.

But regardless of who said it, there is one man who stands out today worthy of this description.

It's West Virginia Sen. Joe Manchin.

Manchin has been a one-man show in the Democratic Party, standing often in solitude, holding feet-to-the-fire of his president and his party's leadership, pushing back on the massive and irresponsible spending avalanche in the Build Back Better act.

Now, Manchin has slammed the door, saying he can't vote for the bill, effectively killing it.

In so doing, Manchin has done a great service to his country and to his party.

Ideologues in leadership in the Democratic Party, intoxicated with the power voters gave them in the last election, lost touch with those same voters.

Last February, immediately after the elections, Democrat voters gave the Democrat-controlled Congress a 61% approval rating, per Gallup. By October, the approval rating for Congress by Democrat voters was down to 33%.

And, of course, President Joe Biden's own approval rating has plummeted from 57% from early last February to 42% by the end of October.

Voters gave Democrats control of Congress in the last election by a tiny eight-seat margin.

Yet, they have been governing like they were voted in in a landslide with a major mandate to transform the United

States into a new secular humanist bastion of socialism.

It's not true, and Manchin has been a bulwark holding fast against this usurpation of power by the far left in his party. As he said in his statement announcing that he will not vote for the bill, "My Democratic colleagues in Washington are determined to dramatically reshape our society in a way that leaves our country even more vulnerable to the threats we face."

The senator also expressed very legitimate concern that it was all being done dishonestly, accusing his colleagues of camouflaging the real cost of the legislation they were advancing.

House Democrats advertised the cost of the Build Back Better act at around $2 trillion.

However, the nonpartisan University of Pennsylvania Penn Wharton Budget Model, run by former government economists, estimated it at more than twice this at $4.6 trillion.

Then the Congressional Budget Office, which answers to Congress, issued its estimate at close to $5 trillion.

The issue is dishonest game-playing by congressional Democrats. Multibillion-dollar programs that clearly will be permanent are scored by those who produced the bill to expire after one year. Informed observers agree that this is ridiculous. The Congressional Budget Office scored the bill, assuming these programs last for the 10-year duration of the projection. As a result, the CBO estimated the cost of the bill at 2 1/2 times more than those who produced the legislation.

Manchin also did voters a great service by calling inflation, which has been one of his great concerns about the bill, "inflation taxes."

Inflation is indeed a tax and also a result of sleight of hand of legislators. How many politicians would specifically legislate $2 trillion in tax increases to pay for a $2 trillion spending bill? Did you say none?

Instead, funds get borrowed and then the central bank prints money to pay the bills.

More money in circulation means every dollar is worth less. Prices go up—inflation.

The latest report of a 6.8% increase in the CPI means a 6.8% reduction in the real income and savings of every American.

All this without even getting into the misguided plans for all these funds. And, hidden in it all, elimination of the Hyde Amendment, which, for almost a half-century, has prevented the use of federal funds for abortions.

Thank you, Sen. Manchin. Every American who cares about saving our country is indebted to you.

What's Jan. 6 Really About?

Jan. 5, 2022

As we await findings and conclusions of the House Select Committee on the Jan. 6 attack, let's take a moment and do our own soul-searching about what is going on.

The House Select Committee is engaged in Washington's favorite pastime—looking for whom to blame. The sidelight of this pastime is the pretense that things that are very complicated can be made clear and simple.

And the other side of the coin of the search for whom to blame is the refusal to step up and take personal responsibility.

The latter, unfortunately, is increasingly becoming a hallmark of today's culture and is exactly the opposite of the personal characteristic that built America.

As I wrote in a recent column, one of the great errors of today's culture is equating the political process we call democracy to a culture that embodies the principles of a free society.

The triumvirate of protection of life, liberty and property—the pillars of a free society—are all under siege today. Unfortunately, the democratic process is, with alarming frequency, now used to undermine these pillars of liberty.

The vast expansion of government power through debt, taxation and regulation amounts to a direct assault on the private property of American citizens.

The storming of the Capitol building on Jan. 6, regardless of if and how it was planned, regardless of the motivations of those involved, put on display disregard for the principles of law and protection of property that are more fundamental than the democratic and political processes.

Unfortunately, the pathology producing this disregard for the fundamental institution of protecting property, for respect and regard for what is not yours, has become widespread. What we learned on Jan. 6 is that this pathology is nationwide, in all political streams, and not limited to the left.

The incident on Jan. 6 was just the latest in many such incidents.

I am not the first to point out that exactly the same behavior was rampant across the country in years prior to Jan. 6, 2021, perpetuated by Black Lives Matter and other progressive groups and justified by the same leaders of the Democratic Party that are now driving the Jan. 6 witch hunt.

In July of 2020, a mob toppled a statue of Christopher Columbus in Baltimore and threw it into Baltimore's Inner Harbor.

When asked about this, House Speaker Nancy Pelosi, who is from Baltimore, responded, “People do what they will do.”

The reporters prodded Pelosi to condemn the mob action, but she refused.

The mob behavior and mentality on display on Jan. 6 was already getting rooted in our country and justified and encouraged by political leaders in the Democratic Party.

Suspicions about improprieties in the electoral process in 2020, which led up to the Jan. 6 incident, were and are quite justified given the closeness of the election coupled with the track record of dishonest behavior in the Democratic Party.

Behind the first impeachment of President Donald Trump was grossly improper and illegal behavior in which the so-called Steele dossier, fabricating evidence of the Trump campaign conspiring with Russia, amounted to the FBI working with the Democratic Party to undermine a Republican president. Where is the investigation of this grotesque incident? All is quiet.

As the core values that were the basis of the founding of the USA are undermined and purged, as eternal truths are displaced by politics, all sense of truth and meaning is being lost. The result is a dangerous tendency to anarchy.

I call on Republicans to take on responsibility for leading the nation back to its core values.

And to advance these truths in our minority communities, where for years the left has co-opted the message of freedom and personal responsibility with a message of blame and victimhood. Releasing these communities from the left will also release us from such close elections.

Sarah Bloom Raskin—Biden's Latest Anti-Freedom Nominee

Feb. 19, 2022

With all the attention directed to President Joe Biden's commitment to nominate a Black woman to replace retiring Associate Justice Stephen Breyer on the Supreme Court, sadly lost is what we expect from our court and what we expect from our nation.

If we have detached from what our nation supposedly is about, what idea could we possibly have about what its top judiciary body is supposed to be about?

But this is what is happening. The American ideal that a just society is a free society is disappearing into the wind. And replacing it is the progressive idea that we give ultimate power to selected men and women to decide what our lives should be about.

Nothing demonstrates this more than the lineup of nominees that Biden has been sending to Congress for confirmation.

Most recent is Sarah Bloom Raskin, whom the president has nominated to be vice chairman of supervision of the Federal Reserve Board of Governors.

Raskin doesn't see her potential new role merely as supervising a smooth-running economy and banking system. She sees her role as prophet and navigator of America's future.

But the difference between today's progressive prophets and the prophets of the Bible is the latter knew they were not God but spokespersons for the Creator.

Raskin is convinced she knows the future. She

questions, for instance, why oil and gas companies received credit and capital infusions from the government during the coronavirus crisis along with other industries.

"The decision to bring oil and gas into the Fed's investment portfolio not only misdirects limited recovery resources but also sends a false price signal to investors about where capital needs to be allocated."

"Why is the Fed Spending So Much Money on a Dying Industry? It should not be directing money to further entrench the carbon economy," reads the headline of her New York Times article.

Based on what does Raskin declare a death sentence on the multitrillion-dollar oil and gas industry?

In April 1977, President Jimmy Carter made the same prediction. He spoke to the nation, announcing that we are in an "energy crisis," that the world is running out of oil and gas, and that the only way to transition to a new world with energy alternatives would be building and investing in major new government programs.

The result of Carter's vision that big government was the answer to our challenges was multibillions of dollars in wasteful government spending and years of delay in the country making adjustments to new realities in energy—adjustments that could only be achieved by letting free markets work.

The crisis then, like today, was not a crisis about natural resources but a crisis in governing, where too many Americans bought the distortion that they needed much more, not much less government.

Carter was a one-term president, and by 2019, the United States was energy-independent, producing more oil and gas than it consumed.

Meanwhile, Raskin's husband, Rep. Jamie Raskin, has been hit with an ethics violation charge for failing to report the sale of stock by his wife, cashing in for $1.5 million, in a firm under supervision by a federal agency that she used to lead.

I am reminded of the quote of Lord Acton, "Power corrupts ... "

Corruption and political power are bedfellows. One follows the other.

It's not the job of our politicians or our government to decide what America's future should or should not look like. It's not their job to decide which industries will flourish and which will fail.

Let me remind all of the critically important phrase in the preamble to our constitution, explaining why it was created and adopted: "to secure the blessings of liberty."

The job of our politicians and our government is to work to "secure the blessings of liberty."

Return of the 'Evil Empire'

March 2, 2022

Regardless of what any American feels about what steps we should take in response to Russian President Vladimir Putin's aggressive incursion into Ukraine, for sure most are appalled by what he has done.

As Putin moves to regain Russian control over nations that once were part of the Soviet sphere, we ought to think about the circumstances under which the Soviet Union collapsed to consider how it all might be reversed.

In March 1983, President Ronald Reagan spoke to the National Association of Evangelicals in Orlando, Florida, and delivered what would famously become known as the speech in which he called the Soviet Union the "evil empire."

Discussing America's efforts to confront the Soviet Union's nuclear arsenal, he said: "I urge you to beware the temptation of pride ... declaring yourselves above it all and label both sides equally at fault, to ignore the facts of history and the aggressive impulses of an evil empire ... and thereby remove yourself from the struggle between right and wrong and good and evil."

Reagan spoke more than powerful words of truth that day. He spoke almost as a prophet.

He noted further: "While America's military strength is important, let me add here that I've always maintained that the struggle now going on for the world will never be decided by bombs or rockets, by armies or military might. The real crisis we face today is a spiritual one; at root, it is a test of moral will and faith."

Some eight years later, the Soviet Union, which for

years during the Cold War was thought to be the superpower rival to the United States, collapsed. There was no war. There was just resolve and Reagan's unwavering commitment to the principles he articulated that day in 1983.

And eight years after that speech, in 1991, Ukraine, now under siege by Putin, was freed from subjugation under the Soviet regime and declared its freedom, independence and sovereignty.

As Putin tries to reverse history, it is upon us to not forget that Reagan declared the global struggle as first and foremost a spiritual struggle, a struggle of good against evil.

As Americans watch events unfold in Ukraine, we must refocus on what is going on in our own country. If we lose a sense of the importance and relevance of Reagan's words as they apply at home, we surely will not know how to relate to events as they transpire in the rest of the world.

And there is plenty of reason to believe we are losing that perspective at home.

We see a direct correlation within our own borders, in our own country, of the decline in faith in the eternal principles that keep us free, and with this decline, Americans are gradually but decisively choosing to abandon their freedom.

In a survey published at the end of last year, Gallup reported that 69% of Americans self-identified as Christians in 2021, compared with 90% who self-identified as Christians in 1971. Twenty-one percent said they have "no religion" in 2021, compared to 4% in 1971.

In 1965, 70% of Americans said religion is "very important" to them. By 2021, this was down to 49%.

Coincident with the decline of the importance that

Americans give to religion, Americans have turned their lives increasingly over to government control.

In 1950, government at federal, state and local levels took almost 23% of the American economy. In 2020, this reached almost 45%.

Turning back again to Reagan's words, "But we must never forget that no government schemes are going to perfect man." Our struggle, said Reagan, is about good and evil.

It's no accident that as America retreats in this struggle, as Americans increasingly believe that government can perfect man and as we relinquish our freedom, that despots like Putin will step forward and try to move the world back to a darker time.

A Morally Weak Biden Invites Putin's Advances

March 9, 2022

I wrote last week about the collapse of the Soviet Union as result of the strength, moral clarity and leadership of President Ronald Reagan.

I quoted Reagan's observation that the ultimate battle we fight, around the world and at home, is one of good and evil.

This battle never ends. Evil always seeks to advance, constantly in search of the retreat of the presence of good, as it seeks opportunities for expansion.

There simply is no other way to understand the horrible realities we confront today.

Russian President Vladimir Putin is an evil man. A murderer and a thief. He chose to advance his outrageous and murderous agenda because he understood that opposite him in the world stood weakness and moral relativism, not strength and moral clarity.

While Putin utilizes Russia's prodigious production of oil and gas as a major weapon in his war of aggression, the Biden administration is fighting its own war against America's oil and gas industry.

I wrote recently about Biden's nomination of Sarah Bloom Raskin to be vice chair for supervision at the Federal Reserve Board of Governors. Raskin is a leading voice to shut down America's oil and gas industry, which she called "a dying industry."

Under President Donald Trump, America's oil and gas industry was booming. However, President Joe Biden has reversed everything.

The Biden administration returned the United States to the Paris Agreement on climate change, from which Trump withdrew.

Biden canceled the Keystone XL pipeline that would have delivered 830,000 barrels per day of Canadian crude oil to the United States.

And the Biden administration has committed to blocking any new oil and gas development on federal lands. One of the first victims has been suspending oil and gas leasing in Alaska's Arctic National Wildlife Refuge.

Now, as Americans see prices at the gas pump skyrocketing, and as Biden and Democrats worry about the fallout of this in an election year, the Biden administration is turning hat-in-hand for supplies to socialist despot Nicolas Maduro in Venezuela, who ruined his own country and was sanctioned by Trump.

Biden also is turning to Gulf producers Saudi Arabia and the United Arab Emirates to increase production.

Aside from the rocky relations we now have with Saudi Arabia as the result of misguided Biden diplomacy, the Saudis and Emiratis are concerned, as The Wall Street Journal points out, about alienating the Russians, who now are a force in the Middle East.

How is it that the Russians have become power brokers in the Middle East?

Israeli leader and former Soviet dissident Natan Sharansky writes in The Wall Street Journal that the Russians stepped in as a force in the Middle East to fill a strategic vacuum left when the Obama administration, of which our current president was a part, chose to ignore its threat to stand against Syrian dictator Bashar al-Assad's use of chemical weapons against his own citizens. Then the Obama administration followed up with its ill-conceived nuclear deal with Iran, which Trump pulled out of and now the Biden administration is working to renew.

Iran poses a threat to Gulf oil producers such as Saudi Arabia and the UAE and also to Israel, which it threatens to destroy.

Sharansky notes that after Obama's retreat, the Russians set up a military base in Syria and now broker its air space. Israel is dependent on Russian goodwill to allow them to counter Iranian aggression in Syria, a direct threat to their security.

Two seats on the board of American's largest oil company, ExxonMobil, were gained last year by Wall Street climate change activists committed to transform the oil company to “clean” energy.

Among Wall Street climate change activists is Larry Fink, CEO of BlackRock, the largest money manager in the world.

Perhaps our president and these billionaire leftists can explain their logic to the Ukrainian citizens now being murdered by Putin.

Clarence and Ginni Thomas, American Patriots

March 23, 2022

Supreme Court Associate Justice Clarence Thomas is once again in the crosshairs of liberals.

This has been going on since his confirmation hearings in 1991, when President George H.W. Bush had the temerity to nominate a Black conservative to take the Supreme Court seat of Thurgood Marshall.

Thomas' confirmation hearings provided a laboratory showing how low liberals are willing to go to try to discredit a conservative, even more so one who is Black.

Now liberal journalists are having their most recent field day because it happens that Thomas' wife, Ginni, is a conservative like him, is an American patriot like him, and is personally invested, like her husband, in safeguarding our Constitution's integrity, written, as its drafters wrote in its preamble, "to secure the blessings of liberty."

Clarence Thomas does it as the court's longest-sitting justice and perhaps its most principled and consistent conservative. Ginni Thomas does it as a conservative activist, involved with a number of conservative organizations in Washington.

For years, liberals attempted to diminish Thomas as a lackey of the late justice Antonin Scalia. Now, as Thomas shines as the court's leading conservative voice, they want to diminish him as a lackey of his wife.

The sparks were fanned, hoping to create a forest fire, about alleged conflicts of interest in a New Yorker article by liberal muckraker Jane Mayer, who has made a career of hatchet-job journalism aimed at conservatives.

Mayer's article leads with her concern about politics finding their way into the Supreme Court, as evidenced by "a recent Gallup poll" showing "the Supreme Court has its lowest public-approval rating in history."

That poll, from last September, shows the court's approval rating at 40%, down from 62% in 2001.

But equally germane, and of course of less interest to Mayer, is Gallup polling from the same date showing Americans' trust in media standing at 36%, the second lowest on record.

Liberal journalists only look for smoking guns when conservatives are the target.

Where were all the liberal journalists when The New York Post broke the story 17 months ago about emails on Hunter Biden's laptop showing he was doing business deals, profiting on his vice president father's position? He even cut his father a piece of one of the deals. The story went unreported through the presidential election. Only now is The New York Times reporting it as real.

How about President Joe Biden's nominee for vice chairman of Supervision of the Federal Reserve Board, Sarah Bloom Raskin? Her husband, Rep. Jamie Raskin, was hit with a House ethics violation for late reporting of a $1.5 million stock sale by his wife in a firm where she may have had a conflict of interest.

We could, of course, discuss America's favorite power couple, Bill and Hillary Clinton, now worth tens of millions despite careers in politics and public service.

The point is, there are no bureaucratic ethics rules that displace what is the real driver of what matters—personal integrity.

There is no decision that Clarence Thomas has ever made on the Supreme Court than cannot be traced directly to his rigorous and principled scholarship and commitment to the U.S. Constitution. Period.

Similarly, Ginni Thomas, who sat on the board of my organization CURE for some 15 years, is motivated by one thing—preservation of our nation as a free nation under God.

The real bottom line is one liberals don't want to hear. The way to limit questions about ethics in government is to keep government limited and small. It's exactly what America's founders had in mind and the exact opposite direction in which liberals have taken our nation.

We owe thanks to Clarence and Ginni Thomas for their relentless struggle to preserve the integrity of our Constitution and the principles that keep our nation free, despite being under endless siege by the liberal media.

The New York Times, Left-Wing Propaganda Machine

April 27, 2022

The New York Times demonstrates why Gallup polling late last year showed only 36% of Americans saying they trust media a "great deal" or "fair" amount.

Times reporters have brought fire to the feet of House Minority Leader Kevin McCarthy, reporting on a recording of private remarks that McCarthy made to other Republicans in the days following the Jan. 6 storming of the Capitol.

In those remarks, as reported by the Times, McCarthy was critical of President Donald Trump, telling Republican colleagues that he believed Democrats had votes to impeach him, in which case, "It would be my recommendation that he resign."

The Times produced the recording after a McCarthy spokesperson denied that his boss said "he'd call Trump to say he should resign."

Taking words out of context to achieve something other than capturing truth is what, unfortunately, defines much of our left-wing union media today, particularly The New York Times.

I wrote in my own column then that, considering the circumstances of what appeared to be certain impeachment, Trump should consider resigning. I called it a "Masada moment," referring to the band of Jews 2,000 years ago, trapped on a mountaintop by Roman troops, who decided to take their own lives rather than being captured by the enemy.

My advice, and it appears what McCarthy had in mind

then, was that a Trump resignation with only 10 days left in his presidency would deprive Democrats of the political objectives they hoped to achieve with impeachment.

The point was to minimize political costs, not repudiate Trump.

If anyone doubts that The New York Times is about a political agenda rather than delivering truth, they should compare how the Times has covered the McCarthy affair to the story about Hunter Biden's laptop.

The Times reporters get big headlines in their breathless delivery of the McCarthy story, which is included in an upcoming book they are publishing.

In contrast, the Times reported on March 16, 2022, confirmation of the authenticity of Hunter Biden's emails, showing his extensive business dealings trading on the position of his vice president father. This a mere year and a half after the New York Post broke the story in October 2020.

Can anyone doubt that The New York Times, along with left-wing social media brethren, withheld this blockbuster story a month before the presidential election?

And can any thinking person not appreciate that this alone could have made all the difference in the razor-thin margins that delivered the election victory to Joe Biden?

Now the New York Post has just dropped another bombshell.

After reviewing White House visitor logs, the Post reports "Hunter Biden's closest business partner made at least 19 visits to the White House and other official locations between 2009 and 2015, including a sitdown with then-Vice President Joe Biden in the West Wing."

It appears that President Biden, who has said, "I have never spoken to my son about his overseas business dealings," may have lied.

Is this a big story? I think so.

As the Times plays this down, it insults our intelligence, focusing on McCarthy and diminishing the truth that what someone speculates about in private—particularly an influential political player—may diverge from what they decide to say publicly.

When President Ronald Reagan proclaimed his 11th commandment—"Thou shalt not speak ill of a fellow Republican"—surely, he was talking about what is said in public. Reagan understood the critical importance of party unity.

Under Trump's leadership, our economy was growing at a pace not seen in years. Black and Hispanic unemployment rates reached all-time lows. A historic peace between Arab nations and Israel was achieved.

Now we are buried in debt, inflation and phlegmatic growth, and Russia has invaded Ukraine.

Delivery of good information to voters is critical in a democracy.

We are paying a dear price for not getting it.

Gun Laws Will Not Fix a Problem of Culture and Spirit

June 1, 2022

Once again, the nation has witnessed a horrible, pointless act of violence, with innocent children the victims.

And, once again, we hear from liberals that the answer is gun control.

If we look at what generally characterizes the mindset of those—generally young men—who commit these acts, we see what generally characterizes the mindset that has taken hold of our whole culture.

Victimhood, blame and denial of personal responsibility.

Can this be an accident?

Kudos to The Wall Street Journal for having the courage to point to these incidents as signs of a "social and spiritual" problem in the country. "The rise of family dysfunction and the decline of mediating institutions such as churches and social clubs have consequences."

The signs of a society that is sick are all around us: the collapse of family, the collapse of interest in marriage and having children.

In 2021, 107,000 Americans died from drug overdoses, an all-time high and a 15% increase over the previous year.

According to the National Institute of Mental Health, the suicide rate in the U.S. increased 35.2% from 1999 to 2018.

Suicide was the second leading cause of death among young people, ages 10-34, and the fourth leading cause of death among individuals ages 34-44.

A characteristic common to suicides and mass killings is that the perpetrators are disproportionately men.

Men—generally young men—commit indiscriminate mass murder, and men take their own lives at a rate almost four times higher than women.

So, men demonstrate in a most unpleasant way another truth that our liberal friends want to deny. Men are different from women—not just in physical makeup but also in spiritual, psychological makeup.

For whatever reason, our increasingly Godless, materialistic, morally empty culture seems to take a particularly heavy toll on men.

American Enterprise Institute scholar Nick Eberstadt has looked into the recent phenomenon of prime-age men—ages 25-54—who have bailed out of the labor market. These are men who have stopped working and seeking work. The official label is NILF—not in the labor force.

According to Eberstadt, the total number of NILF men held steady in the 1940s and 1950s at around 1 million. Then in the late 1960s it exploded. There are now 7 million prime-age men who have withdrawn from the workforce.

According to the Federal Reserve Bank of St. Louis, the labor force participation rate of men—the percent of working age men in the work force—was 86.2% in January 1950. In April 2022, it was 68%.

The labor force participation rate for women has almost doubled over the same period—33.4% in January of 1950 to 56.7% in April 2022.

We've gone from a culture centered on church to a culture centered on government.

According to Gallup, in 1950 over 70% of Americans

belonged to a church. In 2020, it was 47%. Among those born between 1981 and 1996, it's 36%.

Over the same period, take of all levels of government from our GDP went from 22.6% to 43.4%.

Sanctity of life was devalued with Roe v. Wade. Military conscription was abolished around the same time, erasing any personal responsibility, beyond paying taxes, that men have to serve.

In this vacuous culture of entitlement and meaninglessness, lost young men periodically make their presence known through violent expressions, sometimes directed at others, sometimes toward themselves.

I do not pretend that this is simple. I certainly agree that security measures should be taken, particularly in schools.

George Washington warned the nation in his farewell address that there is no freedom without faith, tradition and personal responsibility.

The same liberals that have helped wipe this out now want more government in the way of new gun laws to solve what is a cultural and spiritual crisis.

SCOTUS Decisions Will Change Political Landscape

July 6, 2022

With the Supreme Court concluding one of the most historic and consequential terms in its history, it leaves in its wake consequences and implications for the direction of our country.

One very important result may well be a movement of Black and Hispanic voters to the right.

It is reasonable to conclude that conservatives are happy with where this court has taken us and liberals are not happy.

More specifically, those who believe in the original vision of the country, that it is about individual liberty and that the Constitution is designed to limit the federal government to few and well-defined areas, are happy.

And those who believe that the vision of the founders is no longer relevant today, or that the country was flawed from the beginning and their job today is to fix those flaws, are not happy.

To continue to drill down, many may conclude that this recent court session will deepen the divide between those already on the right and those on the left.

However, decisions of this court bear directly and positively on Black and Hispanic realities and challenges, and it is most reasonable to conclude the political result will be migration of Black and Hispanic voters to the right.

For sure Blacks and Hispanics will hear otherwise from propogandists on the left.

Most of the headlines have been focused on the

Dobbs decision, which overturned Roe v. Wade.

But there were other critically important decisions with far-reaching implications.

In the case of Carson v. Makin, the court found that the state of Maine was in violation of First Amendment protection of “free exercise” of religion where state funds used to pay tuition for public and private schools could not be used for religious schools.

In Kennedy v. Bremerton, the court ruled that Bremerton School District violated free exercise of religion and free speech protections of the First Amendment when Bremerton High School fired its football coach for praying at the 50-yard line at the conclusion of football games.

In New York State Rifle and Pistol Association v. Bruen, the court found a New York State law requiring “proper cause,” that is, a special reason to carry a handgun, in violation of the Second Amendment guarantee of the right to bear arms.

As Justice Brett Kavanaugh asked in the hearing of the case, “Why isn't it good enough to say I live in a violent area and I want to defend myself.”

For Black Americans, who live in some of the most dangerous communities in the nation, the court's decision guaranteeing them the right to defend themselves is important and good news.

For Black and Hispanic Americans, whose children are disproportionately trapped in failing public schools, the court's clarifying protections and guarantees that strengthen the ability for parents to choose where to send the children to school is very good news.

The court's decisions firming up religious freedom protections of the First Amendment and disabusing the faulty notion that the U.S. Constitution is indifferent to sanctity of life and provides for abortion rights will move Blacks and Hispanics to the political right.

Black and Hispanic voters are beginning to see what the cultural chaos of the left has done to their families and communities.

The recent election of Mayra Flores as a Republican and the first Mexican-born member of Congress is case in point. She garnered 51% of the vote in a district in Texas that has never before elected a Republican. She ran as a candidate raised with "strong conservative values that focused on faith, family and hard work."

Her campaign poster branded "God, Family, Country" in both English and Spanish.

I truly believe the recent Supreme Court session will sit well in America's Black and Hispanic communities and gives good reason to expect strong implications for change in the nation's political landscape.

In Washington, Honesty Is Such a Lonely Word

Aug. 3, 2022

A favorite game of politicians, when reality does not conform to the facts they want, is to simply redefine reality.

Democrats want big government, a lot of spending and taxation, the former of which we are now paying for in inflation, so the new strategy of Democrats is to now claim that spending and taxes reduce inflation.

We now have the Senate moving legislation with a price tag of $433 billion in new spending and $327 billion in new taxes, and it's called the Inflation Reduction Act.

It's like McDonald's serving up a new Big Mac with more beef, more cheese and more sauce, and calling it the Weight Watchers Special.

Our president and Congress are imploding in the polls, and what we get from them are word games.

A commonly accepted definition of recession is two consecutive quarters of economic contraction.

The Commerce Department just reported that the U.S. economy contracted 0.9% in the second quarter. This follows a contraction of 1.6% in the first quarter.

Recession?

Our president says no way. Our Treasury Secretary, Janet Yellen, who apologized recently for being wrong last year, denying that inflation was on its way, held what the press called a "rare stand-alone news conference" at the Treasury Department, to assure us we are not in a recession.

It's reminiscent of comedian Groucho Marx, who quipped, "Who are you going to believe—me or your own eyes?"

On a similar note, the House has passed the Respect for Marriage Act, which now will be considered in the Senate.

The Respect for Marriage Act would codify into federal law the legality of same-sex marriage.

This is in reaction to a note by Supreme Court Associate Justice Clarence Thomas in his concurrent opinion in the recent Dobbs decision overturning Roe v. Wade, suggesting that the Obergefell decision, in which the court legalized same-sex marriage in 2015, should be readdressed.

Why is this called the Respect for Marriage Act and not called the Redefine Marriage Act?

It's simply more of the Washington word-game culture, which we now see in government spending and taxing suddenly being about reducing inflation, and consecutive quarters of economic contraction not necessarily being about recession.

To call this legislation the Redefine Marriage Act would be honest, something simply unheard of in Washington.

It is important for same-sex marriage advocates to call this the Respect for Marriage Act, because this suggests that, for those few thousand years in which no one questioned that marriage is between a man and woman, we disrespected marriage.

Now, in our new enlightened age, we understand the truth that marriage includes vows between individuals of the same sex, and thus we now respect this sacred institution.

A recent New York Times poll indicated just 13% of Americans are happy with how things are going in our country.

It's not such a great surprise. Why are Americans so dissatisfied?

Billy Joel had a hit song years ago called "Honesty."

"Honesty is such a lonely word / Everyone is so untrue / Honesty is hardly ever heard / And mostly what I need from you."

As we move into elections during these chaotic times, we might recall the words of one of the nation's founders, Thomas Paine, who observed, "We have it within our power to begin the world over again."

Those who aspire for political office and power might consider that many among the 87% who are not happy with our country today and where they see it headed, know that truths exist—truths upon which a great nation was built—and despair how they have disappeared in our public life.

Leaders who have the courage to be honest, despite how challenging this can be now, will wake up a lot of souls in our nation who recall and long for better days.

T.W. Shannon, a Leader We Need in Washington

Aug. 10, 2022

A runoff election will take place in Oklahoma Aug. 23, which will decide who the Republican candidate will be to run for the Senate seat held by James Inhofe since 1994.

Thirteen candidates ran in the primary. But no one got 50% of the vote, hence the Aug. 23 runoff.

Leading the field is Rep. Markwayne Mullin, who received the endorsement of former President Donald Trump and received 43.6% of the vote in the primary. Running second was T.W. Shannon, who got 17.5% of the vote, and who will face off with Mullin Aug. 23.

A poll one week ago in Oklahoma City by News 9/News on 6 showed Mullin at 57.1% and Shannon at 32.4%. Shannon still lags significantly, but since the primary, he has picked up support disproportionately greater than Mullin.

It is clearly a challenge for Shannon to close this gap by Aug. 23, but it's not impossible.

Which is the point of this column.

I happen to know T.W. Shannon. He is a friend and serves on the board of my organization, CURE.

It is because I know Shannon and his family so well that I know his extraordinary leadership and personal characteristics that make his presence in the U.S. Senate so important in these particularly challenging times.

At the age of 34, Shannon became the youngest speaker of the Oklahoma House of Representatives in history and the first Chickasaw and African American to hold this post. And, in his becoming speaker, T.W. became the first African American Republican to head a legislative body since Reconstruction.

Shannon is also a businessman and banker and is CEO of the Chickasaw Community Bank. He assumed leadership of Black Voices for Trump after the passing of Herman Cain.

But most important, he is a man of principles, and the principles that drive his vision are the principles that drove those that founded our nation.

At a time when we have so badly lost our way, when our nation's future is uncertain because the pillars of limited government and family have been so badly compromised and lost, we need leaders who see our problems clearly and will not waiver in leadership to get our nation back on track.

Shannon is running on what he calls the 3 C's: Christianity, Capitalism and the Constitution.

Some bristle when a candidate is upfront about his Christianity. But one famous Republican who did not was President Ronald Reagan, who quoted William Penn saying, "If we will not be governed by God, we must be governed by tyrants."

Which brings in capitalism and the Constitution.

The Constitution was written to ensure that the power of government was defined and limited so that in a nation under God, men could be free. Capitalism is about private property and unleashing individual initiative and creativity.

These three pillars built the greatest nation in history.

But we have lost our way. Government at local, state and federal levels is now taking almost 50% of the American economy.

Congressional Democrats are about to pass into law the deceptively titled Inflation Reduction Act. This amounts to hundreds of billions in new spending and taxes driven by those in Washington deciding who winners and losers in the U.S. economy will be.

Contrary to the claims of Democrats, University of Chicago economist Casey Mulligan, who was chief economist of Trump's council of economic advisers, says the law will cut employment by 900,000, GDP by 1.2%, average household income by $1,200, and cause increases in inflation and the deficit.

Black conservatives like T.W. Shannon are so deeply committed to our founding principles because they know how badly their communities have suffered as a result of departure from these principles.

We have today two Black Republicans in the House and one in the Senate.

We need the passion and commitment of more Black conservatives like T.W. Shannon in national leadership.

Are We Headed for a Civil War?

Aug. 24, 2022

I wrote a column in 2011, as the presidential politics of the upcoming year were starting to unfold, with the headline "Why 2012 looks a lot like 1860."

The deep fracturing of the American electorate—remember the Tea Party?—leading up to the 2012 presidential election was starting to look like what happened in the presidential election in 1860, which occurred amid another massive splintering of the American electorate.

The issue of slavery in the 1850s—whether or the extent to which it should or could be tolerated in America—tore apart the fabric of common values in the nation, and the result was collapse.

There were presidential candidates in 1860 running on four different party tickets—the newly formed Republican Party, the Constitutional Union Party, and Northern and Southern parts of a split Democratic Party.

Abraham Lincoln, the Republican candidate, emerged victorious with just 39.82% of the popular vote. Immediately upon the Lincoln's declared victory, seven Southern states seceded from the Union.

Soon there would be a bloody civil war.

A vibrant, free and democratic nation thrives with differences of opinion. But there is a difference between differences of opinion on specific issues of policy and fracturing of discourse because of absence of common ground of values and principles.

For a nation to function, there must be some common denominator of shared values and principles.

This common denominator of shared values and principles is dangerously eroding today, and animosities are sharpening and deepening.

Am I predicting another civil war? God forbid.

But the depth of animosities now is looking less like the healthy discourse of a free country and looking more like unraveling of our social fabric. It's dangerous, and we should be aware of what is going on.

A new survey released by Pew Research Center bears out this trend, showing animosities between those identifying with the two parties getting increasingly sharp and increasing numbers of Americans, particularly younger Americans, not happy with either party.

Per the Pew report, in 1994, 21% of Republicans had a "very unfavorable" view of the Democratic Party. Today it is 62%. In 1994, 17% of Democrats had a "very unfavorable" view of the Republican Party. Today it is 54%.

Seventy-two percent of Republicans now, compared to 45% in 2016, say Democrats are more dishonest than other Americans. Sixty-three percent of Democrats, compared to 42% in 2016, say Republicans are more dishonest than other Americans.

According to the survey, in 2022, 27% of Americans now have unfavorable opinions of both parties compared to 6% in 1994 who held unfavorable views of both parties.

This is all consistent with a new survey from Gallup showing that more than half, 52%, of young Americans born between 1981 and 1996 identify as independents.

Forty-four percent of those born between 1960 and 1980, 33% of those born between 1946 and 1964, and 26% of those born between 1928 and 1945 identify as independents.

Just as the presence of slavery challenged the core values and beliefs on which the nation was founded, so today issues such as abortion, sexual identity, and the nature and existence of marriage and family are dividing the common ground on which we stand.

Related to this is the core question of government and its role in the lives of private Americans.

When our divisions become so deep that civil discourse can no longer mend what has unraveled, we need to tread carefully.

Another recent Gallup poll shows 53% of Americans saying they worry "a great deal" about crime and violence.

How can a nation remain intact when large parts of the population have absolutely nothing in common with each other regarding how they see the world?

Limited government and individual freedom are the classic American answers. Unfortunately, we seem to be going in the opposite direction.

Biden About 1619, not 1776

Sept. 7, 2022

President Joe Biden travelled to Philadelphia, to Independence Hall, the place where the nation's founders signed the Declaration of Independence, to make his case for "The Continued Battle for the Soul of the Nation."

Indeed, the president, in his remarks, said we are at an "inflection point" regarding where we stand and the path we'll take for the future.

It is one of those rare moments when I agree with our president.

We are in a tug of war for our future.

Biden presented himself, and the political factions he represents, as those dedicated to saving and preserving the nation's founding principles.

The threat, per Biden, is "Donald Trump and MAGA Republicans," who "represent an extremism that threatens the very foundations of our republic."

But the woke crowd that Biden represents doesn't see the beginning of American history with the signing of the Declaration of Independence in Philadelphia in 1776. They see the beginning of American history with the arrival of slaves to the state of Virginia in 1619.

They see America as a place of oppression that needs to be fixed. Not as the first nation in the world to be founded, under God, on the principles of liberty.

Our president knows that if he conveyed imagery consistent with the values he really represents, the state of his party in upcoming elections would be even worse than it now is.

Biden's performance in Philadelphia, as most appreciate, was politically contrived, because polling shows that former President Donald Trump is a polarizing figure. Democrats want to focus attention on him rather than on what they are about and what those who identify with MAGA really want.

It's not about any one individual but about the struggle for the high ground.

The inflection point is whether America will be secular, socialist and woke or the free nation under God, as conceived by its founders.

Our president cannot even accurately read our own Declaration of Independence, which he described as "an idea unique among nations: that, in America, we're all created equal."

But this isn't what it says. It says "all men are created equal"—not just in America.

It is not about politics. It is about a nation under God that embodies universal truths. And that the job of government is to preserve our God-given rights to "life, liberty and the pursuit of happiness."

Biden left God out of the equation, and he left the role of government out of the equation, which, per the Declaration, is to secure individual liberty, not to exercise power to decide who has what.

The MAGAites that bother Biden so are a nationwide movement to recapture exactly those principles that the nation's founders declared in Philadelphia where Biden stood and spoke.

It is no accident that Biden declares "MAGA Republicans do not respect the Constitution" but with one swipe of the presidential pen, he just wiped out somewhere between a half-trillion to a trillion dollars in student loan obligations that are now on the shoulders of American taxpayers.

Constitutional scholar Jonathan Turley at George Washington University writes that the president's constitutional authority to do this is dubious at best. “His administration,” writes Turley, “is rushing to get money out the door in October, a month before the midterm elections.”

Turley continues, “The Supreme Court has repeatedly found that President Biden has violated the Constitution and overreached in his use of unilateral executive authority. Biden has, arguably, the worst record of court losses in the first two years of any recent presidential administration.”

Trump captured the presidency in 2016 as a complete political outsider because a massive part of America was and is concerned about losing their country.

Half the nation's economy is now being taken by government at federal, state and local level.

This is not the America of 1776. We are indeed struggling for our nation's soul.

Time for a Commitment to America

Sept. 28, 2022

Republicans are gearing up for elections in November by drawing a clear line in the sand between their party and Democrats.

Republicans have rolled out what they call Commitment to America. And this is exactly what it's about.

Our country embodies a worldview, and it is that worldview, and the principles that capture that worldview, that made and makes America a great nation.

The deep tear in our national fabric today is about a large part of the nation—those who support and vote for Democrats—that does not buy into the American dream.

The stark differences are evident in new polling from The Wall Street Journal.

When asked if you agree that America is the greatest country in the world, 91% of Republicans agree, and 6% of Republicans disagree. In contrast, only 61% of Democrats agree that we live in the greatest country in the world, and 34% disagree with this proposition.

What are the driving factors behind this deep contrast between the take of Republicans and Democrats on our nation?

I would call this a deep difference in belief in freedom.

The new Wall Street Journal poll shows a stark difference between Republicans and Democrats regarding whether freedom works.

Regarding the proposition "If people work hard, they are likely to get ahead in America," 85% of Republicans agree, and 13% disagree. However, only 53% of Democrats agree with this proposition, and 46% disagree.

If you don't believe that an individual holds his or her own fate in his or her own hands, then you cannot believe that freedom works. If you cannot believe that freedom works, so you don't buy into the American ideal.

This is where we are as an electorate.

The nation's founders were clear in the Declaration of Independence. All men are endowed with the right "to life, liberty, and the pursuit of happiness," and "Governments are instituted among men" in order to "secure these rights."

That's it. That's the vision of America toward which the founders aspired.

Individual freedom is the core pillar of American reality. Government is there to protect individuals and enable them to live free lives.

If you don't believe hard work will get you anywhere, so the American dream collapses.

This is the great divide today in our nation.

We might look at the just published 2022 Economic Freedom of the World Report by the Fraser Institute in Vancouver, Canada, to get a sense of human reality and freedom.

The Fraser Institute measures economic freedom in 165 countries around the world. Free countries have limited government and low taxes, less regulation, a legal system that protects life and property, a stable currency, and free trade.

The top 25% of countries in economic freedom have per capita income seven times higher than the bottom 25%, have life expectancy 14 years longer, and income earned by the poorest 10% that is eight times higher.

Our country is moving further and further away from

individuals being able to live freely and control their own life. The result is the inflation we're now experiencing and slow economic growth. Individuals sit by the sidelines, convinced they have no control over their own life, and want to turn it all over to government. It is destroying our nation.

This is what the Republican Commitment to America is about. Restoring the right to life, liberty and pursuit of happiness that once was the American dream.

For most of our history, Americans celebrated freedom. The civil rights movement in the 1960s was about Black Americans protesting their inability to participate fully in this freedom.

But once they got it, many chose to not embrace it and turn their lives over to government.

But freedom is not something we can live without successfully. Democrats want Americans to buy that government power is the answer.

But the data, and human history, strongly suggest otherwise.

Justice Clarence Thomas and Ginni Thomas—American Patriots

Oct. 5, 2022

Supreme Court Justice Clarence Thomas and his political activist wife, Ginni, are a high-profile Washington conservative power couple.

Power couples are a common Washington phenomenon. Each spouse wields political power and influence in a certain arena. Together they concentrate power and influence.

Per Public Citizen, of the 115th Congress, 59% of retiring congressmen remained in Washington, taking jobs as lobbyists or in consulting firms, trade groups or business groups, working to influence government.

So, we have power couples that are in office, that were in office—congressmen and ex-congressmen, federal regulators and former regulators, lawyers, etc.

But there is something very different about the Thomases.

Washington power couples are about money, power and influence.

But the Thomases are about principles.

"America is in a vicious battle for its founding principles," says Ginni Thomas.

Really, if the Thomases are successful in their struggle to restore America's founding principles, the result is less power and influence peddling because the result is much less government.

Those who are concerned about influence peddling in Washington should enthusiastically support the principles that Judge Thomas and his wife, Ginni, stand for. It is exactly what the founders of the country had in mind. Limit influence peddling and corruption by limiting the size and scope of government.

In 1900, total take of government from the U.S. economy was 7.8%. In 2020, this was up to 43.3%.

Those on the left that are so critical of Judge Thomas and Ginni Thomas are also those who support the vast expansion of government that we have experienced and struggle with today. This wholesale expansion of government is exactly what the founders did not want for the very reasons we see today.

What about those who argue that Justice Thomas should recuse himself from cases in which his wife has been politically active?

The rules for recusal, as I understand them, are far from black and white. It is very much a subjective decision on the part of the judge to recuse him/herself.

A key issue is it that it is forbidden for a judge to discuss a pending case with a third party.

Ginni Thomas categorically rejected that such discussions ever occur between her and her husband in her recent voluntary testimony before the House Select Committee on Jan. 6.

"I can guarantee that my husband has never spoken with me about pending cases at the Court," she told the committee. "It is an iron clad rule in our home."

But perhaps most importantly, Thomas noted "It is laughable for anyone who knows my husband to think I could influence his jurisprudence—the man is independent and stubborn, with strong character traits of independence and integrity."

It should be clear to anyone who has followed Judge Thomas over the years that this is true.

He is a man of deep principle who loves America and is very serious and committed in his Christian faith.

Bottom line on the whole thing is that Judge Thomas and his activist wife are the solutions we need, not the problem. We are getting the problem from big-government leftists who view Judge Thomas and his wife with such animosity.

We should also give Ginni Thomas credit for her activism for American principles.

It is ironic the criticism she gets from the left, from the feminists, who pretend to be advocates of strong and independent women.

This is exactly what Ginni Thomas is. She should be the role model for the left, for professional women and young women who aspire to be professional.

We keep the country free, per the founders, by limiting government. The source for guidelines for ethical behavior is in the very Christian principles that the left has worked so hard to purge from our nation.

This is exactly what Judge Clarence Thomas and Ginni Thomas bring to the table, for the benefit of all of us.

We Need Republicans to Deliver Our New Leadership

Oct. 19, 2022

As November elections approach, the glaring and deeply troubling headline I see is Americans becoming increasingly alienated from their own country.

There has never been a greater need for a new generation of leaders to restore clarity about American principles and plant them in American hearts and minds.

The Wall Street Journal reports that all branches of the U.S. military are coming up short in recruiting goals.

The U.S. Army will fall short by 25%, meaning 20,000 soldiers. The Air Force and Navy are also falling short.

The WSJ offers various technical explanations as the source of the recruiting problems facing the U.S. military. But most troubling is the observation that, per surveys, "fewer than one in 10 youth are inclined to serve."

It makes sense to expect that kids growing up in a country where they are taught that they live in an evil, unjust, racist nation will have diminishing enthusiasm to put on the uniform, no matter how much they are paid.

A Gallup poll from June showed only 38% of our citizens saying they are "extremely proud" to be an American. This is the lowest since Gallup first did this survey in 2001, when 55% said they are "extremely proud."

On a similar note, a new Gallup survey shows trust in all branches of our federal government has cratered.

The percentage expressing trust in our judicial branch stands at 47%; in our executive branch, 43%; and in the legislative branch, 38%.

It is the first time all three branches of government fell below 50% in trust.

Gallup notes that when it first did this survey in 1972, at least two-thirds expressed trust in each branch of the federal government.

This is a leadership crisis.

Former Democratic Party congresswoman and presidential candidate Tulsi Gabbard drew attention with her announcement that she is pulling out of the Democratic Party.

In an interview on Fox with former Republican congressman Trey Gowdy, Gabbard ticked off her complaints about the Democratic Party, including her concern that Democrats do not carry the banner for "individual liberties," "limited government" and our "God-given rights enshrined in our Constitution."

Some have noted the precedent of Ronald Reagan leaving the Democratic Party.

But Reagan left the Democrats and became a Republican.

And Gabbard? She says she is now an independent.

It's tough to fathom the genuineness of Gabbard's disillusionment with her former party, given that she endorsed socialist Bernie Sanders for president in 2016.

Reagan articulated a clear vision of America, about limited government and individual freedom, and then fought to capture leadership in the Republican Party so the party would become the platform for these ideals.

This option certainly is open to Gabbard. But, no thank you. She's an independent.

Americans are disillusioned because too many so-called leaders are playing games with them.

We need leaders who understand and feel, at the deepest level, what our nation is about. A great definition of leadership/heroism that I once read says that it is someone who embodies "by the cast of destiny, the virtue of their whole people in a great hour."

Inflation is a sure sign of a corrupt political culture. It begins with irresponsible government spending and printing of money.

Alongside our corrupt political culture is the corruption of our society with the breakdown of marriage and family, and the disappearance of children.

A free society is not about economic issues or social issues but both.

In Reagan's farewell address to the nation he said, "All great change in America begins at the dinner table."

He knew that in America, the family passes on the values of freedom.

The press wants to focus the upcoming elections on individual races.

This election must be about party. Republicans versus Democrats.

Voters need to turn the country back to Republicans and pave the way for new, great American leaders.

Democrats Must Stop Dividing Our Country

Nov. 2, 2022

As Democrats see the likelihood of the House and the Senate shifting to Republican control, they have rolled out their biggest gun to try to minimize the damage.

Former President Barack Obama, the most popular Democrat in the country, has hit the campaign trail to try to salvage victories in close and critical races.

Obama's headline message has been about the importance of voting. Meaning, turnout is critical for Democrats, and, in particular, high turnout among Black voters.

Certainly, in Georgia, where the Senate race between incumbent Democrat Raphael Warnock and Republican challenger Herschel Walker rides on a razor's edge, the Black vote is critical.

Unfortunately, despite the charisma and charm of the former president, the message he is delivering is destructive for his party and for the country.

He is pitting Americans against Americans. Blacks against whites. The wealthy against the poor.

"In your gut, you should have a sense: Who cares about you?" asks Obama.

Obama emerged onto the national scene as a young Illinois state assemblyman when he addressed the Democratic National Convention in 2004. In that speech, he captured hearts and minds by reminding the nation that we are "E Pluribus Unum. Out of Many, One ... There's not a liberal America and a conservative America ... a Black

America and a White America ... There's the United States of America."

The message of that young idealist, looking to pave a path for his own political ambition, has totally disappeared now that those ambitions have been achieved.

We would like to believe the battle between the two parties is about which carries the best message for all Americans.

But this is not what the Democratic Party is marketing to voters.

Their message is that the two parties represent different groups of Americans. The question is which interest group will prevail at the expense of the other.

Democrats pitch that they represent the interests of low-income, working-class, non-white Americans and Republicans represent rich, white Americans.

Let's hope it does not resonate because it is for sure not true.

The Republican message is that limited government, respect for sanctity of life and Christian values that preserve the traditional family are beneficial for every single American of every economic and ethnic background.

But voters are hearing from our former president that these values, which capture the essence of freedom, undermine freedom.

"Who will fight for your freedom?" he asks. "Is it a bunch of Republican politicians and judges who think they should ... decide when you start a family or how many children you have, who you marry or who you love."

In 2019, 38% of all abortions were Black babies. In Georgia, it was 65%.

How much longer will Black Americans buy these

horrible lies that are destroying their own lives and legacies?

Freedom is about parents controlling where their children go to school and what they learn. This Democrats oppose.

Freedom is about limiting government so the economy grows at a healthy pace, inflation-free. This Democrats oppose.

And freedom is about citizens getting accurate information from their leaders.

Obama attacked Wisconsin Senate incumbent Republican Ron Johnson for telling the truth that Social Security, which affects practically every working American, is broken.

This year, the trustees of Social Security reported that by 2034, just 12 years from now, there will only be sufficient funds to pay 77% of benefits. This is called bankruptcy.

The Congressional Budget Office now forecasts that by 2052, national debt will equal 185% of our GDP.

Debt, bankruptcy and lies do not hold a promising future for any American.

Let's hope that Black Americans do turn out in record numbers and support Republicans in their efforts to deliver the united, free country that we all desperately need.

In the words of our first Republican president, Abraham Lincoln, we pray for a "new birth of freedom."

Kevin McCarthy, a Republican Leader for Complex Times

Nov. 30, 2022

Republicans are rightly wondering what to expect from the upcoming House of Representatives controlled by their party.

Conservatives are chomping at the bit to move a hardcore conservative agenda.

My own beliefs and convictions are known. We need dramatic change to pull the nation out of its fiscal, cultural and moral chaos.

But the phrase the "art of politics" didn't come from nowhere. Politics is indeed an art—the art of knowing what can be done and when.

Even the great conservative icon Ronald Reagan was sometimes not bold. He nominated Sandra Day O'Connor and Anthony Kennedy to the Supreme Court. O'Connor gave us the decision that preserved the use of race and ethnicity in university admissions policy that only now may be overturned.

Anthony Kennedy wrote the opinion in Obergefell v. Hodges that legalized same-sex marriage.

Reagan appointed Alan Greenspan in 1982 to oversee a commission to address the fiscal problems of Social Security. That commission produced reforms keeping the existing system intact and raising taxes. Certainly not what any good conservative should do.

George W. Bush was reelected to his second term in 2004 and ran on reforming Social Security to allow Americans to invest some of their funds rather than paying taxes. Bush controlled the government—he had a Republican Senate and a Republican House. Yet he failed in this attempt for reform allowing personal retirement accounts.

Bill Clinton signed into law the sweeping reform of welfare in 1996, a reform that required work to qualify for welfare, a conservative reform. Yet, with Republicans controlling the House and Senate welfare reform passed and the Democratic president signed it into law.

Our first Republican president, Abraham Lincoln, knew that any successful political leader, regardless of his convictions, cannot divorce from public opinion. Ultimately, politics is about relationships—in this case, the relationship of a leader with voters.

Lincoln knew the importance of heeding public opinion. "A universal feeling, whether well or ill-founded, cannot be safely disregarded," he observed. "In this and like communities, public sentiment is everything. With public sentiment, nothing can fail; without it nothing can succeed. Consequently he who moulds public sentiment, goes deeper than he who enacts statutes or pronounces decisions."

In this sense, Republican leadership must deal with diversity of opinion in the public at large, but also with diversity of opinion within their own party.

The recent support of 12 Republican senators for legislation to codify into law same-sex marriage raises deep questions about the conservative state of affairs of the Republican Party.

Recent polling reported in The Economist points to the Republican Party being more fractured than Democrats. "For most of the policies we surveyed, more than three-quarters of Democratic supporters took the same line as the majority of Democratic lawmakers, as reflected in their voting records. It's a different story for Republicans." The survey shows divergence in opinion among many Republicans from their party on issues such as "guaranteed family leave, national marijuana legislation, free pre-school, codifying the right to gay marriage, universal health care, and government funding for free community-college tuition."

At the same time, the Republican Party, in the upcoming Congress, will be the most diverse ever. Republicans will have at least five Black members in Congress, the most since the 1870s. There will be a record number 11 Hispanic Republicans and 42 women.

These Republican inroads in diversity helps take race and gender off the agenda and allow focus on the issues of concern to all Americans.

It will take seasoned and skilled Republican leadership to move the country, in these complex times of diversity of opinion, race and ethnicity, toward our country's ideals of traditional values, limited government, open markets and e pluribus unum.

Regarding the race for House speaker, I have known Kevin McCarthy, a fellow Californian, for many years and believe he has the leadership skills for these times.

Race

Can Republicans Get Elected in Nonwhite America?

March 13, 2019

The Pew Research Center has produced a projected profile of what the American electorate will look like ethnically in the 2020 elections.

The portrait shows a continued trend of America becoming an increasingly nonwhite nation and electorate.

Pew projects that 66.7 percent of eligible voters in 2020 will be white. In the presidential election in 2016, 71 percent of voters were white.

In 2000, 76.4 percent of eligible voters were white, 10 points more than Pew projects for 2020. When President Reagan was elected in 1980, 88 percent of the electorate was white.

A number of factors are driving the ethnic changes of the country. One, of course, is the large Hispanic immigration of recent years.

But another key factor is fertility rates. Whites are having fewer children than blacks and Hispanics.

The political implications of these changes are profound.

Nonwhite Americans vote disproportionately for Democrats. So, if voting patterns of nonwhite Americans stay consistent, every year it will become more difficult to elect Republicans, as ethnic and racial minorities become an increasingly larger percentage of the electorate.

In 2016, Donald Trump won 58 percent of the white vote. However, he lost every other ethnicity by large margins.

He won 8 percent of blacks, 29 percent of Hispanics and 29 percent of Asians.

Not surprisingly, this picture translates into the makeup of today's 116th Congress.

Racial and ethnic minorities now hold 116 seats in the current Congress, compared with the 63 seats they held in the 107th Congress in 2001.

And, again, the political implications are profound. Ninety percent of these seats held by racial and ethnic minorities are Democrats.

The last election added nine members to the Congressional Black Caucus, bringing it to 55 members, the largest it has ever been in history. The CBC today is more than 50 percent larger than where it stood in 2001.

This now makes the Black Caucus a formidable left-wing bloc to be reckoned with.

This was on display recently in the failure of the House Democratic leadership to censure Rep. Ilhan Omar, as originally intended, for her anti-Semitic remarks.

Even though it is reported that Omar was prepared to accept the House resolution initially put forth by House Speaker Nancy Pelosi, the CBC pushed back against this and, together with other far-left-wing elements in the Party, succeeded in getting a revised, much-watered-down resolution.

Is it inevitable that the nation will move left as the country becomes less and less white?

Not necessarily—if Republicans do their work.

In a January Gallup poll, 22 percent of blacks self-identified as conservative and 31 percent as liberal. This compared with 13 percent of all Democrats who self-identified as conservative and 51 percent as liberal.

Blacks are more conservative and less liberal than the typical Democrat.

The fact that that only 8 percent of blacks voted Republican in the last presidential election while 22 percent identify as conservative advertises an underlying opportunity for change among blacks.

This in contrast to Hispanics, 29 percent of whom identified as conservative in the Gallup poll, and indeed, 29 percent of Hispanics voted Republican in the last presidential election.

A sluggish, slow-growing economy is the last thing that low-income Americans need. But this is exactly what they will get when things get larded down with the big-government spending and wealth redistribution programs that Democrats want.

Low-income Americans need jobs and opportunity, like we're seeing now, as the economy has shifted gears over the last two years as a result of tax cuts and deregulation.

Whether it's an open dynamic economy, or a flexible education system where parents have control over their child's education, Republicans need to get aggressive in selling their program in minority communities.

There's plenty of opportunity to change mindsets for the better.

Oberlin College's Day in Court

June 12, 2019

For those who despair that the rule of law in America is being crushed by liberal fake news, we have encouraging news out of Ohio.

A jury has ruled that Oberlin College, one of the nation's most left-wing institutions of higher learning, must pay the proprietors of Gibson's Bakery in Oberlin, Ohio, $11.2 million in damages for libel, slander and other disruptions that the college caused in the business by encouraging false charges of racism.

The day after the 2016 presidential election, an Oberlin student entered Gibson's Bakery, near the college campus, and slipped a bottle of wine into his coat.

Allyn Gibson, whose great-great-grandfather founded the business, told the young man that he was going to call the police. When he took out his phone to photograph him, the youth slapped the phone out of Gibson's hand and ran out of the store, with Gibson in pursuit.

When the police arrived on the scene, Gibson, who is white, was on his back being beaten by the youth and two of his friends, all of whom are black.

Nine months later, the three youths pleaded guilty to misdemeanor charges and read a statement saying that Gibson's behavior was justified and not racially motivated.

But in the interim, student protests were held outside Gibson's store, and pamphlets were distributed accusing the store of racism.

The school's dean of students was present at these protests. She claims she was there to supervise, not to protest. However, it was reported that she, too, distributed the pamphlet.

The school canceled business with the bakery, resuming again later.

The college administration claims that it cannot control the free speech of its students and that damages caused by students cannot be ascribed to the college.

The New York Times quotes famed First Amendment lawyer Floyd Abrams saying, "The notion that uninhibited student speech can lead to vast financial liability for the universities at which it occurs threatens both the viability of educational institutions and ultimately the free speech of their students ..."

The college administration wants us to believe it was doing what so many schools on the left have been criticized for not doing: protecting free speech.

But is this really what was going on?

After the incident occurred and the perpetrators charged and arrested, Oberlin's president and its dean of students sent out an email to the student body saying: "This has been a difficult few days for our community, not simply because of the events at Gibson's bakery, but because of the fears and concerns that many are feeling in response to the outcome of the presidential election. We write foremost to acknowledge the pain and sadness that many of you are experiencing. We want you to know that the administration, faculty, and staff are here to support you as we work through this moment together."

Clearly, the college administration has a political agenda that it is not afraid to convey to its students.

This agenda encourages, explicitly or implicitly, student behavior—inspired by this left-wing agenda—to which school administrators clearly are sympathetic.

When students initiate acts consistent with this, is this called protecting free speech?

A real environment in which free speech is encouraged is an environment of neutrality and intellectual humility, in which there is conviction that there is truth to be discovered, and that it is vital to hear all points of view in order to approach that truth.

This is not what is going on at Oberlin or at other similar highly politicized left-wing colleges and universities.

They indoctrinate rather than teach, and they inspire intolerance rather than understanding.

And thus, people get hurt. Like the proprietors of Gibson's Bakery.

Oberlin College is paying the price now, as it should.

Maybe, hopefully, this will encourage the real thought, intellectual responsibility and free speech so woefully absent there and at other colleges and universities.

American Flag Stands for Freedom, Not Racism

July 10, 2019

A new Gallup poll shines a spotlight on the deep political divide in America and surely points to what the upcoming presidential election will be about.

Gallup asked, "How proud are you to be an American?"

Seventy-six percent of Republicans said "extremely proud" compared with 22 percent of Democrats.

Broken down by age, 63% of those over 65 said "extremely proud," and only 24% of those 18 to 29.

This tells us something about Nike's recent move to pull its Betsy Ross flag sneakers from the marketplace, having taken guidance from its ex-football star anti-hero, now-Nike corporate spokesman, Colin Kaepernick. Kaepernick claims that America's first flag is associated with the era of slavery.

Analysts say, according to the Wall Street Journal, that Nike's "core customer base ... starts with American males in their early teens." And, "80% of the sneaker industry's most committed enthusiasts are under the age of 35."

Estimates are that Kaepernick's net worth is $20 million, and his Nike deal will add millions of dollars a year. At age 31, it seems that Kaepernick is not doing badly in the USA.

Does this mean he shouldn't speak out if he sees things that are wrong? Of course not. The issue is spin.

Is Kaepernick—and Nike—delivering a message to young men, particularly young black men, that will make their lives better?

Is a football star worth tens of millions helping our youth by telling them that they live in a nation that is inherently racist?

The operative question is whether it's true.

One of today's headlines is immigration. There are millions who want to come here. There is no country in the world where more aspire to be than the USA. Yet only 24% of those 18 to 29 who were born here feel "extremely proud" of their country? What gives?

Freedom is not about being born into a perfect world. Freedom is about being born into a world where you have the power to fix things.

America has a painful history on race.

But America is comprised of many individual Americans, and in a free country, everyone cannot be painted with the same brush.

Betsy Ross, the seamstress who made America's first flag, was born into a family of Quakers and was educated in Quaker schools. The Quakers were the first group in America to formally protest slavery and the slave trade.

In 1775, they were leaders in forming the Pennsylvania Abolition Society.

On Feb. 12, 1790, a petition arrived to the very first session of the U.S House of Representatives from the Pennsylvania Abolition Society urging measures "for promoting the abolition of slavery and ... discouraging every species of traffick in the persons of our fellow men."

The petition argued that slavery and the slave trade were incompatible with the values that drove the American Revolution.

The petition arrived under the signature of Benjamin

Franklin, a signatory of both the Declaration of Independence and the U.S. Constitution.

The floor debate that followed was the first public debate in Congress on slavery.

As we know, the issue pushed on. More than 700,000 died in a civil war over it some 70 years later.

The American flag made by Betsy Ross, and the one we have today, stand for this struggle and for the principles articulated in the Declaration of Independence that Benjamin Franklin signed.

The truth and power of those principles of freedom is what made us and makes us great, despite the presence of evil.

Let's not make the grave error of thinking that what needs to be eliminated are the principles rather than the evil.

Technology and the internet give us unprecedented power to seek truth. America's youth should be using these tools to look for it, to use their own power to think for themselves, not be seduced by the distortions of confused demagogues.

Understanding Why 'The Squad' Screams 'Racism'

July 24, 2019

Unfortunately, the U.S. House of Representatives is starting to look more and more like America's universities.

Freshmen show up not to learn but to teach. They think they already know it all and see their personal mission is to set straight the faculty, the university administrators and the world.

So we see it with "The Squad," the now-famous far-left freshmen four in the House—Alexandria Ocasio-Cortez, Ilhan Omar, Rashida Tlaib and Ayanna Pressley—who believe they have been elected to a first term in Congress to reinvent what they think is a failed America and set straight the leadership of their party and the nation.

Fortunately, most Americans do not share this highly vocal four's negativism about America. In a new Gallup poll, 70 percent agreed with the statement "If you work hard and play by the rules, you will be able to achieve the American dream in your lifetime." Even a significant majority—61 percent—of households earning less than $40,000 agreed.

It goes without saying that immigration is a high-priority issue on the national agenda because millions from around the world want to come here. There is no more sought-out destination than the USA, and the reason is that no nation in the world offers more opportunity.

So why is this dubious group of naysayers commanding such attention?

The first rule on the list of Rules for Radicals, authored by famed left-wing community organizer Saul Alinsky, is

"Power is not only what you have but what the enemy thinks you have."

Our age of technology and social media adds immeasurable power to Alinsky's advice to gain attention way beyond the support you actually have.

Another Alinsky rule, "Ridicule is man's most potent weapon," provides the ammunition.

These four young freshmen Democrats have no interest in a public discourse of deliberation where we soberly seek what is true and what really works. Their only interest is selling their dogma.

So, following the advice of Alinsky, they get attention not by developing quality ideas for public policy reform and engaging in thoughtful discourse about these ideas but through sensational hype of dogma and character assassination of those who disagree.

As a result, the discussion is not about the merits of the socialism they are selling, about their big-government answers to health, housing, education and lifting up the poor, but about answering their charges that anyone who does not agree with them is a racist.

Attacking the messenger, rather than discussing the message, is a well-established tactic of those whose aspiration is political power rather than seeking truth.

Demagoguery is an age-old threat to freedom and the democratic process. There will always be those who long for power and will try to get it with heat rather than light.

There is only one weapon I am aware of to fight this. And that is doing the hard work to inform people and get the truth to them.

The opposition to socialism, support for freedom, is not about being racist.

It's about believing in human potential, the uniqueness of every single person, and that no system serves human potential better than freedom.

This is not dogma. There's tons of research and data that supports this conclusion.

And it is this that has made and makes the USA so great.

The task is particularly formidable among our youth, where so many have abandoned traditional faith, and among our poor, where the harshness of life increases susceptibility to political demagoguery.

It is no contradiction to say our country and its tradition of freedom is what makes us great but to also be open and honest about how we have problems.

Most of these problems—fiscal problems and social problems—are manifest in areas where we have departed from our tradition of freedom and allowed big-government answers into our lives.

Don't agree? This is the discussion we will have in 2020.

Impeachment About Ideology, Not the Constitution

Nov. 7, 2019

Two American women of color.

Two diametrically opposed views about America.

This clash of worldviews helps us to understand that what is going on in our nation is not a legitimate impeachment process but an attempt to wipe out a sitting president for personal and ideological reasons.

Rep. Rashida Tlaib was sworn in as a freshman Democratic congresswoman for Michigan on Jan. 3, 2019.

At a reception following the event, Tlaib, speaking about the president of the United States, said, "We're gonna impeach the (expletive)."

It had to be unprecedented that a newly elected representative publically used that kind of language about the nation's president and expressed intent to impeach him, with no support from leadership of her own party.

Were there grounds for impeachment? No. The alleged basis was the Mueller investigation, which subsequently found that allegations that President Trump and his campaign conspired with Russia to interfere with the presidential election were false.

What happened to the sacred principle of innocent until proven guilty?

Tlaib had already convicted Trump. He's guilty for being Donald Trump and for what he stands for. The law is irrelevant.

Months later she held a press conference calling President Trump a racist and again calling for his impeachment. She noted: "I represent the third-poorest congressional district in this country. ... I was elected to fight for them."

The Bureau of Labor Statistics just issued its October jobs report, which the Wall Street Journal called "impressive." "The current job market is attracting middle- and working-class workers who have been on the sidelines for years," reported the Journal.

And, black unemployment ticked down a notch to 5.4%, another new historic low.

But just as legal facts mean nothing to Rep. Tlaib, economic facts mean nothing.

Let's now turn to another American woman of color, former South Carolina governor and former U.S. Ambassador to the United Nations Nikki Haley.

She recently spoke at a dinner at Washington's American Enterprise Institute.

Haley, who as Republican governor of South Carolina had the Confederate flag removed from the grounds of the state Capitol, said at AEI: "when we retreat into identity and grievance politics, we make the choice for victimhood over citizenship. By constantly blaming others, we reject personal responsibility for ourselves, our families and our communities."

Are you listening, Congresswoman Tlaib?

Haley spoke about her parents, who immigrated to the U.S. from India: "We were different. We stood out. And my family felt the pain of being judged by our difference. ... But my parents refused to let it define them. They chose citizenship over victimhood."

Haley quoted Lincoln, who, in 1862 when the country was torn apart in civil war, called America "the last best hope of Earth."

She added: "President Trump is a disruptor. That makes ... some people very mad. But if we are a country that lives by the rule of law, we must all accept that we have one president at a time and that president attained his office by the choice of the American people."

Haley hailed the American freedom and exceptionalism enshrined in our Declaration of Independence and Constitution, and noted how, at the UN, representatives from despotic countries would approach her in private and express admiration for our country.

Rashida Tlaib is a poster child for her party. Despite the Russia conspiracy charges discredited by the Mueller report, Democrats have not given up looking for an excuse to impeach a president they hate. Now we have the ridiculous claims from a tainted whistleblower about a conversation Trump had with the president of Ukraine.

It's not about Russia or Ukraine. It's about Nikki Haley or Rashida Tlaib; loving our free country or hating it; citizenship or victimhood; rule of law or guilty until proven innocent.

I meet so many wonderful Americans in my travels around the country.

I'm optimistic we'll make the right choice.

Trump and Black Outreach

Nov. 20, 2019

President Donald Trump recently launched his black-outreach operation—called Black Voices for Trump—in Atlanta. The objective, of course, is to move more African American voters to the Republican Party. There is good reason to believe Republicans can attract more than the 8% of the black vote they got in 2016.

The headline, logically, is the good economic news—a robust economy that has produced a historically low black unemployment rate.

However, religion is also a subject that should get more attention from Republicans.

A new survey from the Pew Research Center focusing on the role of religion in society shows an enormous disconnect between the religious attitudes and behavior of blacks and their political behavior.

Looking inside the Democratic Party, 66% of white Democrats say churches and religious organizations "have too much influence in politics," compared with only 30% of black Democrats who have this opinion.

Thirty-seven percent of black Democrats say churches and religious organization "do not have enough influence in politics," compared with 10% of white Democrats.

Forty percent of black Democrats feel it is a "bad thing" that religion is "losing influence in society," compared with 23% of white Democrats.

The 37% response by blacks that churches "do not have enough influence in politics" is identical to the response of Republicans.

In a Pew survey of last year, 75% of blacks, compared with 49% of whites, said religion is "very important."

Given that roughly 8 out of 10 blacks identify as Christian, according to Pew, how can we understand their disproportionate support for a Democratic Party that views the importance of religion so differently than they do?

The huge migration of black voters to the Democratic Party came with the civil rights movement. In 1964, Lyndon Johnson won 94% of the black vote, compared with John Kennedy, who got 68% in 1960.

Since 1964, 85 to 90% of the black vote has gone to the Democratic presidential candidate.

But the country and the Democratic Party have changed dramatically since 1964.

The civil rights movement was a religious, moral movement to end racial discrimination and achieve equal rights under the law.

The civil rights organization that Dr. Martin Luther King Jr. founded was called the Southern Christian Leadership Conference.

According to one historical account: "One of his (King's) most trusted aids urged him to drop the word Christian from the new organization. It was argued that such an explicit religious reference would alienate Northern liberals, whose support would be crucial in the years ahead. King was adamant, however, and the word Christian remained."

King's famous "I Have a Dream" speech was less a political speech than a pastor's sermon.

In 1964, less than 10% of babies born were born to unwed mothers, compared with more than 40% today. Seventy-five percent of American adults over 18 were married in 1964, compared with 50% today.

In 1973, the Roe v. Wade decision made legal abortion part of American cultural reality.

Religion and politics parted company, with the Democratic Party leading the way to the secularization of America.

The moral wasteland capturing America today disproportionately hurts poor communities, whether we are talking about what children hear in the broken public schools they are forced to attend or the impact of a prevailing culture of meaninglessness on the traditional family.

The conservative majority we now have in the Supreme Court—thanks to President Trump—may well find, during this term, the Blaine Amendments in the constitutions of 37 states to be unconstitutional. This major roadblock to parents using public funds to send their children to religious school will be gone. It would be an Emancipation Proclamation in education for black children.

The Democratic Party of today is no home for blacks. Republicans need to do the work to get to black voters the truth that they can find a home in the Republican Party.

The Pivotal Black Vote

Dec. 11, 2019

Some polls in recent weeks have provided an encouraging picture for President Donald Trump of strengthening support among black voters.

I like these kinds of reports. But I wonder how much of reality they are really capturing.

The Wall Street Journal, for instance, reports on new polling from the Kaiser Family Foundation showing outsize support from blacks for "Medicare for All."

According to this report, 74% percent of blacks compared with 69% of Hispanics and 44% of whites support a single-payer health care plan.

Even when told that there would be a high likelihood that such a plan would mean eliminating private insurance and raising taxes, a large majority of blacks still support the idea.

This isn't exactly the kind of polling data I anticipate from a population that is supposedly discovering that socialism is not a good idea.

Additional recent polling from The Economist/YouGov on Dec. 1-3 gives more reasons to question that there are seismic changes taking place in black political attitudes.

The pollsters asked, "Are you better off now than you were four years ago?"

Among all respondents, 46% said that they are better off now, and 32% said they were better off four years ago.

However, among blacks, only 30% said they are better off now, and 42% said they were better off four years ago.

Given the headlines about a robust economy and

historically low unemployment rates, you have to wonder what black voters are thinking.

Black unemployment is now at a historically low 5.5%. This is 4 full percentage points lower than the 9.4% unemployment rate where black unemployment stood exactly four years ago. Such a change is transformational. Yet it doesn't seem to have impacted black political thinking.

Hispanics also do not seem to be swept away by the good economic news. Despite Hispanic unemployment now at 4.2%, 2.2 percentage points less than it was four years ago, only 37% say they feel better off now, and 39% say they were better off four years ago.

In contrast, 50% of whites say they are better off today, and only 29% say they were better off four years ago. White unemployment now stands at 3.2%, 1.2 points less than four years ago.

Layering on to the sobering news about black attitudes toward those now in charge in Washington, according to The Economist/YouGov poll, 71% of blacks compared with 50% of the general population say the country is "on the wrong track."

And 73% of blacks compared with 45% of the population at large say the House should impeach President Trump.

I think all of this should ring a loud wake-up call for Republicans, and for blacks and Hispanics.

Republicans should wake up to the fact that very good economic news that positively impacts all Americans does not seem to be moving black and Hispanics voters to a more positive attitude toward President Trump.

Blacks and Hispanics should wake up to the fact that if, indeed, they get the country larded down with the big government they seem to want, they, their children and their grandchildren will pay a dear price.

Thirty-one percent of blacks and 38% of Hispanics are under the age of 21 compared with 23% of whites. The burdens of increasingly large government spending, and the debt that goes along with this, will fall disproportionately on those parts of the population that are now the youngest—African Americans and Hispanics.

And the costs of an economy that grows more slowly, the inevitable result of expansion of government, will also fall disproportionately on those who most need economic growth—African Americans and Hispanics.

As I have been saying for many years, Republicans need to communicate more effectively with our minority communities about public policy ideas. If they don't, our entire country could wind up paying a great price in 2020.

Clarence Thomas in His Own Words

Jan. 29, 2020

It has been said that the very moment a man finds himself, he finds God.

This captures the story of Supreme Court Associate Justice Clarence Thomas, a man of deep faith whose youthful struggles with racism caused that faith to be shaken but who later returned to it, more deeply and more resolutely because of his great character and refusal to settle for anything but truth.

The new film "Created Equal: Clarence Thomas in His Own Words" will be released in theaters nationwide Jan. 31, exquisitely timed with Black History Month. But this is also a time of great tensions and divisions in our nation, with race continuing to be one of the main issues dividing us.

Thomas published his memoir, "My Grandfather's Son," in 2007, which tells the story of his journey from beginning life dirt-poor in Pinpoint, Georgia, to his confirmation as U.S. Supreme Court associate justice in 1991.

Now filmmaker Michael Pack delivers Thomas' remarkable story to us in his own words, bringing to the screen exclusive interviews with Thomas and his wife, Virginia Thomas, in which they speak their minds.

Judge Thomas strikes a strong personal note with me because I know well what he means when he talks about being attacked for being black by not acting and saying what is expected from a black person.

I was in the early days of my own work in policy activism when Democrats brought Anita Hill into Thomas' confirmation hearing. I helped organize a large group of black pastors to come to Washington from around the country and demonstrate support for him.

When Branch Rickey, president and general manager of the then-Brooklyn Dodgers, recruited Jackie Robinson to be the first black in Major League Baseball, Rickey warned Robinson that he would be challenged to focus on the game and not react to the racist jeers that would come not just from the stands but from his own white teammates.

"They'll taunt you and goad you," Rickey warned. "They'll do anything to make you react. They'll try to provoke a race riot in the ballpark."

Justice Thomas had to stand the same test.

Except this time, it was not whites trying to drive a black man off the field. It was liberals, black liberals and white liberals, trying to drive a black conservative off the field.

Thomas describes what he had to endure: "(Y)ou're not really black because you're not doing what we expect black people to do."

And with regard to what the left was trying to achieve with Anita Hill, he said: "People should just tell the truth: 'This is the wrong black guy. He has to be destroyed.'"

This circles back to Thomas' similarities with Jackie Robinson. Both men drew their strength from their deep faith to stand with integrity in the face of merciless attacks.

Thomas talks about the restoration of his Catholicism after his youthful rebellion and black radicalism: "I asked God, 'If you take anger out of my heart, I'll never hate again.'"

Anger and hate are just other forms of slavery. Other people are controlling you.

Thomas became a free man once his faith was

restored.

Thomas is now the most senior associate justice on the Supreme Court and has become one of America's great conservative elder statesmen. His opinions over these years have already created a legacy of finely and rigorously reasoned jurisprudence, faithful to the core principles on which America was founded.

When Thomas was sworn in, after enduring what no man or woman should have to endure in his confirmation hearings, in his speech he alluded to Psalm 30, which reads: “I will praise you, Lord, for you have rescued me. You refused to let my enemies triumph over me. ... Weeping may go on all night, but joy comes with the morning.”

What better way to pay tribute to America and black history than going to see this important new film?

President Trump Is Paving the Way. Republicans Must Follow Up With Black Voters

Feb. 12, 2020

The disproportionate number of African American special guests hosted by President Donald Trump at the State of the Union address made clear how very serious he is about courting the support of this community.

The question, of course, is whether meaningful change in how African Americans vote is possible or is just wishful thinking by Republicans.

Since 1964, Democrats have picked up an average of 90% of the black vote in every presidential election, and Republicans have picked up an average of 10%.

Have the Democrats served the black community so well that they deserve such disproportionate support?

I say no way.

The Council of Economic Advisers published a paper a few weeks ago titled "The Blue-Collar Labor Boom Reduces Inequality."

It highlights the incredible economic achievements among lower-income families during the Trump administration.

"(A)verage wage growth for African Americans has outpaced wage growth for white Americans," it says.

Per the data reported, "Nearly 2.5 million people were lifted out of poverty in 2017 and 2018, and the poverty rates for African Americans and Hispanics both fell in 2018, reaching new historic lows."

We're seeing historic increases in net worth among

the bottom 50% of households. Employment has surged, and unemployment has reached all-time lows.

In other words, we've got real evidence that what I have been talking about for 20 years is true. That is, the path to opportunity and achievement for low-income Americans is the same for everyone else: more individual freedom.

How do Republicans translate this into votes?

In my organization, Center for Urban Renewal and Education, we've been looking at recent polling data to see what it tells us about why African Americans vote overwhelmingly for Democratic candidates every presidential election.

One thing that jumps out from the data is how different black voters are from typical Democrats.

Per Gallup, 49% of all Democrats define themselves as liberal. Only 28% of blacks do.

On questions of religion and morality, blacks poll far more like Republicans than Democrats.

One example: Per Pew Research, 55% of blacks say belief in God is necessary to be moral. This compared with 26% of all Democrats and 46% of all Republicans.

The real departure of blacks from Republicans is on questions touching on fairness and inequality.

According to Gallup, 57% of Democrats feel the country is divided into "haves and "have-nots." Twenty-four percent of Republicans believe this, but 70% of blacks do.

And, per Pew, 39% of whites compared with 66% of blacks say economic inequality is a major problem in the country. And 48% of whites compared with 74% of blacks say government should be doing more to solve problems.

President Trump ticked through much of the good economic news for low-income Americans in his State of the

Union address.

Then House Speaker Nancy Pelosi ripped up the speech. And Michigan Gov. Gretchen Whitmer, in the Democratic reply to the State of the Union, called President Trump “dishonest.”

Democrats will deny what is happening. They know that black voters have been listening to their big-government-dependence message for half a century. And the results have been dismal.

Republicans have already got black voters on board with them regarding the importance of religion, faith and morality.

But they've got a big job to change black attitudes about reliance on big government.

Republicans need to get into the trenches and present the case for freedom. The advantage they have is truth and plenty of glowing data from the last three years.

President Trump's outreach to African Americans in the State of the Union was a great start. In addition to highlighting the great economic news, he showcased education opportunity scholarships, opportunity zones and criminal justice reform.

President Trump is laying the groundwork for a sea change in African American politics. Republicans need to follow up.

Will African Americans Abandon Biden for Bernie?

Feb. 26, 2020

Democrats appear to be walking the same walk that Republicans walked in 2016.

They want something new and completely different.

Former Vice President Joe Biden must be in shock that he is taking a far back seat to a 78-year-old socialist who recently had a heart attack.

He may not even be able to rely on black voters, whom he assumed would be there for him.

According to a new Wall Street Journal/NBC poll, Biden and Sen. Bernie Sanders are running neck and neck with black voters in the upcoming South Carolina primary, where 60% of Democrat voters are African American.

Influential Congressional Black Caucus member and House majority whip James Clyburn of South Carolina was circumspect on "Meet the Press" when Chuck Todd pressed him regarding an endorsement of Biden.

We get a hint on what voters are feeling by looking at Gallup polling on whether voters are satisfied or dissatisfied with the direction of the country.

Gallup has been asking this question since 1979. The average over the entire period, from February 1979 to January 2020, has been 37% expressing satisfaction with the direction of the nation.

Good news for President Donald Trump is that the figure recently jumped to 41%, the first time since July 2005 that it is over 40%.

The average for former President Ronald Reagan's

second term, 1985 through 1988, was 54%. The average for former President Barack Obama's two terms was 24%.

It shows why Biden has been such a flop. Although Obama had high personal ratings with the American public, the public's sense of the state of the nation under his stewardship provides a far different picture.

Taking voters, certainly black voters, for granted just isn't going to work anymore.

Americans sense that there has been something very wrong in the country, and they want very clear answers from candidates on what they think is wrong and how they plan to fix it.

We're just not going to get by anymore as half-free and half-socialist. To paraphrase Abraham Lincoln, we're going to become all one or all the other. I discuss this in depth in my new book, "Necessary Noise."

In 2016, Republicans went out of the mainstream and picked Donald Trump to clean up the Washington swamp. Democrats went for the establishment candidate and lost.

Now Democrats want to move left from the murky middle as Republicans move right.

Polling of black voters shows they feel that the country is unfair and that more government is needed to fix this.

According to Gallup, 70% of blacks feel the country is divided into "haves" and "have-nots," and 57% of blacks self-identify as "have-not."

In polling by the Pew Research Center, 66% of blacks say economic inequality is a major problem in the country today. And 74% of blacks, compared with 48% of whites, say "government should do more to solve problems."

Regarding government-run health care, Bernie

Sanders' flagship, 66% of black Democrats, per Gallup, express preference for a government-run system.

Bernie Sanders is serving it all up, clear as day for all to see.

Turn your whole life over to the government.

So in November, Americans may have a clear and stark choice.

Blacks will have a chance to decide whether being free or living under government dictate is the best way to deal with the opportunity problem they perceive.

Truth is that blacks have been living disproportionately under government dictate since the 1970s. And today, average black household wealth is one-tenth average white household wealth.

Apparently, many African Americans feel that this gap persists because we don't have enough government in our lives, rather than too much.

It looks like bye-bye, Biden. Americans want vision and leadership. Now the question is whether we look to freedom or the other way.

Today's Great Black Dilemma

March 11, 2020

I was proud recently when Marc Little, chairman of my organization, the Center for Urban Renewal and Education, stood behind President Donald Trump at a White House event for Black History Month and prayed for him.

Then a parade of black liberals did their thing in the media to try to deflate and devalue this important event. Their actions help us understand why so little progress has been made after more than half a century of civil rights activism.

CNNs Keith Boykin called the black Christians grouped around the president "Uncle Toms." Chris Redd of "Saturday Night Live" called them "White House negroes." And Spike Lee mocked them, writing, "We Gonna Pray Fo' You Massa."

How can we miss the irony of black liberals, their lives dedicated to keeping blacks on the government welfare plantation, using insulting plantation imagery to attack conservative black Christians working for freedom and better lives for African Americans?

The Economist magazine last year ran an article with the headline "The black-white wealth gap is unchanged after half a century."

"(I)n 1962," the article reports, "two years before the passage of landmark civil-rights legislation ... the average wealth of white households was seven times greater than that of black households. Yet after decades of declining discrimination and the construction of a modern welfare state, that ratio remains the same."

The article fails to mention that total spending on government anti-poverty and welfare programs over these years is estimated at $20 trillion.

Why do significant gaps in wealth and income persist between black Americans and the rest of the country?

Racism?

Americans recently elected a black man as their president twice.

In the elections of 2008 and 2012, Barack Obama received almost 80 million votes from white Americans.

Between 1967 and 2015, the percentage of marriages that are interracial or interethnic couples increased by five times.

Why are blacks still inclined to attribute the challenges they face to racism? Because that's all they hear from left-wing black media moguls who are in business to get a rise out of people, rather than enlighten them.

A major theme being peddled in the current Democratic presidential campaign is that wealth is evil. Candidates are tripping over one another to see who can come up with a better tax on wealthy Americans.

But is punishing wealth and achievement the answer for improving the lives of black Americans or any Americans?

According to one study, 69% of those on Forbes Magazine's list of 400 wealthiest Americans are self-made. And 20% grew up poor.

Dr. Ben Carson, now secretary of housing and urban development, rose from a Detroit ghetto; he was raised by a single mother and later became a world-renowned neurosurgeon. His story, how his mother made her sons turn off the television and read at least one book every week, should be read by every American child.

Surely, if blacks continue to buy the lie that the poor are poor because the rich are rich, 50 years from now there will still be no change in the wealth gap between black households and the rest of the country.

It's so easy to hate. It's so easy to blame others for your problems. And it's so hard to take responsibility for your life, regardless of the circumstances.

But hate, blame and mockery are the meal ticket of black liberals.

So for them, conservative black Christians standing by the president, standing at the seat of power, is a red flag. The idea that freedom, faith, family, marriage and personal responsibility are the path to the good life is the last thing they want to see legitimized.

Once, the great challenge that black Americans faced was the scourge of racism and the acts of evil white men.

Today's great challenge for blacks is to shake off the culture of the welfare plantation and the destructive rhetoric of evil black liberals who want to keep them there.

Will the Real Racists in America Raise Their Hands?

Jan. 6, 2021

While sitting in the Delta lounge in the Atlanta airport waiting for my flight back to Washington, a white gentleman approached me and struck up a conversation.

Politics was on his mind, and seeing me, a black woman, he was sure that he had found a kindred spirit to share his hopes that Democrats will prevail in both U.S. Senate runoff races in Georgia.

I politely straightened him out, leaving him a bit in shock that he had incorrectly assumed that seeing the outside of me was sufficient information to know what is going on inside of me.

There is a word for this: stereotyping.

Is this gentleman a bad man? I don't know.

But he is proof of the horrible success of the perception of racism industry that has been damaging our country since the 1960s. The result is today's identity politics, diversity politics and all the politics of the left that promote the notion that what is relevant is the outside of a person, what he or she looks like, not what is going on inside the person.

With all the screaming about racism, a huge story of recent months hardly received any attention. Maybe because it doesn't fit into the story that our left-wing media want to report about what they call racism.

Several months ago, the Census Bureau issued its annual report called "Income and Poverty in the United States: 2019."

According to the report, real median black household income in 2019 was up 7.9%—the largest annual increase in median black household income in history. This put the increase in black household income in 2019 1.1 points higher than the 6.8% increase for the nation as a whole.

Further, for the first time ever, the percentage of high-income black households exceeded the percentage of low-income black households.

In 2019, 29.4% of black households had income of $75,000 or more, compared with 28.7% of black households that had income of $25,000 or less.

In 1967, per the Census Bureau, 9.1% of black households had income of $75,000 or more, and 44.5% of black households had income of $25,000 or less.

Contrary to what blares out daily from liberal media, African Americans are not getting a raw deal in our country. In fact, as this new data from the Census Bureau shows, African Americans are systematically getting ahead and improving their lives.

One area of enormous improvement is in education achievement, which no doubt is a major factor in the improvement in income of black households.

According to the Census Bureau, in 2019, the black high school completion rate was 98% of the national average. Back in 1980, it was about 75%.

In 2019, 29.6% of blacks ages 25 and above completed four years of college. In 1980, this stood at 11.6%.

The rejoinder from the left is yes, but black average incomes still lag behind white average incomes.

My answer is that what drives human achievement is the same for everyone. It comes from lofty goals and a sense of each individual that it is up to them, their character and hard work to achieve those goals.

Teaching black children that they are living in a racist country and that they have no chance without government intervention, without diversity politics, without receiving special treatment because of their race destroys that child's sense of humanity, personal uniqueness and personal responsibility.

We have two competing cultures in America today. One culture says that life is, by nature, hard and that achievement comes from diligence, good character and struggle. The other culture says that life is only hard if it is unfair, and that life can be made fair and easy through politics.

The latter is the culture of the left, which damages the very individuals it pretends to help.

If we want to build a more perfect union, believe that every person is unique and that what people look like tells you nothing about who they are.

Reparations Don't Buy Justice, Dignity or Freedom

Feb. 24, 2021

The issue of reparations to Black Americans as payment for damage done as a result of years of legal slavery and subsequent discrimination is back on the table.

The House Judiciary Committee just held hearings on H.R. 40, which would establish a commission to look into ways in which African Americans could be compensated, including possible payments of trillions of dollars to individuals.

The commission would examine the role of government in supporting the institution of slavery, "discrimination in the public and private sectors against freed African slaves and their descendants" and "lingering negative effects of the institution of slavery ... on living African Americans and on society."

My ancestors were slaves. And my life as a young woman was a mess.

Was my life a mess because my ancestors were slaves? I don't think so.

My life was a mess because I lived a wanton, irresponsible existence, defined by promiscuity, petty crimes and scamming the nation's well-meaning but totally confused welfare system to the greatest extent of my ability.

Did I need reparations to turn things around for me? Certainly not. I needed a wake-up call, which, to my great gratitude, I got, from a few church-going black Christians who told me the way I was living was unacceptable.

I went to church, took back responsibility for my life

and turned my circumstances around.

The problem with the idea of reparations is it redirects attention away from exactly where attention is needed: on individuals' personal responsibility for their own unique lives.

And it redirects attention in such a way to encourage individuals to believe that some abstract, collective entity from the past is the cause of all their individual problems in the present.

Compensation for damages is a basic legal principle.

It's about personal responsibility. Individual A sues individual B for damages caused. Exactly what the damages were and exactly how B injured A must be shown in a court of law.

Today, only a small fraction of our population has ancestors who were around before 1865 when slavery was legal. The idea of collective guilt, with no specific individual identified as causing the damage and no specific individual showing how he or she was damaged, doesn't fly.

If there is any legitimate claim of collective guilt, it is the guilt of original sin, which we learn in the book of Genesis. Every man and woman is imperfect and responsible for fixing themselves—and, by doing so, helping to fix the world.

There is no word more frequently used in political discussions than "freedom." But rarely discussed is what gives meaning to the word "freedom," and that is understanding that individuals have free choice—the power and responsibility to choose how to live.

Only when we understand that there is good and evil, that there is sin, does free choice have meaning. It means individuals have the power and responsibility to choose how to live—that their individual choices matter.

Driving the push for reparations are policies on race that obliterate this key idea that every individual, regardless of circumstance and history, is unique and has free choice. The political idea of freedom becomes irrelevant because free choice becomes irrelevant.

So-called critical race theory says everything is about culture. Because, per their claim, the USA is about what they define as white culture, the cultural script needs to be rewritten to make things fair for those who are not white. Put politicians in charge of making things fair.

No, I am sorry; I always thought the problem with racism is it denies the uniqueness, dignity and personal responsibility of each individual.

If the ideal we seek is a free country with free citizens, then commissions such as that proposed in H.R. 40, which pretend to be about justice but are really about a left-wing agenda to put government in charge of our lives, are not the way to go.

I'm With Israel and Against Critical Race Theory

May 19, 2021

In 1867, American writer Mark Twain visited the Holy Land. He recorded his impressions in a book titled "The Innocents Abroad."

Twain was appalled when seeing the abandoned and desolate land that was the home of the Bible.

"The further we went, the hotter the sun got and the more rocky and bare, repulsive and dreary, the landscape became," he wrote. "There was hardly a tree or shrub anywhere. Even the olive and the cactus, those fast friends of a worthless soil, had almost deserted the country."

Some 15 years later, Jews began a movement to return to and restore their ancient homeland.

They started rebuilding under horrendous and challenging conditions.

By November 1947, as Jews continued their process of building and Arabs continued their process of hating, the United Nations gave the green light to establish a Jewish state and an adjacent Arab state.

Jews accepted the U.N. partition of the region, declaring the new state of Israel in May 1948, but the Arabs rejected the plan and attacked the newly declared Jewish state. Israelis fought and miraculously prevailed in its War of Independence, and the project of rebuilding the ancient homeland moved forward. Now it is an officially recognized member of the community of nations.

Compared with the desolation described by Mark Twain, Israel today is a modern miracle, with per capita GDP (gross domestic product) higher than that of Great Britain, France, Italy and Spain, according to the World Bank.

As of 2019, Israel had a per capita GDP of $43,589, much higher than that of its immediately adjacent neighbors: Jordan's was $4,405, Egypt's $3,019, Syria's $2,037 (as of 2007) and Lebanon's $7,584.

Per Statista, Israel has the highest per capita venture capital investment in the world.

During its short history, from its founding in 1948 with a population of 806,000 to today, with a population of 9,291,000—slightly more than the population of New York City—Israel has produced 12 Nobel Prize winners.

All this while fighting three major wars and dealing with endless terrorism.

According to Freedom House in Washington, D.C., Israel is among the freest countries in the world by measurement of political and civil rights.

Commentary from America's left and left-wing media says that Israelis oppress Palestinians under horrible conditions, and these Palestinians have no choice but to periodically explode with violence like we are now seeing, with missiles being hurled from Gaza into Israel's civilian population centers.

Palestinians in Gaza do live in horrendous conditions, but not because Israelis force them to. They choose to.

Israel unilaterally pulled out of Gaza in 2005 and left it under complete Palestinian sovereignty.

The Palestinians could have started building, putting in place infrastructure for political and economic freedom that would allow them to produce the kind of miracle the Israelis have produced.

But instead, they put Hamas terrorists in charge, who

started shooting missiles into Israel.

In a hard and imperfect world, it's so much easier to hate and blame than to take personal responsibility to create and build.

We see the same in our own country.

We have Black Lives Matter and a political left embracing critical race theory, which peddles the distortion and lie that American history is about a dominant, oppressive white class rather than an ongoing struggle for all to take personal responsibility to prevail under freedom.

Worse, those who choose to buy into the great lie that their lives are about what others do, rather than what they themselves choose, get paid off politically or in lawsuits resulting from inevitable tragedies that emerge from this culture of irresponsibility.

Similarly, Palestinian terrorists get paid off by sponsor-terrorist nations such as Iran, and through massive foreign aid from confused, left-wing-dominated Western countries.

Subsidizing blame and irresponsibility produces squalor.

A culture of hard work and personal responsibility, despite a world that is often unclear and often seems unfair and unjust, produces miracles like the modern state of Israel.

Destroying Black Babies and Families With Federal Dollars

June 2, 2021

If there is one reason why problems associated with race in America persist, it is because we pretend to address problems caused by one sin by exchanging them with other sins.

President Biden has just issued a proclamation recognizing 100 years since the race massacre that occurred in the Greenwood District in Tulsa, Oklahoma, in 1921.

Greenwood was a wealthy Black neighborhood, a center of Black business, known as Black Wall Street, that was ravaged in two days of rioting by white racists. It resulted in the death of hundreds and the loss of property of thousands.

It is indeed another tragic and painful memory of race relations in our nation's history.

The proclamation issued by President Biden states, "The Federal Government must reckon with and acknowledge the role that it has played in stripping wealth and opportunity from black communities."

I totally agree. What offends me is that Biden's administration enthusiastically continues federal policies that damage Black communities, while it pretends it is addressing the problems.

As a starter, let us consider that at the same time the president issued this proclamation, he sent an unprecedented $6 trillion federal budget to Congress that, for the first time ever, omits the longstanding Hyde Amendment.

The Hyde Amendment, passed in 1976 and named for its sponsor, Illinois Rep. Henry Hyde, prohibits use of federal funds to pay for abortion, except in cases of rape or incest or when the mother's life is in danger.

Every federal budget since the Hyde Amendment was passed has included a rider with this provision—except this year's, thanks to President Biden and his party.

So, while Biden issued one proclamation recalling the tragedy of a massacre of Black Americans, he now wants new federal policy that would use federal funds to subsidize another massacre.

Abortion policy in our nation amounts to nothing short of a massacre of and tragedy for Black Americans, born and unborn.

According to National Right to Life, 62.5 million unborn children have been destroyed in the womb since Roe v. Wade legalized abortion on demand in 1973.

Per the most recent data from the Centers for Disease Control and Prevention, about one-third of all abortions are done on Black babies. Given this, we can estimate that since 1973, some 21 million Black babies have been destroyed in the womb.

Despite the words in the president's new proclamation indicting the federal government in causing damage in Black communities, this is exactly what he wants now: to bring the federal government in to fund the abortion massacre.

But the damage done by abortion to Black Americans goes beyond this massacre of unborn Black children. It has tangible, damaging effects on the well-being of the Black family.

Why, after all these years, do poverty rates persist so

much higher, on average, in Black communities compared with national averages?

Data shows a compelling correlation between family structure and incidence of poverty.

Per the Census Bureau's "Income and Poverty in the United States: 2019" report and per Statista, the incidence of living under poverty is more than four times higher for Black families headed by a single woman than for Black families headed by a married couple. And 41% of Black families are headed by a single woman.

Per data from Pew Research Center, in 1970, three years before the Roe v. Wade decision, around 10% of Black adults over 25 had never been married. By 2012, this had more than tripled, to 36%.

Abortion undermines the values of the traditional family. And traditional family values provide the offramp from the cycle of poverty.

The persistence of problems in Black communities stems from federal policies that pretend to fight the sin of racism with the sins of the destruction of life and family.

Now President Biden not only wants to continue this destruction; he wants to use our tax dollars to subsidize it.

The State of Black America

June 9, 2021

Listening to all the rhetoric in the popular media, you would think America is the most unfair, racist nation in the world. You would think that Black Americans are uniformly living in oppression and poverty, with no hope for the future, save the federal government arriving on the scene to their rescue.

Sorry, liberals, to trouble you with facts. But indeed there are facts. And the facts tell a far different story than what we are hearing.

Let's start with the most recent annual report of the Census Bureau: Income and Poverty in the United States: 2019.

According to this report, annual real median household income in the U.S. increased 6.8% in 2019, the largest annual increase recorded by the Census Bureau going back to 1967.

Black median household income in 2019 increased 7.9%, the largest on record and, per American Enterprise Institute economist Mark Perry, "almost nine times the average annual increase of 0.90% over the last half-century."

Moreover, in 2019, 29.4% of Black households had income of $75,000 or more, compared with 28.7% of Black households that had income of $25,000 or less. This was the first time, ever, that the percentage of high-income Black households exceeded the percentage of low-income Black households.

In 1967, 44.5% of Black households were low-income, compared with 9.1% high-income.

Last September, the Federal Reserve published its Survey of Consumer Finances, published once every three years. The survey covers the three-year period 2016-2019, just prior to the onset of the pandemic.

Over this period, per the report, Black net worth increased 32.1%, Hispanic net worth increased 63.6% and white net worth increased 4%.

Business equity among Blacks increased 138%.

How about other measures of achievement?

Per the Census Bureau, in 2019, 88% of Blacks had a high school diploma, 98% of the national average. In 1950, the percent of Blacks with a high school diploma equaled 50% of the national average.

In 2018, 37.8% of Blacks ages 18-24 were enrolled in college, compared with a national average of 40.9% in this age group.

In the age group of 25-39, 28.4% had a bachelor's degree or higher, compared with 40.5% of the general population.

The high school dropout rate among Blacks in 2018 was 4.9%, compared with a national average of 5.7%.

Am I trying to divert attention from the many real economic and social problems in many Black communities?

Certainly not. But what I do wish to disabuse is the focus on problems in certain Black communities and using this data to generalize about all Blacks. It's certainly false and a distortion, and ironic how often this is coming from those who pretend to be fighting racism.

It certainly is true, again according to the Census Bureau, that in 2019, Blacks, who constituted 13.2% of the population, represented 23.8% of those living below the poverty line.

But is this about racism? The data tells us that this is about family breakdown, not racism.

And the problem of family breakdown is afflicting the whole nation. It just happens to be hitting many Black communities particularly hard. Poverty is excessive in households of all races that are headed by single women. Blacks just happen to have a very high percentage of households headed by single women.

But, according to Statistica, only 6.4% of Black households headed by a married couple live in poverty.

So, enough of racist generalizations about Blacks. And enough of the distortions that Blacks have not been gaining ground in our free country and that where we do have problems, we need more government.

Black progress and achievement since the 1960s have been substantial.

Where problems exist, and where progress is disappointing, invariably, government has been the problem, not the solution.

The Perverse Agenda of Black Lives Matter

July 21, 2021

Since the new wave of race consciousness that has been sweeping our country, precipitated by the graphic video of the killing of George Floyd by police officer Derek Chauvin, something very strange has happened.

Somehow, what is perceived as a problem has become widely understood to be the solution. And it is endangering our country.

If there remain citizens in America who, because of race or any other reason, are deprived of the benefits and protections of a free society, we should work to bring those benefits of freedom to them.

The answer is not to abandon the principles that make us a free country.

But this is what is happening. Those who are the loudest and most aggressive about what is supposedly wrong don't want a free country. Their complaint is not about absence of freedom, but who has power and who will be in charge and running the show.

Nothing could make this clearer than the recent bizarre statement of Black Lives Matter about the current civil unrest in Cuba.

Cuba is an unfree country. It has been run by communists for years. And, like all countries that are run by communists, the people there live deprived and oppressed.

This is not rhetoric. This is fact.

Freedom House in Washington, D.C., is a nonpartisan organization that rates all the nations in the world according to how free they are. They rate nations according to political rights and civil liberties.

Cuba ranks as one of the world's least free countries. Out of a possible score of 100, Cuba scores 13. In political rights, out of a top score of 40, Cuba gets a 1. On civil liberties, out of a possible score of 60, Cuba scores 12.

Yet, Black Lives Matters writes, "The people of Cuba are being punished by the U.S. government because the country has maintained its commitment to sovereignty and self-determination."

As the information from Freedom House shows, the only sovereignty and self-determination that exists in Cuba is in the hands of the communist despots who run the place.

Yet, in the opinion of Black Lives Matter, the suffering of the Cuban people is not due to the despots running Cuba, who deprive them of their freedom, but it's caused by the free country, the USA, that is its nearby neighbor to the north.

We don't see many Americans fleeing to live in Cuba. But, per the Pew Research Center, there are over 2 million Cuban Americans who left Cuba, or whose family left Cuba, to come to live in a country that is free.

Moreover, per a survey done by Pew in 2020, 58% of Cuban Americans identify as, or lean toward, Republicans, compared with 38% who identify as, or lean toward, Democrats.

Cuban Americans know what oppression is about, and it's why they care so much about being free Americans.

"Since 1962," says Black Lives Matter, "the United States has forced pain and suffering on the people of Cuba by cutting off food, medicine and supplies."

Yes, the United States maintains an economic

embargo on Cuba. Why should our nation provide sources of revenue that will only go into the coffers of the communists who control everything? But, as The Wall Street Journal's Mary O'Grady points out, contrary to BLM's distortions, “food and medicine are exempt” from this embargo.

The one thing that Black Lives Matter gets right is that almost a third of Cubans are Black and brown. Yet, somehow, Black Lives Matter thinks they will enhance the lives of these people of color by supporting oppressors rather than bringing them more freedom.

And, indeed, Black Lives Matter has the same anti-freedom agenda in our country.

The question is why this perverse group has so much credibility and power? What is wrong with our political and business leaders that support these enemies of human freedom?

Cancel Culture and Wokeness Will Destroy Our Country

Aug. 11, 2021

The enabling tool of what we call "cancel culture" or "wokeness" is language.

People are put in categories to which names are assigned, and this supposedly captures who they are and what should be done with them politically.

Unfortunately, the whole business of racial identification and categorization is not about advancing the quality of the human condition and human dignity but about progressive politics.

The left puts people in racial categories as instruments toward their political agenda.

In 1977, the Federal Interagency Committee on Education produced a five-race classification for the American population: American Indian or Alaskan Native, Asian or Pacific Islander, Black, White and Hispanic.

These categories, over time, continued to undergo changes and refinements.

The Hispanic category emerged in the 1970s, and the legislation described this group as "Americans who identify themselves as being of Spanish-speaking background and trace their origin or descent from Mexico, Puerto Rico, Cuba, Central and South America, and other Spanish-speaking countries." So, an American with roots in Spain and an American with roots in Peru wind up in the same category because their country of origin was Spanish-speaking.

Hispanic is neither race nor ethnicity. It is a category of political design, including individuals from 20-plus countries, with no commonality other than the language their grandparents spoke.

In the 2020 census, there are 19 different possibilities for self-categorization.

In both the white and Black categories, filers are now asked to respond to additional questions regarding their country of origin.

The strangest part of the emergence of this movement as a political force is that it constitutes everything that supposedly is undesirable that we want to eliminate. Racism.

Is it any less racism if I conclude who a person is and what they are about based on whether they are white or Black?

Yet, here we are with a good part of our nation mobilized, adopting the disease that we all thought we were trying to eliminate as its cure.

Last weekend, I came across a beautiful short video of the great Nobel laureate in physics, Richard Feynman, talking about knowledge.

Feynman began his legendary career working on the Manhattan Project, which developed the first atomic bomb, and finished as a member of the commission that investigated the cause of the fatal explosion of the space shuttle Challenger in 1986.

The video starts with the headline "Names Don't Constitute Knowledge."

Feynman recalls walking through a park with his father and his father telling him the names of different birds in different languages. In the end, notes Feynman, you know what different people around the world call the same bird, but you know absolutely nothing about the bird.

Consider what Feynman tells us in his observation that "names don't constitute knowledge."

If we look in the Bible in the Book of Genesis, it says, "God had formed out of the ground every beast of the field and every bird of the sky, and brought them to the man to see what he would call each one; and whatever the man called each living creature, that remained its name. And the man assigned names to all the cattle and to the birds of the sky."

Man does not create reality. He just names it.

Politics is the opposite. Rather than naming a reality that precedes him, of which he is a part, the progressive political man pretends to create reality with his language and names.

America was founded to be a free nation under God. Our government was not designed to replace God, but to be subservient to God.

The so-called enlightened theory of wokeness will reduce America to a weak, balkanized country where everyone is at his neighbor's throat, rather than unique individuals cooperating in unity to produce greatness.

Speech must be free—not politically canceled—and used in the pursuit of truth.

Corporate Social Justice Programs Don't Work

Sept. 1, 2021

According to a new report from The Washington Post, America's corporations have committed “at least” $49.5 billion to the cause of “racial justice” since the George Floyd murder last year riveted our national attention on race.

This amounts to a little over $1,100 for every Black man, woman and child in America.

Or, from another perspective, about $16,500 for every Black household earning $25,000 or less.

But we're not talking about corporate America, despite their deep concern for racial justice, just simply giving black Americans cash. As much as they undoubtedly care about these Black citizens, they would never trust them to just take the money and spend properly.

These corporate executives nationwide have concluded that they can justify taking a huge chunk of their shareholders' funds—an amount equal to the entire economy of the state of Alaska—and spend it in a way that will produce more racial justice.

It is reasonable to ask why they believe they can achieve this.

It goes against all experience we have had with government.

The federal government has been spending trillions since the war on poverty began in the 1960s—$20 trillion, by some estimates—and the incidence of poverty over these years has hardly budged.

Apparently, these corporate executives feel they have

some insight that has eluded politicians all these years.

A large percentage of these funds is earmarked for loans and investments in housing and business loans.

According to the report, $28 billion flows from a pledge by JPMorgan Chase to move 40,000 families into home ownership over the next five years.

But, again, special loans and grants to encourage minority home ownership are nothing new.

Government has been doing this for years, causing more damage than good.

Most should recall that we had a major financial crisis in our country in which we saw a collapse in financial markets in 2008 that was the worst since the Great Depression.

According to research at the American Enterprise Institute, this collapse was driven by the bursting of a highly inflated bubble in housing prices, the result of widespread deterioration in lending standards driven by government affordable housing goals and mandates.

Black citizens, who these government programs were designed to help, were disproportionately hurt when housing prices collapsed as a result of the plethora of bad loans.

The great mystery is why the principles that made and make our country great are nowhere to be found in the various ideas and programs being promoted with this vast sum of funds.

Why have so many in corporate America signed off on left-wing dogma that American principles—principles of protection of life, of liberty, of property—are the problem rather than the solution?

A healthy portion of American Blacks are doing very

well because of these American principles.

Per the Census Bureau's recent annual report—Income and Poverty in the United States, 2019—a larger percentage of Black households, 29.4%, were earning $75,000 or more than the percentage earning $25,000 or less, 28.7%.

Those left behind need liberation from government control of their lives. Less government-created ghettos from federal housing programs, more freedom from failing government schools and from broken government entitlement programs such as Social Security.

I started promoting the idea 25 years ago of releasing low-income earners from the Social Security payroll tax and allowing them to invest those funds in a personal retirement account. Back then, the Dow Jones Industrial Average stood at 10,000. Today, it stands at 35,000.

The very naysayers I heard back then are the ones bleating today about unfairness and the wealth gap.

Rather than betraying the tradition of free enterprise capitalism that built corporate America, America's corporations should be promoting these values. This is the path to more prosperity, more justice, for all Americans.

The New Victim of Cancel Culture: Science

Oct. 13, 2021

Cancel culture has reared its ugly head once again, and this time in a new and unprecedented way.

A lecture by a physicist was canceled at one of America's premier institutions of science, MIT, for reasons having nothing to do with the subject of the lecture. The lecture was canceled not because of its scientific content but because of the politically incorrect views on diversity of the scientist scheduled to give the lecture.

Dorian Abbot is a professor in the department of the geophysical sciences at the University of Chicago. He has an undergraduate degree in physics from Harvard and a Ph.D. in applied mathematics from Harvard.

Abbot was scheduled to give the annual John Carlson lecture at MIT's Lorenz Center in the department of earth, atmospheric and planetary sciences. The topic was to be "climate and the potential for life on other planets."

But this lecture will not take place.

In August, Abbot and Ivan Marinovic, an associate professor of accounting at Stanford University's Graduate School of Business, published an opinion piece in Newsweek entitled "The Diversity Problem on Campus."

Abbot and Marinovic argued that the politically correct regime now taking control of America's universities, which they identify as "DEI"—diversity, equity and inclusion—is undermining the mission of what universities are supposed to be about. That mission is, per Abbot and Marinovic, "the production and dissemination of knowledge."

When universities no longer look for the "most talented and best trained minds" in hiring, and politically motivated criteria drive hiring practices, the university's "core business"—the "search for truth"—is undermined.

They propose that "MFE"—merit, fairness and equality—be adopted as the regime to define hiring practices to displace DEI. MFE is about hiring based on individual merit and qualifications alone.

Abbot is now paying the price for publicly expressing such heresy.

Twitter outrage descended on the administration at MIT, and Abbot was disinvited.

So now academic speech is not just about what is said but who is saying it.

Abbot and Marinovic were right on target in their Newsweek essay, suggesting that the DEI politically correct regime carries forward everything about racism that we supposedly have been trying to get rid of.

Racism is all about obliterating individuality and making predetermined judgments about who any individual is based on socially defined characteristics of the group to which they are assigned.

How can any Black child in America not be injured when they are not taught that they are special and unique human beings but that what is most important is their color.

It doesn't matter whether they are being rejected because of their color or accepted because of their color. Their humanity is being undermined.

Science advances when we recognize that truth is bigger than and beyond any single human mind. Truth is discovered, piece by piece, through humility and hard work, not political arrogance, pretending we already know it.

We might recall that modern science only emerged some five centuries ago. It wasn't all that long ago that most believed that the sun moved around the Earth rather than the other way around. Scientists such as Nicolaus Copernicus and Galileo Galilei, through honest observations, concluded the prevailing view was wrong. This was politically incorrect then; they were attacked, and their books were banned.

One famous graduate of MIT was the great Nobel laureate physicist Richard Feynman.

Feynman observed, “Reality must take precedence over public relations, for nature cannot be fooled.”

The increasing deference of reality to public relations, meaning suppressing what is true to serve what the politically correct want to be true, is destroying our national integrity, hurting the very people that supposedly we are trying to help, and threatening the future of our nation.

Political correctness is undermining personal responsibility and personal development. Now it is threatening to undermine science and truth.

MIT should step up and apologize to Dorian Abbot.

Give America a New Birth of Freedom in Virginia

Oct. 27, 2021

The joke goes that a slip of the tongue for a politician means that they accidentally said what they actually believe.

Now Democrats are trying to clean up the mess created by Virginia Democratic candidate for governor, Terry McAuliffe, when he said in a debate on Sept. 28, "I don't think parents should be telling schools what they should teach."

McAuliffe's 5-point lead over his opponent, Republican Glenn Youngkin, who has made parental control in education a central issue in his campaign, has disappeared.

Big-name Democrats, including former President Barack Obama, are now showing up in Virginia with a mop and pail. Vice President Kamala Harris sent a video to over 300 Black churches statewide, urging support for McAuliffe. According to some opinions, Harris' politicking for McAuliffe in churches violates either or both the Johnson Amendment, which prohibits tax-exempt entities such as churches from electioneering, and the Hatch Act, which prohibits federal government officials from using their position to influence the outcome of an election.

Former Democratic Virginia Gov. Douglas Wilder, Virginia's first Black governor, has weighed in saying he believes churches will jeopardize their tax-exempt status if they show Harris' video.

McAuliffe followed up with an ad claiming what he said is being misconstrued and that he really meant the opposite.

Comedian Groucho Marx once quipped "Who are you going to believe—me or your own eyes?"

Panic among Democrats is well-founded in that Blacks constitute approximately 20% of voters in Virginia and can make all the difference in the outcome of the election. And Blacks poll strongly in favor of parental choice in education.

In 2018, Republican candidate Ron DeSantis defeated Black Democratic candidate Andrew Gillum by less than 40,000 votes in the gubernatorial election in Florida. One reason was DeSantis got 18% of the vote of Black women. This was most likely Black mothers expressing appreciation for the 100,000 low-income children attending private schools through tax-credit funded scholarships provided through the Step Up for Students program.

If anything positive has come out of COVID-19, it has driven home to many parents the implications of government and politically controlled schools.

Given the central importance of education to a child's future, more parents are becoming aware of grave implications of losing control of when and where their children are taught, how they are taught and what they are taught.

McAuliffe's accidental moment of truth put out for all to see what Democrats are really about. They are casting a wider and stronger net of government and political control of almost every aspect of our lives. The core American value of freedom has all but disappeared.

More Black parents are sensitive to the crisis in the Black family. Do they really want progressive politicians defining sexuality for their children? But this is what is happening.

Thirty states and the District of Columbia mandate sex education in public schools.

Log onto the website of either of the major teachers unions—National Education Association and American Federation of Teachers. Both include the commitment to LGBTQ values.

What about Black parents, or parents of any ethnicity, that reject this worldview? What about Black parents, or parents of any ethnicity, who want their child's education about sexuality to be defined by traditional biblical views of love and marriage?

In a recent Pew Research survey, 59% said Americans disagree on "basic facts."

In a country where there's not even consensus about what reality is—what is true and what is false—how can we possibly have a government-controlled education system? How can parents allow progressive bureaucrats to determine the worldview conveyed to their children?

A wake-up call, a new birth of freedom, is long overdue in America.

Virginia is a good place to start.

Dusting off Dr. King's Great Message

Jan 12, 2022

We celebrate Dr. Martin Luther King Jr. Day on the third Monday of January—this year, Jan. 17.

On Aug. 28, 1963, King delivered one of the great speeches in American history, popularly known as the "I Have a Dream" speech. It is a speech that must be dusted off and studied anew today, because it contains the very message that our nation sorely needs to hear and digest now. A message that has been tragically lost and buried and replaced with great and destructive distortions.

Two things jump out when reading through that speech.

One is how this Black preacher captured in his words that day the heart and soul of America.

Second, how King's great message that day stands in total contrast to the rhetoric peddled by today's progressives as the remedy to our racial strife.

The indictment of the woke movement is that America is the problem.

King offered up America as the solution.

He talked about the "magnificent words of the Constitution and the Declaration of Independence."

"I have a dream that one day this nation will rise up and live out the true meaning of its creed: 'We hold these truths to be self-evident, that all men are created equal.'"

The problem, as King explained, is not America or the eternal truths that were brought to bear in its founding.

The problem was the failure of the nation to live up to the challenges of its great founding principles.

This was the heart of King's message that day.

He appealed to the nation to realize the dream of its founding fathers. Not to crush it and bury it, as we hear today.

The problem is not white people.

"The marvelous new militancy ... must not lead us to a distrust of all white people," he said.

And, of course, the most memorable and oft-quoted line of the speech, "I have a dream that my four little children will one day live in a nation where they will not be judged by the color of their skin but by the content of their character."

What has happened instead? Where has this great message of King gotten lost?

In the name of racial justice, our race campaigns today are defined by selection and placement based on race, based on the color of skin, and not based on the content of character, as King implored the nation to do.

King's speech is divided into three parts.

Part one is an appeal to the nation to live up to its great founding principles.

Part two is an appeal to Black Americans to rise up and act accordingly in the noble cause of the pursuit of liberty and justice. Let's not drink "from the cup of bitterness."

Part three is an appeal to the ideals of the Christian soul of the nation.

He quoted the prophet Isaiah that "the crooked places will be made straight ... and the glory of the Lord shall be revealed, and all flesh shall see it together."

Biblical truths and ideals have been sadly lost to wokeism, which has for all practical purposes become a religion in itself.

Let's honor Dr. Martin Luther King Jr. now, as we come out of COVID-19 and enter 2022, by revisiting and taking to heart the great truths he spoke on that summer day in Washington, D.C., 1963. Great truths that have very sadly been cast to the side and replaced with the religion of politics and power.

Let us honor King by seeing America as he presented it then, as embodying the ideals of a free nation under God.

And then we can join hands and sing, as King appealed, "the words of the old Negro spiritual: Free at last! Free at last! Thank God Almighty, we are free at last."

Supreme Court Nominees—Race Can Be Relevant

Feb. 2, 2022

"Mr. Biden's campaign promise that he'd appoint a black woman to the Supreme Court is unfortunate because it elevates skin color over qualifications."

Thus, The Wall Street Journal editorial page captured, in one sentence, the sentiment of many if not most of right-of-center white Americans about the president's campaign pledge, which he appears to have every intention to fulfill.

But, no pun intended, is it all really so black and white?

May we ask if ever there might be justification for taking race and gender into consideration as deciding factors in making a Supreme Court nomination?

I believe we can answer this question by looking at the one Black justice on the Supreme Court, Associate Justice Clarence Thomas.

Thomas is now the longest serving sitting justice on the U.S. Supreme Court. When he was nominated by President George H.W. Bush in 1991, there was never any question that Bush would nominate an African American to replace the legendary Thurgood Marshall.

This was clearly a "Black seat" on the Supreme Court, and it would stay that way.

However, race is not a reality with one dimension. Despite what some might think, Black reality is as multifaceted and complex as is all of human reality, and the views of Black Americans cover the full scope of the political spectrum.

And thus, Bush did indeed appoint a Black man to

replace Marshall. But this Black man was a conservative.

And Clarence Thomas has shown himself to be a brilliant conservative addition to the court. Had not Bush felt it politically important to replace Marshall with an African American, our country would be the worse off for not having given this African American the opportunity to shine and contribute immeasurably to our nation.

But the other side of this coin is to note the irony that the then-chairman of the Senate Judiciary Committee through which Thomas' nomination had to pass was our current president, Joe Biden.

The then-Sen. Biden presided over a confirmation hearing that he allowed to be transformed into a carnival of pornography, allowing Anita Hill to make shameful public accusations about Thomas that had no place in a Senate hearing, and that defamed Thomas such that one wonders if full recovery in the court of public opinion is ever possible.

In a recent documentary, Thomas spoke about what happened and how, under Joe Biden's chairmanship of the Judiciary Committee, liberals sought to destroy him because he is a conservative: "People should just tell the truth: This is the wrong Black guy. He has to be destroyed. Just say it. Then now we will be honest with each other."

In fact, the track record of liberals toward minority Americans who are not liberal is not pretty.

Janice Rogers Brown, a conservative/libertarian African American woman who served as a justice on the Supreme Court of California, was nominated by President George W. Bush to the U.S. Court of Appeals for the District of Columbia Circuit. Senate Democrats blocked her nomination for two years until she was finally confirmed in 2005.

Miguel Estrada is a distinguished Honduran American attorney who arrived as an immigrant without being able to speak English and wound up graduating, magna cum laude, with a Juris Doctor degree from Harvard Law School. Democrats blocked Bush's nomination of Estrada to the District of Columbia Circuit Court of Appeals because he is a conservative.

The point is our country has a complex history and cultural reality in addition to its ideals.

Among our ideals should be mutual human respect and decency.

There can be justification to Biden's commitment to nominating an African American woman to the court.

South Carolina Republican Sen. Lindsey Graham has signed off on the impressive credentials of one such candidate—South Carolina federal district Judge J. Michelle Childs.

Let's give Childs, and the process, the respect they deserve.

Learning the Lessons of Black History

Feb. 16, 2022

February is Black History Month.

Why do we need Black History Month? Why don't we set aside special occasions to observe the history of other ethnicities in our country?

My answer to this question is that Black history tells a uniquely important story in our nation. It is a story that no other race or ethnicity shares. It is a story that must be grasped and understood if we are to understand our country as a whole, where it has been and where it needs to go.

Unique among a large percentage of Black Americans is a history in which their ancestors did not choose to come to America. They were brought here by force and enslaved. No other ethnicity shares a history in which their ancestors did not come here by choice.

According to the 1790 Census of the United States, of a population of 3,893,635, 17.8%, or a total of 694,280, were slaves.

In a nation founded on the principle of human liberty, almost one-fifth of the population were slaves. How should we understand this?

Some want to tell us that slavery is not just a stain on American history but that it defines America and American history. That America is a nation founded in racism and evil and that the task today is to reinvent and recreate the nation.

This is what "wokeness" and DEI—diversity, equity and inclusion programming—is about.

Those who have declared that the nation was evil at its birth now want to seize control and put themselves in charge of deciding what it should be about and what it should look like.

This is a great and dangerous distortion, doomed to add on to, not erase, the sin at America's founding.

The proclamation from the White House noting National Black History Month 2022 says, "Our nation was founded on an idea: that all of us are created equal and deserve to be treated with equal dignity throughout our lives."

This, I think, is false.

Our nation was not founded on an idea. An idea is a product of thought.

When slave trader John Newton, composer of the haunting hymn "Amazing Grace," had the horrible confrontation with himself, realizing the grave sin he had committed, he wrote "I was lost, but now I'm found. / Was blind, but now I see."

Newton did not discover he had a bad idea and decide to replace it with a better idea.

He realized that there is truth in the world, which he gravely violated.

The ideals upon which our nation was founded were rooted in divine principles and recognition that all are created equal because all are the product of the same Creator.

It is for this reason that those who signed the Declaration of Independence concluded saying, "With a firm Reliance on the Protection of divine Providence, we mutually pledge to each other our Lives, our Fortunes, and our sacred Honor."

"Sacred" is not about ideas. "Sacred" is about faith and divine truth.

The presence of slavery at our nation's founding was about Man's ability and willingness to sin.

Slavery was the symptom, not the cause.

Black History is documentation that even in a great nation, sin was present.

The Creator gave man the ability to choose. This is why freedom is important. Men cannot be denied their ability to choose. But they also cannot escape their responsibility to choose good over evil.

This is the lesson we must learn from Black History.

We will not live right, we will not treat our neighbors right, until we recognize that we all are the results of the same Creator.

America is in crisis today because recognition of that Creator has been widely purged.

And like the plantation owners that usurped truth, so today we have a new generation of usurpers.

This is what we must recognize and fix.

Blacks Saying Bye-Bye to Biden

Feb. 23, 2022

A new report from Pew Research shows that the sharpest drop in approval for President Joe Biden is among the Democratic Party's most loyal and consistent supporters—Black protestants.

In March 2021, shortly after he took office, Biden's support among Black protestants stood at 92%. By January 2022, this was down to 65%, a drop of 27 points.

Over the same period, overall national approval for the president, per Gallup, was down from 54% to 40%—14 points. About half the drop among Black protestants.

Other polls among all Black voters tell the same story.

An NBC poll shows Black approval for Biden dropping from 83% last April to 64% now. A Quinnipiac University poll shows Black approval during Biden's first year in office dropping from 78% to 57%.

What's going on? Should Democratic strategists be worried that a sea-change is occurring among voters on whom they could always most depend?

Trying to define some new grand reality is always a dangerous game in political analysis.

But what we can do is note two major areas of great concern to Black Americans where they have reason to be dissatisfied with the leadership they see in Washington.

One is inflation.

The president and his Federal Reserve chairman bear responsibility for the new round of inflation now rearing its head and disrupting American lives.

The Wall Street Journal recently noted in an editorial

that the now 7.5% annualized increase in the price level is the worst in 40 years. During January "some 73% of the items saw annual price rises of 3% or higher" and "some 55% of items saw inflation of 5% or higher."

A Gallup poll in December showed that 71% of households earning $40,000 per year or less reported hardship as result of price increases; 28% reported "severe hardship"; and 42% reported "moderate hardship".

These are households that are disproportionately Black households. According to Statistica, whereas 37% of all American households earn $50,000 or less, 55% of Black households are in this income category.

The Wall Street Journal calls this new round of inflation the result of a "historic policy failure" at the White House and the Federal Reserve.

But also, prominent Democratic Party economists and businessmen are calling out this administration.

Wall Street businessman Steven Rattner, who was counselor to the Treasury secretary in the Obama administration, wrote a piece recently in The New York Times titled "Biden Keeps Blaming the Supply Chain for Inflation. That's Dishonest."

Rattner calls on the president to set a priority for reducing spending and the deficit, the complete opposite direction in which they have taken things, despite many warnings.

The terrible irony is that a major rationale for all the spending was to allegedly help the very low-income Americans who are now being hurt.

The other issue is COVID-19.

According to the Kaiser Family Foundation, after adjusting for age differences, the incidence of hospitalization due to COVID-19 has been almost three times higher among Black than white Americans. And the incidence of death almost twice as high.

A new Gallup survey shows 69% of Black Americans reporting being "very stressed" or "somewhat stressed" because of threat of COVID-19 infection, compared with 57% of white Americans.

Morning Consult reported that in the three weeks following Biden's announcement of federal rules mandating vaccines, Black approval for Biden's handling of the crisis dropped nine points from 70% to 61%. Among unvaccinated Blacks, Biden's net approval—approve less disapprove—dropped 17 points.

One might say that the Biden administration has been operating in a fashion detached from the very real and challenging realities—day-to-day life and the cost of living, and health concerns during a terrible pandemic—with which Black Americans have been struggling,

Good reason to believe this is what is causing Biden's approval ratings with Blacks to plummet.

Gibson's Bakery Scores a Victory for Truth

April 6, 2022

Periodically, in what seems like a never-ending assault on our basic values and the rule of law, good news emerges.

The good news now is the unanimous decision of a panel of three judges on an Ohio Court of Appeals, supporting a jury decision in favor of Gibson's Bakery in its case against Oberlin College.

Gibson's Bakery sued Oberlin College for libel, intentional infliction of emotional distress and intentional interference with a business relationship, because of the school's involvement and support of student demonstrations accusing the bakery of racial profiling and discrimination.

The decision is worthy of our attention because it shows just how troubling the situation is at our colleges and universities.

As our nation leans increasingly to the left, as our most basic values—now called conservative values—are being pushed out the door, while they are displaced by the chaos of moral relativism, some bold individuals—in this case, the proprietors of Gibson's Bakery in Oberlin, Ohio—refuse to be intimidated and concede.

And that refusal has paid off for the Gibson family and for all Americans who care about truth.

Oberlin College now must pay $33 million in punitive damages and $11 million in compensatory damages to Gibson's Bakery.

In brief, a Black student from Oberlin was chased down by the son of the store's proprietor when he saw him shoplift a bottle of wine.

The student, and two of his friends who then got involved, were arrested by the police and all subsequently pleaded guilty.

But the incident set off student demonstrations outside this mom and pop bakery, started by David Gibson's great-grandfather in 1885.

The owners were branded racists, and flyers were handed out claiming that the store had a history of "racial profiling and discrimination."

Hopefully, the lawsuit filed and won by the Gibson family will put a damper on the casual use of these horrible accusations.

The snapshot we now have of the academic and social reality at Oberlin College, which has a reputation as one of the nation's premier liberal arts colleges, is deeply troubling.

Oberlin is now on the line for millions of dollars in damages because its own school administrators are so self-absorbed in their own liberal dogma that they can no longer think clearly, honestly and objectively.

The college maintains a website dedicated to the case, and now, even after they have experienced such a devastating defeat in court, they are still in denial about what happened.

Particularly troubling is that the school administration refuses to accept that this case was not about the First Amendment but about their support of their own students to libel the Gibson family.

Over the years, I have spoken at almost 300 colleges and universities, and I have watched and experienced these campuses taken over by dogma and left-wing activists.

In a study published in 2020 by the National Association of Scholars, 12,372 college and university faculty were surveyed regarding political affiliation.

Over the full sample, 8.4 were registered Democrat for each registered Republican. At Oberlin College, this ratio was 10.8 to 1.

Given that over the whole American population, the ratio of those identifying as Democrat to Republican is about 1 to 1, we get a picture of the incredibly distorted reality that has captured higher education.

In the last presidential election, former President Donald Trump won the vote of those with no college degree, 50% to 48%. However, he lost the vote of college graduates 43% to 55%.

The nation is indebted to the Gibson family for refusing to be intimidated by left-wing dogmatists at Oberlin and for standing hard and fast for what is true.

But despite this important victory, we remain with a big problem that young Americans are getting college degrees and learning how not to think.

Freedom Is Rooted in Sanctity of Life

May 11, 2022

In 1955, an unmarried pregnant University of Wisconsin graduate student left her home and traveled to San Francisco to a doctor who took in unwed expectant mothers, delivered their babies and helped arrange adoptions.

The baby son she delivered and put up for adoption grew up to become the legendary business and technology entrepreneur Steve Jobs.

Had it been 1975, rather than 1955, there is a reasonable chance there would have never been a Steve Jobs. In 1975 America, after Roe v. Wade became law and where values markedly changed such that a young Catholic woman felt less shame to be unmarried and pregnant, Steve Jobs' mother could well have wound up in a Planned Parenthood clinic.

Looking around at the impact of laptop computers, iPhones, social media and remote work, it's hard to imagine what our lives would be like today had that one genius not been born.

But the preciousness of every human life depends not on whether that life is a potential Steve Jobs. Each brings their own unique and invaluable gifts to the world.

As the left goes berserk over the leaked Samuel Alito opinion pointing to the overturning of Roe v. Wade, we should consider that we'll never know the gifts of the 63 million children obliterated since the 1973 Roe v. Wade decision.

The Kaiser Family Foundation reports in 2019 that

38% of abortions were given to Black women. Using this figure, 24 million Black babies—roughly half the current Black population—were removed by abortion since 1973.

The United States in 1955 was a nation before the passage of the Civil Rights Act. There was segregation; there was racism; and there was poverty.

But today, many years later, we still have poverty, and our public discourse is still dominated by allegations of racism.

According to the rhetoric on the left, there was nothing good about the America of 1955.

But this is not true.

The state of faith and, because of this, the state of marriage and childbearing, was far healthier than today, both among whites and among Blacks.

According to Gallup, as we show in the "State of Black America" recently published by my organization, CUREPOLICY, in the early 1960s, 70% of Americans said religion was "very important" in their own lives. By the late 1970s, this was down to 52%.

In 1955, the national fertility rate—the average number of children birthed by women of child-bearing age—was 3.42. Today, this is down to 1.78. The rate needed for a population to replace itself and not shrink is 2.2.

In 1960, 9% of Black adults and 8% of white adults had never been married. By 2012, this had increased to 36% among Blacks and 16% among whites.

In 1960, less than 5% of white babies were born to unwed mothers. By 2010, this was up to 29%. Among Blacks, in 1960 a little over 20% of babies were born to unwed mothers. By 2010, this was up to 72%.

The secularization of the country in the 1960s did not

produce more freedom. It produced more dependence on government.

Blacks, in this regard, have been hurt the most.

In 1950, the federal government took 15.3% of the national economy. By 2020, this was up to 32%.

President Joe Biden, now presiding over a nation drowning in debt, inflation and sclerotic growth, said the other day that "The MAGA crowd is the most extreme political organization that has existed in American history."

If an aging America without married fathers and mothers and without children is where you think our future lies, so Biden is your man.

In 1956, 39% of Blacks voted for the Republican presidential candidate Dwight Eisenhower.

We're going back to the future. More Black Americans, and all Americans, are seeing that rooted in the American ideal of freedom is sanctity of life and family.

Black Conservatives Convene for a 'New Birth of Freedom'

May 18, 2022

Recent remarks by Supreme Court Justice Clarence Thomas, noting the institutional damage caused by the leak of Justice Samuel Alito's opinion on Roe v. Wade, have gotten exhaustive coverage in the press.

But, not surprisingly, the venue where Thomas made these remarks has gotten little attention by these same journalists.

The event was a convening of the nation's leading Black conservative intellectuals—from academia, policy institutes, media—to focus on, as explained in a press release from one of the institutional sponsors, the American Enterprise institute, why "despite decades of affirmative-action programs, wealth-redistribution schemes and other well-intentioned government efforts, racial gaps in educational achievement, employment, income, family formation and crime persist."

The venue, Old Parkland in Dallas, was provided through the generosity of Texas businessman Harlan Crow.

The Old Parkland Conference was inspired as a reconvening of a similar effort organized by economist Thomas Sowell in December 1980 at the Fairmont Hotel in San Francisco—a pioneering effort, the first of its kind.

At that time, in 1980, Sowell was already making his mark challenging what had become conventional wisdom that it was essential for government to play the central role in dealing with challenges facing Black Americans.

Sowell, who began his career seeing the world from

the perspective of the left, changed. He was once asked in an interview what drove his transformation in perspective from left to right, and he answered, "Facts."

The Old Parkland Conference was organized by four of the nation's leading conservative Black thought leaders—Brown University economist Glenn Loury, Jason Riley of The Wall Street Journal, Ian Rowe of the American Enterprise Institute and Shelby Steele of Stanford University's Hoover Institution.

Three days of speeches and panels covered the gamut. Why do the gaps persist? Speakers assess the current realities in education, law enforcement and crime, government programs such as affirmative action, and the role of culture and the persistence of social inequality and claims of racism.

Sowell, now 91 years old, did not attend this reconvening of his effort of 40 years ago.

Looking over those who presented at the 1980 Fairmont Conference, we see greats who no longer are with us. Greats like the late economist Walter Williams and economics Nobel laureate Milton Friedman.

The topic of Friedman's presentation then says it all. "Government is the problem."

However, one attendee of both events—last week's Old Parkland Conference and the Fairmont Conference in 1980—is Clarence Thomas, who attended in 1980 as a young congressional aide.

I was honored to be invited to participate and reconnect with admired friends with whom I have worked toward common goals over many years.

It reinforced my own sense of mission.

The analysis and conclusions of Sowell and others 40

years ago at the Fairmont Conference were correct. They saw then that human lives are not liberated by government programs and politics, and they saw then that this approach would make lives worse, not better.

This is indeed what happened.

I began my work in the 1990s inspired to bring the success of a capitalist America to the failures in low-income communities caused by socialism.

What we have today, unfortunately, is the reverse. Mainstream America is looking more like our poor communities destroyed by socialism than the other way around.

The work must continue.

The special responsibility of Black Americans, with their unique and troubled history, is to show that evil occurs because men sin. Not because the vision of American freedom is flawed, as we hear almost daily from progressives.

In many ways, the country is in worse shape today for everyone than where things stood in 1980.

More government, slower growth, family breakdown.

The answer can only be to seek, in the words of Abraham Lincoln, "a new birth of freedom," for every American of every background.

The State of Black America

May 25, 2022

I am so pleased and proud that the first annual edition of the "State of Black America" (Encounter Books), published by my organization, CURE, Center for Urban Renewal and Education, in conjunction with the Claremont Institute has just been released.

CURE was founded to provide a platform for an alternative vision of what "Black America" is about and what the real challenges are of our citizens of color.

Heretofore, the left has dominated the discussion concerning Black Americans. The left has dominated the discussion to such an extent that too many Americans of all backgrounds believe that the view from the left captures all chapter and verse of who Black Americans are and what ideas and policies will best serve them.

Too few understand and appreciate that even the term "Black America" is no more an accurate depiction of the realities of individual Black Americans than the term "white America" captures the realities of individual white Americans.

The politicization of race, and the formal incorporation of racial and ethnic labels in American government and law, is itself a victory of the left.

Reducing any human being to a racial and ethnic label, even under the guise of helping, results in the treatment of a disease amounting to a continuation of the disease itself.

Now, with the publication of CURE's first annual edition of "The State of Black America," conservatives push back and move to recapture the high ground in the policy discussion regarding Black Americans, who they are and what they need.

This collection of essays and analyses, compiled and edited by Dr. William B. Allen, resident scholar at CURE, professor emeritus of political philosophy at Michigan State University and emeritus dean of James Madison College at Michigan State University, starts with ideas and moves on to data that strike at the heart of left-wing conventional wisdom about Black Americans and their role in and relation to our nation's history.

There are few of any political orientation who do not agree that problems of race continue to plague us.

Where left and right part company is defining what those problems are and how best to address them.

Most fundamentally, concerning our nation, the difference of opinion is whether our nation is a vessel in need of repair, or whether the vessel itself is fundamentally flawed and needs to be replaced.

And left and right part company on the question about the extent to which the vessel, the nation, is even relevant and whether today the issues lie with individuals taking responsibility for their own lives.

In CURE's "State of Black America," leading scholars from academia and policy institutes take on these hard questions regarding our nation's history and examine with rigor the struggles from a nation founded on the ideals of freedom that permitted slavery to the Civil War and the 13th, 14th and 15th Amendments to the Constitution—dealing with equal protection and forbidding of slavery—to the welfare state and today's attacks on our culture and policing.

The annual surveys from organizations of the left, like

the National Urban League's "State of Black America," seek more government in every area of the lives of Black Americans as the answer to what will improve their lives.

As conservatives, we see the secret and success of America in its founding as a free nation under God and see the ongoing task as perfecting this ideal rather than departing from it.

Fix our national institutions to conform to our ideals of freedom, and appreciate that eternal truths—the responsibility of every individual for their personal choices and the sanctity of life, family and property—transcend race and ethnicity.

This is the important bottom line of CURE's first annual "State of Black America." Get the full story and details; it is recommended reading.

Why Are Blacks Still on Board With Biden?

July 20, 2022

New polling from Pew Research and from NY Times/Siena College, released a few days apart, cast similarly dismal pictures regarding the popularity of President Joe Biden.

Overall approval for Biden from NY Times/Siena College stands at 33% and from Pew 37%.

However, both polls show approval for the president much stronger than the national average among minorities.

The NY Times/Siena college poll shows Black approval for Biden at 62%, which, according to the Times, is higher than "any other race or ethnicity, age group or education level."

Per Pew, Black approval for Biden stands at 57%.

However, Pew also shows a marked difference in approval for Biden from all minority groups, compared to white voters.

White approval for Biden stands at 30%, Hispanic 47%, and Asian 45%.

Why the difference between whites and minorities?

One obvious answer is that the white figure includes a larger percentage of Republican voters.

But this still leaves a very important question that everyone, certainly leaders in the Republican Party, should be asking.

Why do minorities disproportionately lean Democrat?

Current polling shows the issues most on the minds of voters are inflation and the economy.

Inflation is nondiscriminatory. Every American is being hit by the same price increases in the supermarket, at the gas pump, in housing and across the board.

Given that everyone is concerned about our dismal economy, why should approval ratings for the performance of our president be so different for whites and for minorities?

Let's focus on Blacks because the difference is most pronounced here.

According to survey data from the last few years compiled by my organization, CURE, there is a very large gap in attitudes among Blacks, compared with whites, regarding the most basic functioning of the country.

Many more Blacks than whites see racism still as a major problem. According to Gallup polling from last year, 84% of Blacks, compared with 59% of whites, believe racism is widespread.

Only 31% of Blacks, compared with 62% of whites, believe that Blacks "have an equal chance of getting a job for which they are qualified."

And, particularly telling, 74% of Blacks, compared with 48% of whites, think "government should do more to solve problems."

Responses in the new Pew Research polling about what's causing this latest round of price increases show how little so many Americans understand about how our economy functions.

Most do not understand that inflation is caused by government spending and printing excessive amounts of money. Most, 49%, said it is business taking advantage of the current economic situation to raise prices.

Bottom line is that in order for the Republican Party

to attract more minority voters, Republicans need to do a much better job going into minority communities and educating these voters about what is actually going on in the country and what it means to them.

Low-income Americans are disproportionately minority Americans. They need an economy that functions properly, an economy where prices are stable and an economy that is growing at a healthy pace.

They must understand that economic opportunity comes from economic growth, not from government programs. Minorities must understand that limited government, not bloated government, allows robust growth.

As I recently wrote, the latest round of Supreme Court decisions protecting life, strengthening our Second Amendment right to bear arms and bolstering parents' ability to choose where to send their child to school are overwhelmingly in the interests of minority Americans.

In a nutshell, where the crucial battle for minority voters has been lost over the years is allowing these voters to believe that freedom is not in their interest.

Ironically, the Civil Rights Movement was about freedom. It then got diverted by the left to big government and socialism.

In order to get the nation moving again, we need all Americans on board.

We need to get the crucial message of freedom to our minority citizens.

Goodbye Affirmative Action, Hello Individual Freedom and Dignity

Nov. 9, 2022

The Supreme Court just heard arguments in the case Students for Fair Admissions v. Harvard and Students for Fair Admissions v. University of North Carolina.

It's about affirmative action—universities using race and ethnicity in their admissions policies.

Students for Fair Admissions argues that both universities violate the U.S. Constitution in their discriminatory admissions policies. They discriminate against Asian Americans in favor of whites, Blacks and Hispanics and unlawfully discriminate to achieve diversity that could be achieved in a race-neutral fashion.

Consensus is that Students for Fair Admissions will win this case and racial discrimination in university admission programs will be gone.

The decision will likely overturn Grutter v. Bollinger, which, in 2003, authorized universities to discriminate as an input factor in pursuit of diversity goals.

This will be a victory for those who see affirmative action as a mistake of the civil rights movement, inconsistent with its goals and the Constitution.

Let's recall again the words of Dr. Martin Luther King Jr. in his great "I Have a Dream Speech" in 1963. "I have a dream that my four little children will one day live in a nation where they will not be judged by the color of their skin but by the content of their character."

Next year it will be 60 years since that speech. Would King have thought that more than a half-century after he spoke those words that we would be still so far from that dream?

One reason is the Civil Rights Act of 1964, the crown jewel of the movement King led.

The act went way beyond the goal of making discrimination illegal. It was constructed to use government as the means to achieve a just society.

The Equal Employment Opportunities Commission was created, and the door opened for affirmative action, quotas and the acceptance of the principle that it is lawful to discriminate in favor of certain racial groups to achieve social justice.

Not long after came the categorization of the whole American population into racial groups.

By the 1970s, the entire U.S. population was classified by race and ethnicity through a new racial code called Statistical Directive 15.

We were no longer just Americans. Now every American is formally categorized as white, Black, Hispanic, Asian/Pacific Islander and American Indian/Alaskan Native.

Why? We entered a new era in which it was assumed that government force and action were needed achieve social justice, and toward this end, every citizen needed to be put in a racial or ethnic category.

King might as well have said, "I have dream that one day we will categorize every American according to their race and ethnicity and government will use this as basis to decide who should have what."

In the oral arguments in the case against Harvard and UNC, Justice Clarence Thomas questioned what diversity means and achieves. "I've heard the word diversity quite a few times, and I don't have a clue what it means. It seems to mean everything for everyone."

The diversity that really produces benefit in education is diversity of opinion, and Harvard has virtually none. In the most recent annual survey that the Harvard Crimson does of the university faculty of Arts and Science, more than 80% self-identified as "liberal" or "very liberal." Only 1% self-identified as "conservative" and zero as "very conservative."

Chief Justice John Roberts got to the heart of the matter when he observed in Parents Involved v. Seattle in 2007, "The way to stop discrimination on the basis of race is to stop discriminating on the basis of race."

The good news is the Supreme Court seems ready to start turning this around. With the court finding discrimination in college admissions unconstitutional, we'll be taking a major step to restore individual freedom and dignity and end the demeaning, dehumanizing idea of reducing individuals to racial and ethnic categories.

Black Youth Want Freedom

Nov. 23, 2022

Among the key headlines from the 2022 election were gains by Republicans among minority voters.

According to the AP VoteCast survey, Republican House candidates got 14% of the Black vote, almost twice the 8% of the Black vote that Republicans captured in 2020 and 2018.

The difference between the percentage of Black votes that Democrats got compared to Republicans was 68 points, compared to a difference of 83 points in the 2020 election and 82 points in 2018.

This was even more pronounced among younger Black voters, ages 18-44, where the difference between percentage voting Democrat and Republican was 54 points, compared to 76 points in 2020 and 75 in 2018.

The Republican Party is most aggressively taking root among younger Black voters.

Per Pew Research, 28% of Black Republicans are ages 18-29, compared to 17% of Black Democrats and 10% of White Republicans.

My own sense is that younger Blacks are less inclined to think of themselves primarily by race and less inclined to think of their future in terms of racial group identity politics.

Pew Research data shows 58% of Black Republicans say that their race is an "extremely or very important" aspect of their personal identity. This compared to 82% of Black Democrats.

Twenty one percent of Black Republicans, compared to 6% of Black Democrats, say their race is of little or no importance to their personal identity.

Also worth noting is that 50% of Black Republicans live in lower-income households.

So, in general, Black Republicans tend to be younger and poorer.

This makes sense. These younger Black Americans are thinking about their future and have a sense of realism that their future is about their own efforts as opposed to racially driven government programs.

Per Pew, 45% of Black Republicans, compared to 21% of Black Democrats, are more likely to say that the future of Black Americans depends on their own efforts. About half as many Black Republicans compared to Black Democrats—44% versus 73%—see racial discrimination as the main barrier to Black progress and achievement.

So, change is underway, and this is good news. More in the upcoming generation of Black Americans see themselves as the civil rights movement wanted all Black Americans to be seen—as unique individuals.

But this change must be greater and faster to slow and stop the leftward movement of the country.

Per analysis from the Brookings Institution, in 2022, among voters 65+, 76.3% were white; ages 45-54, 68.2% were white; ages 30-44, 62.2% were white; and 18-29, 56% were white.

This demographic snapshot shows the future ethnic profile of the country. It is becoming dramatically less white.

In 2022, 72% of voters were white, and 58% of them voted Republican, accounting for 42% of the overall Republican vote. If the overall profile looked like it does among 18-29 voters, 56% white rather than 72%, with no change in the percentage voting Republican, 58%, white voters would be delivering 32% of Republican votes rather than 42%.

It should be clear that with the percentage of the American population dramatically shifting to non-white Americans, there must be a corresponding dramatic increase in the percentage of non-white Americans voting for Republicans or we can expect the country to continue to transform to big government and moral relativism.

Despite the improvements, 14% of Black voters and 39% of Hispanic voters voting Republican in 2022, this is not enough.

Republicans should be taking a closer look at the positive dynamics driving young Blacks to the Republican Party and use this message to reach more minority Americans.

That is, don't bank your future on racial politics. Every American should be considered a unique individual, personally responsible for their own life. The job of government is to protect life, liberty, property and the pursuit of happiness for everyone.

Why Did Black Georgians Vote for Raphael Warnock?

Dec. 14, 2022

There are plenty of post-mortems about Raphael Warnock's defeat of Republican candidate Herschel Walker in the runoff for the Senate seat in Georgia.

Yes, in the same state, Republican Brian Kemp won a decisive victory in the race for governor.

And, yes, to be kind, Walker was not a great flagbearer to draw voters, particularly Black voters, to the Republican Party.

But let's ask why voters, particularly Black voters, would send Warnock to represent them for another six years in the U.S. Senate.

The Georgia electorate is around 30% Black, and 90% of them voted for Warnock.

What are these Black voters thinking about?

Warnock is a boilerplate Democrat of the left, with an agenda of government spending as the answer to every problem, who is also the address to turn to keep the door open to abortion and the LGBTQ agenda.

Atlanta, which is about 50% Black, has a poverty rate of 18.5% compared to a national average of 11.6%, and among Black adults in Atlanta, 75% are not married compared to 50% of all adults nationwide.

Is Warnock's agenda, pretty much the agenda of his party, really what these folks need?

Let's turn to economist John Cochrane of Stanford University's Hoover Institution. In an essay about the importance of economic growth, he notes that the U.S.

economy averaged 3.5% growth annually from 1947 to 2000. Since then, the average has hovered around 2%.

What if the average growth from 1947 to 2000 was 2% instead of 3.5%, asks Cochrane. He answers that average income in 2000 would have been $23,000 instead of $50,000.

Taking 1.5% off the annual growth rate lops off roughly half the average earning potential of working Americans.

Democrats love to pitch their programs as about rich versus poor, "haves" versus "have nots." But if we are doomed to slow, sclerotic growth, who will suffer the most? The "haves" or the "have nots"?

Check out the latest long-term economic projections from the Congressional Budget Office.

They forecast economic growth over the next 30 years averaging less than 2% per year.

This while the federal government bloats to levels unimaginable in healthier times.

CBO projects national debt, now 100% of our GDP, something not seen since World War II, to 185% of GDP by 2052.

Cochrane notes that the core of economic growth is "productivity, the value of goods and services each worker can produce in a unit of time."

But productivity is declining because an increasing percentage of every income earner's reality is controlled by government. Transfer payments, taxing one set of Americans to make payments to others, now amount to $4 trillion—80% of the federal budget and more than 20% of disposable income (four times higher than in the 1950s).

When people are rewarded for not working, they

don't work.

Today's labor force participation rate—the percent of the population of working age that is either working or looking for work—is now 62% compared to 67% 20 years ago.

So, my fellow Black Americans, Warnock and his party may make you feel good that they will deliver more government money to you that the country doesn't have.

But you buy into this feel-good moment at the expense of the future of your children and grandchildren.

Warnock is a pastor, so he surely read in his Bible that man's punishment for the original sin was work.

The ship is sinking, folks.

And the first to drown will be those low-income Americans who think they will be saved by short-term government fixes served up by the Democratic Party and their faithful servants like Pastor Warnock.

This doesn't let Republicans off the hook. I appeal to Republicans to belly up, finally, to the task at hand, and get these truths to all Americans, and particularly those low-income Black Americans whose votes you so badly need.

About the Author

Star Parker is a leading figure in America's black conservative movement. She is a nationally syndicated columnist, an author and a regular commentator on national television, radio and social media platforms. Currently, Star is host of a weekly national news talk show called "Cure America with Star Parker." Prior to her involvement in social and political activism, Star spent seven years in the grip of welfare dependency before a Christian conversion changed her life. She started a business in Los Angeles, began her activism and began consulting with federal and state legislators on market-based strategies to fight poverty, including federal welfare reforms that passed in the mid-1990s. She founded CURE in 1995 to bring new ideas to policy discussions on how to transition America's poor from government dependency to self-sufficiency. In 2020, Star was appointed by President Donald Trump to the U.S. Commission on Civil Rights California Advisory Committee. She was appointed in 2018 by Senate Majority Leader Mitch McConnell to the U.S. Frederick Douglass Bicentennial Commission. In 2017, Star joined the White House Opportunity Initiative advisory team to share ideas on how to best fix our nation's most distressed communities.

Star holds a bachelor's degree in marketing and international business from Woodbury University and has received numerous awards and commendations for her work on public policy issues. In 2016, CPAC honored her as the "Ronald Reagan Foot Soldier of the Year." In 2017, Star was the recipient of the Groundswell Impact award, and in 2018, Bott Radio Network presented Star with its annual

Queen Esther award.

Serving on the National Religious Broadcasters Board of Directors and their Executive Committee and the Board of Directors at the Leadership Institute, Star is active in helping other organizations that impact the culture, particularly for younger generations.

What Is the CURE for America?
is also available as an e-book
for Kindle, Amazon Fire, iPad, Nook and
Android e-readers. Visit
creatorspublishing.com to learn more.

Made in United States
North Haven, CT
10 November 2026

22091351R00280